Eight Urban Musical Cultures

EIGHT URBAN
MUSICAL CULTURES
Tradition and Change

Edited by BRUNO NETTL

UNIVERSITY OF ILLINOIS PRESS
Urbana Chicago London

LIBRARY OF CONGRESS CATALOGING IN PUBLICATION DATA

Main entry under title:

Eight urban musical cultures.

 Includes bibliographical references.
 CONTENTS: Nettl, B. Introduction.—Blum, S.
Changing roles of performers in Meshhed and Bojnurd,
Iran.—Coplan, D. Go to my town, Cape Coast. [etc.]
 1. Music—Addresses, essays, lectures.
 2. Music and society—Addresses, essays, lectures.
 3. Ethnomusicology—Addresses, essays, lectures.
 I. Nettl, Bruno, 1930–
 ML3547.E4   780'.9173'2   77-25041
 ISBN 0-252-00208-3

To George Herzog

Acknowledgments

I should like to thank the authors of the essays for allowing their work to be included. I am grateful to Alan Merriam, Adelaida Reyes-Schramm, William Kay Archer, Alexander Ringer, the authors of the essays themselves, and of course others too numerous to mention, for the many stimulating discussions which led me to plan this project. And I wish to express my thanks to the University of Illinois Center for Advanced Study, which provided a year's release from teaching during 1973–74 that was in part devoted to the planning of this volume, and to the University of Illinois Research Board for providing secretarial help, the editorial services of a research assistant, and funds for reproducing the music in Stephen Blum's study. Finally, sincere thanks must go to two colleagues, Judith McCulloh and Ronald Riddle, for undertaking the exacting task of copy editing this rather heterogeneous book.

B.N.

Contents

Eight Urban Musical Cultures

Introduction

BRUNO NETTL

This volume presents a group of ethnomusicological studies devoted to the fate of traditional musics in modern cities of developing or recently developed nations of Asia, Africa, and the Americas. Each of the essays deals in the main with one city and attempts to comprehend in one way or another the role of the traditional music of the culture in the processes or changes toward modern, essentially Western, urban life. Each is concerned with the interaction of traditional and Western musics or musical cultures, including musical style and sound, and inseparably associated cultural background, context, and behavior. Each provides a different and, we hope, unique approach. The studies deal with musics of various social strata and with classical, folk, or popular music complexes. As a group, these essays constitute a series of model studies within the broad scope of urban ethnomusicology, a field that is hardly new but whose special problems and contributions have only recently begun to be recognized.

Scholarship in the history of Western music has given much attention to the role of cities. To be sure, most musicological literature is oriented toward the lives of individual artists, the development of genres and forms, the explication of specific parameters of music. But a significant strand in this scholarly tradition deals with cities as units with continuity of tradition. For example, it is easy to find numerous monographic studies on the history of music in specific urban centers, particularly of Germany and Central Europe;[1] and there are many entries under the names of cities in such important reference works as *Die Musik in Geschichte und Gegenwart*,[2] establishing the significance of such

3

urban institutions as schools, cathedrals, palaces, concert halls, and societies of musicians in developing traditions that characterize a given city. (And, to be sure, the historical study of European cities is paralleled by a scholarly tradition of research on the music at particularly prominent courts and monasteries.)[3] But this literature is vast, and it is not our purpose to discuss it here. While no body of theory has been established that sets off the type of development experienced by music in an urban environment throughout history, there is ample recognition that cities have played an important part in the history of Western music; and there are great bodies of data that could provide the raw material for such theory.

There are no similarly developed data for cities in the non-Western world. Cities in Asia and Africa and even in Latin America are in many cases much more recent, although ancient cities with centuries of tradition are found in these continents as well. Detailed historical information, however, is often rather sparse or is exceedingly difficult to acquire. We are talking here essentially about twentieth-century cities.

But there is a more important cause for the neglect of urban music. Ethnomusicologists, the scholars who have been most involved in the study of non-Western musics, have for most of their field's short history avoided studying the music of cities as such. They are only now coming to terms with the obvious fact that much of what they study occurs as a result of the particular characteristics of urban culture. They have only lately recognized that some of the most interesting and significant events in the recent history of world music result from the rapid growth, modernization, and Westernization of cities in the developing or recently developed nations outside Europe and North America.

Ethnomusicology, especially as developed in the schools of E. M. von Hornbostel and Béla Bartók, has concentrated on the rural. There is thus a good deal of generalized belief and theory on what happens to music in a tribal or rural folk environment. A number of works have appeared on "primitive" music.[4] Herzog points out the tendency for rural populations to cleave to their tradition,[5] as does Bartók.[6] The relationship of rural to urban is admitted almost grudgingly; and the flow of folklore and music from city, court, and monastery to the village is embodied in the definition of folklore as *"gesunkenes Kulturgut."*[7] Alan Merriam devotes much attention to the problems of change in the music of contemporary non-Western civilizations, but he hardly mentions the existence of cities and eschews any generalization about the kinds of things that happen in them and as a result of their growth.[8] In this respect he reflects accurately the state of research and thought in his field in the 1950s. Until recently, field research has been concentrated in villages; and when studies of music *have* taken place in a city, they have rarely given much specific consideration to the urban environment as such, but have concentrated rather on enclaves that have preserved authentic rural traditions or maintained ancient classical court musics.

In the period since about 1960, however, ethnomusicologists have increasingly moved their venue of research to the city. Characteristically following the trends of anthropology by a few years, they have begun to approach certain special problems occasioned by urbanization in folk and tribal musics. Attention was first focused on Afro-American music as it moved from the rural South of the United States to cities of the North. Among the early landmarks of this interest was the publication of *Urban Blues* by Charles Keil;[9] various other studies, particularly of jazz music and musicians, followed the same trend. Similarly, studies of the folk music of recently urbanized groups such as the Poles of Detroit,[10] the Hungarians of Cleveland,[11] the Slovaks of Pittsburgh,[12] the Puerto Ricans of New York,[13] and the Jews of Los Angeles were produced.[14] But again, the main thrust of these studies has been the retention of nonurban folk tradition (in itself a phenomenon of enormous interest), rather than the roles of these traditions and the changes they experienced in the urbanization and modernization of their peoples.

In the 1960s a number of studies dealing with the music of non-Western cities did appear that addressed themselves specifically to the role of the urban environment. Among them the most notable are in African studies, an area in which the study of urbanization and its tribal backgrounds has been prominent for some time.[15] Most recently, studies of musicians and their role have appeared,[16] as have studies of the popular musics that have arisen in various parts of the world, combining traditional and Western elements and giving musical expression to the many interrelated strands of culture change.[17]

The special nature of cities has been widely recognized and explicated in works ranging from essentially humanistic historical studies dealing with the city of the West, such as Lewis Mumford's momentous work *The City in History*,[18] to specialized publications on the contemporary world cast in an anthropological context and including special periodicals devoted to the subject, such as *Urban Anthropology*. New disciplines such as urban planning have been created, together with such branches of traditional disciplines as urban sociology and urban anthropology. Such developments testify to the recognition of the particular problems of studying man's activities as determined by an urban environment, the special nature of life in the city, and the need for viewing urban activities in the perspective of the total context of the city.

What is it that sets urban musical culture off from that of villages, small towns, and nomadic life? It is wealth, power, education; it is specialization in professions; it is the interaction of different and diverse population groups, rich and poor, majority and minorities, recent migrant and long-standing urbanite; it is the ease of rapid communication, the mass media, literacy; it is crowding and enormous divergencies in living standards and styles. Translated to musical culture, it is in many cases—though by no means in all cities for all repertories—the patronage of wealthy aristocrats and of government agencies. It is the specialization of the professional musician. It is Western musical notation, recording, radio, television. Perhaps most of all, it is the coming together of different musical styles and genres from many sources. These characteristics of modern urban musical life are not necessarily confined to the city. Professional musicians, specialists in specific instruments and genres, the patronage of wealth, the combination of styles—all of these are found in rural and tribal life as well. But the frequency with which they occur in the countryside is low in comparison with what is almost an inevitability of these characteristics in the city.

Cities in Asia, Africa, and Latin America obviously vary enormously, but many do share certain characteristics that perhaps distinguish them as a group from the cities of traditional Western civilization. Among these traits are the rapidity of their growth and the speed with which they have absorbed some of the features of urban life such as modern technology and the mass media. The cities of Europe, on the whole, grew more slowly and only gradually became transformed by such technological creations as electricity, the automobile, the printing press, the radio, and motion pictures. Elsewhere, this process was telescoped. Cities in North America have indeed experienced periods of rapid growth that might be compared with the burgeoning of cities in Africa and Latin America during recent decades; but American and Canadian cities underwent their most accelerated growth somewhat earlier, in the last decades of the nineteenth century and the first decade of the twentieth, and did not experience the instant technologization of the non-Western world.

Perhaps the most significant concomitant of the rapid growth of cities in what has sometimes been called the Third World is the need for quick absorption of rural populations, which are often of highly diverse culture, economic and social background, and language. No doubt this need has also existed in European cities, but in general their settlers from the countryside have arrived at a slower rate and have had more in common culturally with the already settled urban population. Again, in the United States and Canada, a situation similar to what is now happening in the non-Western world took place decades ago. The composition of Detroit in the 1920s (with the city's many non-English-speaking groups coming substantially from European villages and small towns) and of San Francisco (with its large Oriental enclaves) have had in certain respects more in common with contemporary Third World cities than with London, Paris, and Berlin. (For this reason the essays in this volume include one on San Francisco's Chinese-Americans by Ronald Riddle.)

But what are the musical characteristics that accompany those of demography and culture? And what musicological problems result?

The music of a given population group may be considered as a system. Indeed, one of the contributions of early ethnomusicology was the presentation of samples of the entire repertory of music of a given culture as a single system. In describing the folk music of a particular village, an ethnomusicologist could take into account all the music of the village, including what was indigenous, what came from elsewhere, and what was mixed. Descriptions of the musical behavior of tribal groups were similarly holistic (although, to be sure, music of Western origin that was enjoyed by such groups was usually neglected). This same approach was not, however, followed in studying the music of cities. The reason is, no doubt, that the musical "system" of a city is far more complex, defying quick comprehension.[19]

The idea of a musical culture as a system in which parts interrelate, and in which changes in one part inevitably force changes in the others, is one that should be explored further. Such exploration is in a sense at the base of most of the essays presented here. Thus, the musical culture of modern Tehran consists of over a dozen different and easily separable musics: Western popular; Western classical; a mainstream style of Persian popular music; various styles of Persian rural folk music transported to the city; Arabic, Indian, and Russian musics; and various styles of popular music derived from mixtures of the mainstream and other musics in this list. Although each person may associate himself primarily with one of these, he has access to many. The way in which most of the styles are derived from others in the group or tend to influence each other (mainly via the mixture of styles in the genres of popular music) indicates the profound modification that changes in individual population groups and their musics work on the whole.

The Indian classical music of Delhi consists of various interrelated schools, some of them more and others less obviously cognizant of Western music and musical life. While changes in the styles of Western music are perhaps not likely to produce changes in the sound of Indian music, the ways in which Western musicians and their Indian counterparts who perform Western music make a living has had a profound effect on the way in which the performers of Indian music study, live, and adapt themselves in order to preserve their traditions. Such adaptation is essentially the subject of the studies on Delhi (by Daniel Neuman) and on Madras (by Kathleen and Adrian L'Armand).

What has happened in cities has also happened in smaller communities. A case in point is Browning, Montana, a town of 6,000 whites, Blackfoot Indians, and members of other Indian tribes. Here the population groups are easily identified, as are a variety of musical styles—Western, old Blackfoot, and modern intertribal

Indian. But the performers and audiences of these musics are in part separate, in part overlapping; and the attitudes of the members of a population group primarily associated with one of these styles toward the other musics are part of the rapidly changing picture of this microcosmic metropolis.[20] Stephen Blum's discussion of Bojnurd, Iran, is relevant to this thought.

Thus the presence and interaction of different population groups and their musics in a single, intermeshed set of causes and reactions is a special feature of the musical culture of the rapidly modernized city.

But forces that *oppose* mixing and interaction can also be identified. While the contact of many musics causes them to interrelate and to affect each other, there is also the tendency for cultures and musics whose identity is endangered in this way to withdraw, thus inhibiting change. The results are sometimes labeled as "marginal survivals." A part of a culture unit leaves its center and moves elsewhere, then comprising a margin of population—sometimes far-removed—in respect to that center. For example, in the late nineteenth- and early twentieth-century movement from Poland to North American cities, the dynamics of the immigrants' musical culture became two-directional. The Poles learned the music of other groups around them, both rural and urban. But for a time they also retained their traditional Polish folk music and indeed tried to keep it from mixing with the other musics, holding it intact in stable forms even while their kith and kin in Poland accepted change more readily. The cities of developing nations may at times be a repository of archaic rural materials in addition and in contrast to the mixing that ordinarily characterizes them. But normally it appears to be the mixtures and the changes that hold sway over any stabilizing trends.

A general characteristic of cities is the development of "art" or "cultivated" or "classical" musics, and this is true of Western as well as non-Western cities. The cities that have developed in recent years normally partake of Western art music. Those that have existed for centuries, as in India, now have art-music systems from both their own traditions and those of Western culture. The interaction of the two classical-music systems can be fascinating. Often it takes the form of adaptation of elements from Western music to the traditional—most typically in musical life, in attitudes such

9

as those concerning the status of musicians; but frequently the sound and structure of the music itself are affected. Out of the "art" musics, there often develops a group of popular-music styles in which the interaction of traditional and Western is far more vigorous.[21]

The processes by which this interaction takes place are various, and they overlap and are easily confused. One such process may be labeled Westernization. In its simplest form, the concept is used simply to describe the absorption of Western elements into a non-Western music. Most obvious are the introduction of Western instruments, harmony, and notation, as well as the technologies of recording and broadcasting. Also to be included are Western-influenced melody, rhythm, intonation, use of the voice, and innumerable other parameters of musical structure and musical behavior. A more sophisticated view, however, could define musical Westernization as a process whereby a traditional music is modified so as to become a part of the Western musical system. Thus, the interpretation that a culture gives to a set of changes taking place in its musical structure, as much as the nature of the changes themselves, would determine whether such changes actually constitute Westernization.

If Westernization is the process whereby a music becomes Western through the accretion of Western elements, modernization is the process whereby, through similar additions, a music retains its traditional essence but becomes modern—that is, part of the contemporary world and its set of values. The motivation is opposite to that mentioned above for Westernization; the traditional music is changed in order to remain intact in the modern world, not in order to become a part of Western civilization. The parameters of Western musical culture that are adopted may actually be the same as those used in Westernization, but also include other, quite contrastive ones.

For example, in certain repertories of Arabic and Persian music, the use of larger, more dramatized musical structures, imitating those of the Western symphony and sonata, seem to have been introduced in order to show that the music is capable of the same degree of complexity as Western music; yet the basic sound, in general and in detail, is still "Arabic." On the other hand, as Ruth Katz has shown, younger generations of Jewish-Arabic musicians have incorporated other modernizing elements, by tending to emphasize, in their performances, those features of music that are regarded by the Western listener as typically Arabic—that is, varieties of ornamentation—in order to underscore the music's integrity and its ability to live in a modern context, which includes recording, amplification, and large public performances.[22] Modernization of still another sort is seen in the creation of a modern, pan-Indian style of music, in the North American Plains, which uses singing groups that give public performances for pay, English words in the songs, a highly flamboyant performance practice compared with the more subdued style of the past, and standardization of song forms.[23] Various elements of Western musical behavior are used to "beef up" the traditional music, in order to make it modern and thus competitive with that of the West, but there is no thought on the part of the Indians that this "modern" music is part of the Western musical system.

Thus, two ways in which Western and traditional musics interact, Westernization and modernization, may have the same effect on the sound of the music; but they are motivated differently, and their respective effects are interpreted differently by the cultures in which they take place. This contrast is the main subject of Nettl's essay on Tehran in this collection.

Both types of interaction produce mixtures of Western and traditional elements in musical style and culture. What are the specifically musical techniques that are employed to do this? Ethnomusicologists have made little headway in developing a theory of musical change. The main concept that has been established is syncretism,[24] a technique, as it were, in which those elements of music that are similar or compatible in two musical cultures undergoing acculturation are identified. These elements become the dominant features of a new style that replaces one of those traditional to the cultures involved. The concept was developed mainly in the study of Afro-American musics; harmony, diatonic scales, antiphonal technique, and specific rhythmic approaches, found in both African and Western music, were established as prominent features of the freshly developed musics of the New World. The notion of musical compatibility between two styles whose cultures were in close contact was emphasized.

In an urban context, the use of syncretism as an analytical concept may be rewarding, as indicated in some of the papers presented here. We should add to it the tendency, in some cultures, to select features of an acculturating musical style that are regarded as especially characteristic of that style by the cultures with which it comes into contact. For example, the hallmark of Western musics, in the eyes of many non-Western cultures, is the pervasive use of harmony. There are situations in which harmony and other prominent features of Western music, because of their very prominence, are selected for adaptation into non-Western styles, whether or not they are compatible with the tradition. Examples are found in the film music of India and in modern Arabic café music.

Studies of the interaction of musics in cities, widely and systematically carried out, should provide identification of other techniques used to preserve, abolish, and innovate in the sound of music and in musical behavior.[25] An attempt in this direction is Stephen Blum's essay in this collection, for it examines the changing roles of two types of performers in a basically multicultural and multilingual context in northeastern Iran.

One feature that modern cities appear to have produced, and to have in common, is popular music. Difficult to define, and perhaps definable only in terms specific to the culture in question, this is a genre that seems to have eixsted in at least some cities for a long time. In European cities of the sixteenth and seventeenth centuries, for example, there evidently existed something closely akin to rural folk music but with a special urban flavor, and related to the art music as well.[26] But with the coming of mass audiences, mass media, and amplification, great changes have come about in the musical life of European cities.

In the cities of the developing and recently developed world, popular music has become one of the main sources of both musical change and the combining of musical styles. Indeed, the popular musics of Asia, Africa, and, to some extent, Latin America are the prime venue for the combination of non-Western and Western musics in these cultures. For example, while Indian and Western classical musics in India tend to coexist with almost negligible cross-fertilization, the music of Indian films much more readily mixes traditional classical and folk elements with those of Western music. Indeed, one characteristic of popular music everywhere since World War II, as it appears in the mass media of recording and film, is its tendency to very rapidly combine material from a diversity of sources and particularly from two or more cultures. Even European and North American popular musics participate in this trend, drawing on Western classical, folk, Afro-American (and ultimately African), as well as Latin American elements. If we are to understand the musical culture of the modern city, we will have to devote much attention to the history and anthropology of popular music. Attempts in this direction are provided here by several scholars: David Stigberg, writing on the music of Veracruz; David Coplan, on Ghanaian highlife; and Naomi Ware, on Freetown.

The preceding paragraphs have presented some thoughts about the special contributions of modern cities to the musical culture of the world and about the need for studying them. While the study of cities in the non-Western and developing world and their musical culture inevitably shares method and theory with ethnomusicology at large, there are certain special problems to which the student of this field must address himself, and there are certain contributions he can make. It is for these reasons that it makes sense to regard this area of study as a valid subfield, for which "urban ethnomusicology" is a useful appellation.

The problems to be addressed in this area result from the very nature of the modern city. The mass of data and the complexity of the sociomusical system are quantitatively of a different order from those found in smaller communities, although, to be sure, certain villages and towns provide a microcosm that can be used as training ground and as experimental way-stations for work in larger cities. The ethnomusicologist who is used to working with a single musical style or genre at a time must make special preparations for the greater complexities of the city, and particularly of the city in a Westernizing environment.

Another major problem concerns the clarification of concepts involving the various strata of music in a city. In a rural environment, in the history of Western music, and in the study of the learned systems of Asian music, scholars have been satisfied with relatively simple definitions of folk, popular, and art music, and of such classes as sacred and secular music, largely because they have worked with one of these classes or genres at a time, excluding others. If the interrelationship among these musics is to be comprehended, the concepts will have to be refined, and the differences among the typologies in various cultures will have to be taken into account and compared.

The student of urban ethnomusicology may be able to make major theoretical contributions to the field of ethnomusicology at large, for he will have to deal with problems that have confronted not only this entire field, but also the discipline of musicology, broadly defined. At the same time, because the sociomusical system is in certain respects a smaller and more easily manageable version of the entire social system, and because music lends itself to quantification and to statistical treatment, the urban-oriented ethnomusicologist may be able to make substantial contributions to anthropology.

In addition to the ethnography of music and musical life in cities, these contributions involve a number of other areas, some of them hitherto treated only theoretically or by implication. The study of a community as a musical system involving both the musical artifacts and the behavior of music producers and consumers, already mentioned in several contexts, should perhaps be at the top of this list. It is one area in which urban ethnomusicology is likely to make distinct contributions that cannot be made at all in more traditional types of study.[27] Related is the study of the interaction of a city with its surroundings, already touched upon by the proponents of "gesunkenes Kulturgut" and "marginal survival" many decades ago (and treated in Stephen Blum's essay here); in only a few instances has the relationship between a modern non-Western city and its rural surroundings been probed.[28]

Urban ethnomusicology can make important contributions to the study of change and its processes, because of the rapidity of change in cities as compared to that in the rural musical environment, and because, indeed, many changes even in the village emanate from events in the city. In this connection, the problems of measuring such changes come into the foreground. Ethnomusicologists have been comparing musics since their studies began, but they have made little progress in assessing the amount of difference and in comparing the degrees of similarity among three or more genres, styles, or musical cultures. The need for the development of this kind of methodology is a matter of highest priority, and the mixed urban context should stimulate the development of such methods, to perhaps a greater degree than has the past focus on the rural musical cultures of the world. The cognitive study of folk classifications of music, that is, classifications applied by members of the culture rather than by the investigator, has been touched upon in a number of studies in the past, but never systematically explored; in an urban venue it can be more readily explored than in the rural, because of the need for each member of an urban population to come to terms somehow with a variety of musics and thus to classify them.[29]

Among the possible benefits of urban ethnomusicology is the potential for working in what might be called applied ethnomusicology—involving, for instance, work with the problems of maintaining traditions in the face of modernization, or teaching music in inner-city schools in North America. Many publications touch upon those problems, but only a few address them specifically.[30]

The problems of urban ethnomusicology have long been recognized, implicitly and sometimes explicitly; there is no thought here of the need for a new field or discipline. But there is a need for scholars to view the world's musics in their proper context, and today this is substantially an urban context in which the characteristics of the twentieth-century city, its rapid growth, its cultural diversity, and its inevitable conglomeration of social and musical interactions, are given proper attention.

The essays in this volume are presented as contributions and as stimulus for further discussion and research. We attempt to provide a number of viewpoints, musical and anthropological, a number of types of problems, a variety of musical strata—classical music and musicians, popular music, and folk music—and a number of kinds of cities and geographic areas. Together, these essays present a cross-section of data and thought in urban ethnomusicology.

NOTES

1. See e.g. Arnold Schering, *Musikgeschichte Leipzigs von 1650 bis 1723* (Leipzig: Kistner und Siegel, 1926); Josef Mantuani, *Die Musik in Wien* (*Geschichte der Stadt Wien*, part 3, vol. 1) (Vienna, 1907); and Karl Gustav Fellerer, *Mittelalterliches Musikleben der Stadt Freiburg* (Regensburg: F. Pustet, 1935). These are three examples from a vast range of publications, the majority probably produced by German-speaking scholars.

2. Friedrich Blume, *Die Musik in Geschichte und Gegenwart* (Kassel: Baerenreiter, 1949–).

3. See e.g. John E. Stevens, *Music and Poetry in the Early Tudor Court* (Lincoln: University of Nebraska Press, 1961), which deals with a world-famous establishment; other publications describe more modest courts, e.g. Karl Schweickert, *Die Musikpflege am Hofe der Kurfürsten von Mainz im 17. und 18. Jahrhundert* (Mainz: Wilckens, 1937). Again, these are merely samples from a large list of publications.

4. The idea that nonliterate or tribal cultures had much in common seems to have been widespread for a long time. Thus, there are publications that treat the subject as a unit, such as Richard Wallaschek, *Primitive Music* (London: Longmans, 1893); Carl Stumpf, *Die Anfänge der Musik* (Leipzig: Barth, 1911); Bruno Nettl, *Music in Primitive Culture* (Cambridge: Harvard University Press, 1956); Marius Schneider, "Primitive Music," in *Ancient and Oriental Music,* ed. Egon Wellesz (London: Oxford University Press, 1957), pp. 1–82; Curt Sachs, *The Wellsprings of Music* (The Hague: Nijhoff, 1962).

5. George Herzog, "Song," in *Standard Dictionary of Folklore, Mythology and Legend,* ed. Maria Leach (New York: Funk & Wagnalls, 1950), p. 1033.

6. Béla Bartók, *Hungarian Folk Music* (London: Oxford University Press, 1931), p. 2.

7. The basic assumption behind this concept is that all folklore (the authors concerned with this concept deal with folklore in Western civilization primarily or exclusively) is rural in provenience but derived from urban artifacts that have been handed down to the rural environs of a city (or court or monastery) and have in some respects become debased in the process. See e.g. Werner Danckert, *Das europäische Volkslied,* 2d ed. (Bonn: Bouvier, 1970), pp. 9–10.

8. Alan P. Merriam, *The Anthropology of Music* (Evanston, Ill.: Northwestern University Press, 1964), pp. 303–20.

9. Charles Keil, *Urban Blues* (Chicago: University of Chicago Press, 1966).

10. Bruno Nettl, "Preliminary Remarks on Urban Folk Music in Detroit," *Western Folklore* 16 (1957), 37–42; Harriet Pawlowska, *Merrily We Sing* (Detroit: Wayne State University Press, 1961).

11. Stephen Erdely, "Folksinging of the American Hungarians in Cleveland," *Ethnomusicology* 8 (1964), 14–27.

12. Jacob A. Evanson, "Folk Songs of an Industrial City," in *Pennsylvania Songs and Legends,* ed. George Korson (Philadelphia: University of Pennsylvania Press, 1949), pp. 423–66.

13. Shulamith Rybak, "Puerto Rican Children's Songs in New York," *Midwest Folklore* 8 (1958), 5–20.

14. Samuel G. Armistead and Joseph H. Silverman, "Hispanic Balladry among the Sephardic Jews of the West Coast," *Western Folklore* 19 (1960), 229–44. See also Israel J. Katz, "Towards a Musicological Study of the Judeo-Spanish Romancero," *Western Folklore* 21 (1962), 83–91.

15. See e.g. *African Urban Notes* 5:4 (Winter 1970), a special issue edited by Sylvia Kinney, with eight papers on urban musical traditions. See also Akin Euba, "Islamic Musical Culture among the Yoruba," in *Essays on Music and History in Africa,* ed. Klaus P. Wachsmann (Evanston, Ill.: Northwestern University Press, 1971), pp. 171–84.

16. E.g., David W. Ames, "Igbo and Hausa Musicians: A Comparative Examination," *Ethnomusicology* 17 (1973), 250–78.

17. See e.g. Bruno Nettl, "Persian Popular Music in 1969," *Ethnomusicology* 16 (1972), 218–39; Gerard Béhague, "Bossa and Bossas: Recent Changes in Brazilian Urban Popular Music," ibid. 17 (1973), 209–33; Robert Kauffman, "Shona Urban Music and the Problem of Acculturation," *Yearbook of the International Folk Music Council* 4 (1972), 47–56.

18. Lewis Mumford, *The City in History: Its Origins, Its Transformations, and Its Prospects* (New York: Harcourt, Brace & World, 1961).

19. There are exceptions; e.g. William P. Malm, "The Modern Music of Meiji Japan," in *Tradition and Modernization in Japanese Culture*, ed. Donald H. Shively (Princeton, N.J.: Princeton University Press, 1971), pp. 257–300, discusses many aspects of musical culture from the classical tradition to public school music. It does not deal with a particular city, but its focus is clearly urban. See also Robert Günther, ed., *Musikkulturen Asiens, Afrikas und Ozeaniens in 19. Jahrhundert* (Regensburg, 1973).

20. Bruno Nettl, "Studies in Blackfoot Indian Musical Culture, Part II: Musical Life of the Montana Blackfoot, 1966," *Ethnomusicology* 11 (1967), 293–95, and "Biography of a Blackfoot Indian Singer," *Musical Quarterly* 54 (1968), 199–207.

21. A special issue of *Asian Music* (7:2, 1976), guest-edited by Daniel E. Neuman, contains a number of relevant articles on the ethnomusicology of culture change in Asia. See particularly Neuman's introductory essay, "Towards an Ethnomusicology of Culture Change in Asia," pp. 1–5.

22. Ruth Katz, "The Singing of Baqqashot by Aleppo Jews," *Acta Musicologica* 40 (1968), 65–85.

23. See William K. Powers, "Contemporary Oglala Music and Dance: Pan-Indianism versus Pan-Tetonism," *Ethnomusicology* 12 (1968), 352–72.

24. For detailed discussion of syncretism and literature bearing on it, see Merriam, *Anthropology of Music*, pp. 313–15.

25. Among recent writings on the interaction among musics, see particularly the excellent dissertation by Adelaida Reyes Schramm, "The Role of Music in the Interaction of Black Americans and Hispanos in New York City's East Harlem" (Columbia University, 1975).

26. Among the few books dealing with this interrelationship of folk, urban popular, and cultivated musics, we may mention Walter Wiora, *Europäische Volksmusik und abendländische Tonkunst* (Kassel: Hinnenthal, 1957), as an example dealing mainly with Central Europe and Germany; and Reginald Nettel, *Seven Centuries of Popular Song* (London: Phoenix, 1956), as an example dealing mainly with the English-speaking world.

27. For earlier discussion of music as a system which includes musical sound and musical behavior, see Merriam, *Anthropology of Music*, p. 29; and also a review of this book by Bruno Nettl, *Current Anthropology* 7 (1966), 225, and Merriam's rejoinder, ibid., p. 229. This discussion deals with the "system" concept on the basis of a single style of music and its associated behavior; here we present the idea that an urban context multiplies the components by introducing the interaction of several or many musics.

28. Among the "early" studies in this direction we should mention two dissertations: Robert Stephen Blum, "Musics in Contact: The Cultivation of Oral Repertoire in Meshed, Iran" (University of Illinois, 1972) and Daniel

Moses Neuman, "The Cultural Structure and Social Organization of Musicians in India: The Perspective from Delhi" (University of Illinois, 1974). See also n. 25.

29. For a brief attempt to find out about the folk classification of musics used by members of the educated class in an American city, see Bruno Nettl, "A Technique of Ethnomusicology Applied to Western Culture," *Ethnomusicology* 7 (1963), 221–24. See also Merriam, *Anthropology of Music*, pp. 31–32, 209–10.

30. Among the landmark publications addressing themselves to this problem are many of the essays contained in William Kay Archer, ed., *The Preservation of Traditional Forms of the Learned Music of the Orient and the Occident* (Urbana: University of Illinois, Institute of Communications Research, 1964).

Changing Roles of Performers
in Meshhed and Bojnurd, Iran

STEPHEN BLUM

The several musical traditions cultivated in Khorasan, the north-easternmost province of Iran, bear traces of complex processes of change, extending over many centuries. The available historical evidence does not permit us to speak at any point of a "musical consensus which is in constant interaction with the cultural consensus and the social consensus."[1] To the contrary, analysis of music and its social/historical contexts in Khorasan indicates that specialists in musical performance have long functioned as "intermediaries" between diverse social groups,[2] in circumstances marked by conflict and continual shifts in the distribution of power and prestige. Because they normally work in diverse sets of circumstances, Khorasani performers have learned to control musical techniques that permit a high level of variation, in response to changing demands of patrons and audiences.

In the cities of Khorasan, professional performers find a number of situations in which they can work. In some cases, performers travel widely, moving from towns to villages in the exercise of their craft. Drawing on fieldwork carried out in 1969 and 1972, I will examine the roles of specialists in musical performance in two urban settings: Meshhed, the largest city in Khorasan, with a population of over 400,000 persons; and Bojnurd, a smaller town with perhaps 40,000 inhabitants.[3] I will discuss aspects of the work of two important types of performers active in both cities: (a) the *darvish* and the *naqqāl*, who recite several forms of Persian poetry

Stephen Blum is Associate Professor of Music, York University, Toronto.

in teahouses, in private homes, and on the streets; and (b) the *bakhshi*, who sings various genres of Turkic and Kurdish verse in teahouses and other urban locations, and also travels widely to perform in villages.

The recitation of religious poetry by darvishes and naqqals occupies a prominent place in the musical life of both Meshhed and Bojnurd. The former city functions as an important religious center in many respects, primarily as the burial place of the eighth imam of Shi'ite Islam, attracting a large number of pilgrims annually. The greater concentration of Turks and Kurds in the region of Bojnurd supports a larger number of performances by bakhshis than does the city of Meshhed, where few persons understand Turkic languages. In attempting to work within the particular circumstances that they encounter in both cities, performers make choices that I will describe with reference to a set of six distinctions.

In his pioneering study of the folk poetry of northern Iran, Alexander Chodzko contrasted the values represented in the Persian poetry recited by naqqals in urban teahouses with those embodied in the Turkic narratives sung by '*āshiqs* and bakhshis at gatherings in towns, villages, and encampments:[4]

> The ideal of Rustem [principal protagonist of the *Shāh-Nāme*, the cornerstone of the naqqal's repertoire] is service and fidelity to his crowned master; the ideal of Kurroglou [protagonist of an important sequence of Turkic stories] is the fidelity of a warrior to his knightly word and, above all, a wild, unbounded freedom. . . . It is in this mode of thinking, identical with that of his countrymen, that lies the secret talisman of the sympathy the name of Kurroglou excites, and the popularity it enjoys among the Turkic tribes of northern Persia. According to their opinions, nothing is more natural than for the strong to oppress and plunder the weak.[5]

To Chodzko, the ideals of "manliness" held up by the naqqal's recitations of the *Shāh-Nāme* and other classical poetry did not afford "a faithful picture of the character, manners, and civilisation" of nineteenth-century urban Iranians. On the other hand, popular Persian song (the *taṣnif*), "being an exact expression of the moral state of a nation," accurately mirrored the situation of contemporary Persia—"feeble, disheartened, poor, and enervated." Chodzko heard a superior morality in the folksong of Iranian

Turks: ". . . their warlike life in tents, exposed to inclemencies of weather and incessant danger, keeps up a continual freshness of feeling, and a moral excitement unknown to their degenerate lordlings, wallowing in the corruption of towns and palaces; and has, naturally, cast its congenial hue over their popular songs."[6] In the popular poetry of the Turkmen, Chodzko was particularly attracted by "sentiments of pure morality," religious and philosophical concerns in which he discerned the impress of Shi'ite Islam: "Such poetry is really a blessing of Providence in a country where all other guarantees of social order are either unknown or trampled upon."[7]

The present paper will not attempt to describe the context of European imperialism in which Chodzko formed his assessment of the moral character of Iranians; nor will it trace the stereotyped view of Persian popular music as "enervated" and "sad" through its many subsequent appearances in European and Iranian literature during the past century. Objectionable as it is from many respects, Chodzko's account of his observations and fantasies recognized two complementary aspects of the interaction between settled and nomadic groups throughout the "Turco-Iranian world":[8] (a) the idealizations of tribal life as morally superior that have been held by many nomads, peasants, urban dwellers, and European observers; the corresponding attempts to retain (or to create) distinctive ethnic identities by means of standardized musical and linguistic practices; (b) conversely, the pressures that have pushed nomadic groups to acquire (musical) aspects of urban culture; the principles of "moral ecology" whereby "tribesmen identify with a religion which, through literacy, ultimately must have an urban base."[9] Like the rest of "the main Islamic block between Central Asia and the Atlantic shores of Africa," Khorasan has witnessed a "symbiosis of urban, literate, centrally governed, trade-oriented communities, with tribal ones,"[10] a symbiosis that has continued to shape its musical culture down to the present day. Differences between "Persian" and "Turkic" styles are only a part of the story. Furthermore, urban institutions have not invariably promoted the values of either "Islam" or "literacy."[11] A brief survey of the predecessors of the naqqal and the bakhshi may facilitate an understanding of the roles exercised by these performers in 1969.

The formation of modern Persian literature at the courts of the

Sāmānid rulers in Khorasan (875–999), like the cultivation of poetry in pre-Islamic Arabia, was marked by a division of labor between poet and *rāvi,* the latter serving as a "rhapsodist to whom [the poet] entrusted the task of declaiming the poetry which he had composed."[12] According to legend, Ferdousi was accompanied by his ravi, Abu Dulaf, when he delivered the completed text of the *Shāh-Nāme* to the court of Maḥmud of Ghazna (reigned 999–1030).[13] Although the tradition of public recitation of some genres of courtly poetry (notably the *qaṣide*) was dying out in the latter half of the twelfth century,[14] the principal attribute of a ravi—control of a good memory—has remained one of the essential hallmarks of a public performer in Khorasan down to the present day.

The *Shāh-Nāme* has often been described as the culminating expression of the worldview of "the old Persian landowning classes of eastern Iran, the dihqāns."[15] The mores of the Khorasani dihqan, as described by Arabic geographers of the tenth century, corresponded in many respects to Ferdousi's ideals of "manliness,"[16] which Chodzko found wanting in the comportment of nineteenth-century urban Iranians. With the decline of the dihqans and the collapse of Samanid rule toward the end of the tenth century, the Turkic peoples who entered Khorasan in increasing numbers found the rich land lying between Meshhed and Quchān (among other regions) well suited to a pastoralist way of life.[17] The subsequent process of assimilation, which had earlier roots in the relationships between Iranian agriculturalists and Turks (both nomadic and settled) under the Samanids,[18] took place under the rule of Turkic dynasties. A well-known distich of Manuchehri, a Persian poet active at the court of the Ghaznavid ruler Masʿud (reigned 1030–42), points to one of the immediate cultural consequences of Turkic rule—the coexistence of both Turkic and Persian oral repertoires in the artistic life of the Ghaznavid court:

> Be rāh-e turki mānā ke khubtar guʾi
> Tu sheʿr-e turki bar-khvān marā u sheʿr-e ghuzi.
> (In the Turkic mode, so that you might speak better,
> Declaim for me verses in both Turki and Ghuzzi!)[19]

C. E. Bosworth has suggested that the contrast between what Jan Rypka has termed the "feudal epic" of Ferdousi and the "romantic epic" fostered by the Ghaznavid rulers may reflect the "attitudes and requirements" of "the extensive groups of Turks in the Ghaznavid court and army."[20] Just as Rypka believed Ferdousi to have drawn upon "abundant, orally-transmitted sources" of Iranian epic traditions, so Bosworth posits the existence of a "Ghaznavid taste," partially based upon Turkic oral traditions, which shaped the subsequent elaboration of Persian "epic and romantic literature" along two main lines: "One follows directly on from Ferdousi, but with a romantic element injected into the epic, pushing the heroic element further and further into the background; the other stream is that of purely romantic and lyrical idylls in verse."[21]

However this may be, a number of typical distinctions between (and syntheses of) "heroic" and "romantic" ethos continually recur in Iranian folklore and literature from the eleventh century onward. The strong traditions of the Persian heroic epic left little room for Islamic subjects and motifs, which occupy a more prominent position in romantic literature. The didactic intent, the attempt to provide ethical counsel, which characterized much Iranian literature and folklore before the impact of Islam, continued to shape the forms of "romantic" narrative, including the dāstān.[22] Although Turkic traditions of heroic epic were preserved by peoples who remained nomadic (such as the Kirghiz), the Turks of Anatolia, Azerbaijan, Khorasan, and Turkmenistan developed the ḥikāye, a form that alternates third-person prose narration with verses attributed to the protagonists.[23] The 'ashiq and the bakhshi, who performed these tales from the sixteenth and seventeenth centuries onward, are thought to be the descendants of the earlier ozān of the Oghuz Turks.[24] The repertoires of Turkic and Persian folklore share a large number of common subjects and motifs: in Khorasan at the present time, Persian tales recounting the exploits of 'Ali (the first imam of Shi'ite Islam) are known as ghazavot, and at least one Turkic hikaye ("Bābā Roushān") refers to (imaginary) adventures of 'Ali in Central Asia.

Rival groups of Shi'ite and Sunni reciters in Khorasani towns argued about the "excessive" or "appropriate" use of romantic and fantastic elements from an early date. Although Khorasan was a stronghold of Sunnism under the rule of the Seljuk Turks (1038–1158), adherents of the Shi'ite Imāmiyya sect attempted to create "a wide network of propaganda centres." One of the principal techniques of Shiʿite propaganda was the use of a *monāqebi* or *monāqeb-khvān*, "a singer who extols the virtues of ʿAli and his descendents in streets and bazaars." Drawing on the *Kitāb al-naqd* of the early twelfth-century Shiʿite writer al-Qazvini, Bausani speaks of two basic types of material in the repertoire of a mo-naqeb-khvan: (*a*) qasides in praise of the twelve Shiʿite imams that "also contained doctrinal and theological elements" and (*b*) "religious epical songs" or "fantastical tales of the military exploits of ʿAli and his paladins." Bausani quotes passages of the *Kitāb al-naqd* that describe the comparable use by Sunnis of *faẓāʾil-khvāns* who, imitating Shiʿite practice, sang poems presenting Sunni dogmas along with praise of the first two orthodox caliphs, Abu Bakr and ʿUmar:

> . . . they invented false wars and unfounded stories concerning Rustam, Suhrāb, Isfandiyār, Kāʾus, Zāl, etc. [all of whom are personages in the *Shāh-Nāme* and a large number of related poems and narratives] and sent their singers to spread these idle tales (*turrahāt*) in all the bazaars of the country, as a confutation of the bravery and virtue of the Prince of the Believers [ʿAli]. This heretical practice is still observed now, and it is truly a heresy and an aberration to sing the praises of Zoroastrians in the holy Nation of Muḥammad (blessings! on him!).[25]

For such reasons was public recitation of Ferdousi's text and/or its offshoots shifted from the courtly ravi to the urban fazaʾil-khvan. The institution of the coffeehouse, already an important center of social life in Qazvin and Isfahān during the reign of Shāh ʿAbbās I (1581–1628), eventually served as a focal point for the types of recitation long heard in streets and bazaars.[26] In 1969 the repertoires of Khorasani naqqals and darvishes embraced narratives concerning both the "false wars" of Rustam and the "true holy wars" of ʿAli, as well as a large number of qasides expounding Shiʿite doctrine and praising the twelve imams. Conflict regarding the merit of each genre has continued in vigorous forms.

Minorsky has associated the variable fortunes of Shiʿite movements in Iran at this time with "the cause of the nonprivileged classes," against the (Sunni) "higher bureaucracy, which had quickly ranged itself on the side of the conquerors at the time of the Turkic and Mongol invasions": "If powerful parties can elaborate detailed systems and maintain purity of line in their doctrines, the opposition, leading a hazardous and hidden life, is forced to accept compromise and varied coalitions. On this account the unofficial Persian Islam has always preserved traces of multifarious contacts as it became more and more heterodox but more popular and accessible to the masses."[27] According to Minorsky, one of the most important aspects of popular Shi'ite religion, ceremonial commemoration of the sufferings of the martyrs, "must reflect the customs of the Dailami mountaineers" who provided the basis of support for the Ziyarid and Buyid rulers of western Iran in the ninth and tenth centuries and who thus "became the second constitutive factor in the formation of the Persian national consciousness" (after the Samanid dihqans).[28] Be this as it may, the "emotionalism" of the Shi'ite lamentations for the martyred imams has been a focus of further conflict in the musical traditions carried by the darvish and the naqqal: present-day performers adopt a wide range of positions regarding "doctrinal purity" versus "accessibility to the masses." The development of Sufic brotherhoods in the twelfth century served to institutionalize some of the practices of wandering ascetics, reciters, and mendicants, who had "exerted a powerful influence on the masses by enlarging Qur'ānic stories with the aid of materials borrowed from all kinds of sources," and who had played an important role in the Islamicization of the Central Asian Turks.[29]

The working conditions that confront the present-day darvish, naqqal, and bakhshi demand subtle adjustments whereby the performer shifts his positions, so that he acts, say, now in a more "orthodox," now in a more "popular" manner. With respect to the general musicological problem of "melody types," analysis of the circumstances of music-making in Khorasani cities provides an essential control over any usage of the concepts "type," "model," or "framework" in the analysis of Khorasani musics.

Many of the concepts by means of which musicologists have distinguished between "oral" and "written" traditions might be read as variations upon Schiller's distinction between "naïve" and "sentimental" poetry.[30] If we believe that an oral tradition makes possible a singer's capacity for spontaneous creation based upon existing models, we may perhaps regard the replacement of an oral tradition by one dependent upon writing as a "disenchantment of the world"—the Schillerian concept that so preoccupied Max

Weber. Yet continued attachment to the many variants of Schiller's distinction, or of Weber's dichotomy between *Gemeinschaftshandeln* ("social action") and *Gesellschaftshandeln* ("rationally regulated social action"), may serve to obscure the distinctions that we encounter in examining changes in the social life of Asian cities.[31] It is particularly difficult to describe the repertoires of the Khorasani darvish, naqqal, and bakhshi in terms of "regulations" or "models" that might be attributed to the constraints of oral as opposed to written poetry, since these performers depend upon the use of written texts.

In an important paper first published in 1929, Jakobson and Bogatyrev discussed many of the methodological problems arising from situations of "reciprocal influence," on an "intensive and habitual" basis, between the oral transmission of folklore and the creation of written literature. They maintained that Saussure's distinction between *langue* and *parole* provides a necessary foundation for the scholarly study of folklore, since the "preventive censorship" exercised by the community (*Gemeinschaft*) and the strict control of "norms and impulses" inherent in oral transmission impose upon folklore the same types of boundaries that define a *langue*: ". . . there are general structural laws which may not be violated by particular languages. The diversity of phonological and morphological structures is limited and can be reduced to a relatively small number of basic types, resulting from the limitations which collective creation places upon the diversity of forms. The *parole* allows for a greater range of variation than does the *langue*."[32] Bruno Nettl has made the closely related point that "because there are mnemonic problems in the oral transmission of music, the material must adhere to certain specifications in order to make retention possible."[33] In commenting upon the Jakobson-Bogatyrev paper, Albert Lord suggested that the general laws and specifications to which "oral epic performance" must conform might involve "something that is neither *langue* nor *parole*," or "something that is both *langue* and *parole* at the same time, under different aspects."[34] Lord nonetheless believed that the complex relationship between "the tradition" and "an individual creator" in performances of Yugoslav oral epic song rested upon principles common to any situation marked by "composition during oral performance": "The oral singer thinks in terms of . . . formulas and formula patterns. He *must* do so in order to compose. But when writing enters, the 'must' is eliminated. . . . When the point is reached that the break of the pattern is made consciously and is desired and felt to be 'right,' then we are in a 'literary' technique."[35] Since Khorasani performers make varied uses of musical "formulas and formula patterns" in singing existing texts, analysis of their repertoires should indicate ways in which constraints of both *langue* and *parole,* and of both oral and written transmission, may intersect.[36]

Jakobson and Bogatyrev drew a sharp opposition between "production on demand [from a patron or a social group]," characteristic of folklore, and "production for the market," practiced by a *littérateur.* This distinction entails a difference in the degree to which the *function* of a work determines its structure: whereas literature may survive without being sold on the market and without fulfilling a specific function, folklore must remain functional in order to be remembered. The "preventive censorship" that shapes each work to the demands of its function also ensures that "any intention toward transformation of his social circumstances (*Milieu*)" remains "utterly foreign" to the folk poet or singer.[37]

Jakobson and Bogatyrev discussed the range of "intermediate types" of folklore falling between those repertoires in which any member of the community might act as either producer or consumer and those "repertoires of folklore belonging to particular groups of professionals, but directed toward consumers who are [socially] distant from the producers."[38] As an example of the latter category, in which a *Gemeinschaft* of performers exercises a higher degree of "preventive censorship" than does the community of listeners, they mentioned the Russian *kaliki perekhozhie* (mendicant singers of religious verses, often organized into guilds), whose activities in some respects resemble those of certain darvish orders in Khorasan.[39] Jakobson and Bogatyrev defined the variable levels of professionalism in terms of the extent to which an oral poet or singer depends upon his performances as a source of income, and the extent to which a group of specialists exerts monopoly control over performances of a particular genre. Both types of distinctions affect the manner in which prestige is ascribed to or achieved by members of darvish orders in Khorasan.

Nonetheless, I do not believe that we can describe the work of

Khorasani performers as primarily "production on demand" (from patrons or from a guild of performers) *or* "production for the market." It is difficult to measure the effects of various constraints—those exercised by patrons, by a group of "like" performers, by actual or potential listeners in the "market." The central problem lies in assessing a performer's perception of and response to various *sets* of constraints. How does a patron state and enforce his demands? (Patrons have often exercised extremely flexible standards of acceptance.)[40] To what extent does conformity with particular standards ensure a performer's initial and continued acceptance in a particular group or guild of performers? (He may need to demonstrate some type of "originality.") What combinations of attributes induce consumers to pay for, or at least to tolerate, the performances offered on a particular market? (Consumers have frequently purchased works that openly defied the consumers' habitual modes of perception.)[41] What pressures does a consumer receive from his "peers" that inhibit his reactions to specific performances?

Performers residing in cities enjoy the prospect of obtaining support from more than one source. Once again, analysis of the working conditions of Khorasani performers should reveal ways in which individuals may deal simultaneously with pressures from several different directions.

The Darvish and the Naqqal

Most darvishes active in Meshhed and Bojnurd describe themselves as members of either the Khāksār or the Ni'matollahi orders. According to Richard Grämlich, Khaksar houses in Khorasan include two in Meshhed, one in Bojnurd, and one in Birjand; Ni'matollahi houses of the Zu'r-riyasatein branch include two in Meshhed, one in Quchan, and one in Torbat-e Heidari.[42] Under different conditions, members of both orders may engage in public performance of certain genres—sung recitation of Ferdousi's *Shāh-Nāme*, of other classical Persian poetry, and of more recent religious verse. In 1969 at least one member of the Ṣafi 'Ali Shāh branch of the Ni'matollahi, temporarily residing in Meshhed before returning to his home in Tehran, recited the *Shāh-Nāme* every day in two teahouses. Another person (probably a member of the same order) was said to perform in a third teahouse only during the nights of Ramaẓān. In conformity with Ni'matollahi strictures against "begging," neither of these men requested money from patrons of the teahouses, although the first named did accept the coins left "voluntarily" on the table before him.

Some members of the Khaksar order (including at least three of my informants in Meshhed and Bojnurd) also recite the *Shāh-Nāme* and other forms of poetry in teahouses. Others perform different genres (*a*) from stationary positions along the street, sometimes attracting a crowd by exhibiting a canvas painting on a religious subject or by displaying snakes and rats to onlookers before beginning the recitation; or (*b*) while walking up and down the streets, perhaps reading the verses from a small notebook, perhaps displaying a veiled painting suspended from the neck, and extending a bowl to receive alms from passersby.[43] In all three cases, a Khaksar darvish may appeal directly for contributions from his audience, without addressing any particular individual, all the while taking steps to "create the illusion of alms being given voluntarily."[44] Nonetheless, such performances are vehemently denounced by many persons as a socially undesirable form of "begging." Street performances occur most often in the least prosperous sections of Meshhed, such as the area around Pā'in Khiābān and Jādde Sarakhs in the northeastern quadrant of the city.

Analysis of the actions, statements, and musical performances of Khorasani darvishes requires attention to the following distinctions:

Amateur versus professional performers

Many darvishes, like other persons who are active carriers of musical traditions in Meshhed and Bojnurd, exhibit great reluctance to identify themselves as "professional performers." The terms *naqqāl* and *Shāh-Nāme-khvun* ("reciter of the *Shāh-Nāme*"), on the other hand, are used as surnames by some persons (and also designate others) who support themselves in part by recitation of the *Shāh-Nāme* and other forms of poetry in teahouses. In 1969 at least ten teahouses in Meshhed, and three or four in Bojnurd, offered daily recitations by a naqqal. Some of the naqqals interviewed in the two cities had engaged in formal study under older

29

practictioners of the art as a means to a professional career. Others had acquired their skills in recitation as part of a much broader education, a period of "service" (*khedmat-gozāri*) under a master, in preparation for assuming membership in a darvish order. The terms with which a naqqal describes his teacher might refer to the latter's role as a performer, to his other low-status jobs (if any), or to his spiritual attainments as a darvish.[45]

A darvish need not pursue any particular occupation and (unlike a naqqal) may enjoy a relatively high social status. Both Ni'matollahi and Khaksar informants agreed that the former order includes many "important men" (*bozorgān, rejāl*). A darvish who does recite poetry in public and who occupies or aspires toward a high social status may choose to emphasize his freedom from economic constraint and/or the greater distinction of his order (or his mode of performance) in comparison with others. One naqqal, a Ni'matollahi of the Safi 'Ali Shah branch, insisted that his order was "distinct (*mojazā*) from the Gunabadi or the Khaksar" precisely because the latter "do not have a good reputation (*ṣurat*)."[46] He attributed the low status of the Khaksar to the fact that "their hierarchy (*selsele*) includes those poor men (*faqir-hā*) who attract a circle [of onlookers: an activity termed *mo'areke-giri*]. Their path is begging (*gedā'i*)." The prestige of the Khaksars also suffered, in the eyes of this informant, from popular belief that "one group smokes opium and hashish" and from conflicts with the sheikhs and *akhunds* (religious authorities) of Meshhed.

Three naqqals associated with the Khaksar order did in fact describe their work as a means of gaining sustenance:

> My voice has been ruined by reciting the *Shāh-Nāme* every day in the teahouse, but I must do this to earn my bread.

> Suddenly, I saw that this work was better than poverty. My eyes and heart were opened. [This informant had previously worked as a rug-weaver.]

> I go wherever I am invited to recite religious poems. I also go to sessions (*majāles*) [of religious recitation in private homes]. I chose to earn my living working in coffeehouses. I don't have any other place to work, except the coffeehouse and the radio.

The last informant described himself as "a merchant (*tājeri*) who can recite whatever type of poem is requested." Despite his affiliation with a darvish order, his attitude resembled that expressed by a fourth naqqal who was *not* a darvish: "I sell speech (*sokhan*); I must find goods (*matā'*) so that I can sell them." Both men regarded the profession of *naqqāli* as requiring a broad repertoire, which might accommodate the tastes of many types of listeners: "It is necessary that every odor remain in the chest of a singer." The "professional" demands upon a darvish who hopes to earn an income through recitation of poetry also include possession and maintenance of an agreeable singing voice.[47] According to one naqqal in Bojnurd (not himself a member of a darvish order): "There are not any important darvishes in Bojnurd. . . . Darvishes recite religious poems in coffeehouses and collect money. They stay ten days in each city. They recite the works of Maṣnavi [*sic*], Moulavi, Sa'di, Hāfeẓ. They sing very well. If they don't sing well, no one will give them ten *shāhi* [one-half of one rial, the smallest legal Iranian coin]. Those darvishes who aren't addicted to opium sing better than the others. Addicts don't have good voices. Their voices die."

Teahouses and the streets provide different "markets" that darvishes, like other types of performers, may choose to exploit. In the former case, a performer must obtain the approval of the proprietor of the teahouse, who thus exercises a measure of control over the types of recitation offered under his auspices. Some proprietors have long-standing agreements with one or two naqqals, who recite at specified hours every day. In other cases, performers appear at unpredictable intervals. A blind *nei* player and singer whom I encountered in the bazaar of Bojnurd spoke of his desire to return to Meshhed after collecting 50 tomans ($6.50) by singing the *ghazals* of Shems Tabrizi (Moulavi). In his judgment, this repertoire was appropriate only to the teahouse, and he sang or played very different items as he sat on the streets of the bazaar.

Private versus public performance

A darvish, although he does not necessarily earn an income as a professional performer, is nonetheless one who publicly pursues a particular way of life or mode of conduct, whereas a *sufi* adheres in principle to a set of beliefs or doctrines; the distinction involves "the difference between theory and practice," with some form of prescribed actions in public situations implicit in the role of a darvish.[48] Every darvish has to some degree gained entry to the traditional wisdom transmitted by his master (*morshed* or *ustād*). He may or may not deem it desirable (or possible) to pass on in his turn a part of this wisdom, through particular circumstances of public performance. Similarly, the functions of the various types of gatherings in a *khuneqāh* (the meeting-place of a darvish order) determine the extent to which attendance is restricted to members of the order.[49]

Just as a master exercises discretion in judging the "readiness" of any pupil to receive instruction, so may a darvish assess the "worthiness" of his listeners in the teahouse, as he selects the repertoire and modes of performance for any particular occasion. A member of the Ni'matollahi order stated that "if the customers are worthy, I recite some good (*hesābi*) poems [before beginning recitation of the *Shāh-Nāme*]. I sing for people within the limits of what is appropriate to humans." A member of the Khaksar order, on the other hand, spoke of singing ghazals "to attract the attention of customers," in preparation for his subsequent recitation of the *Shāh-Nāme*. Although both spoke of "customers," the attitudes and practices of the two performers differ in (*a*) the degree to which the moral quality of the singer's verses *demands* the attention of listeners, and (*b*) the extent to which the singer actively *solicits* the interest of his (potential) audience.

The differences between the two attitudes rest on opposing concepts of "public" performance. Darvishes and naqqals may actively seek to dissociate themselves from one or the other frame of reference. A performer may take great pains to avoid giving the impression that he is "soliciting the attention of an audience"; his musical choices may insist upon the *distance* between sounds and potential listeners, saying, in effect, "This lies (somewhat) beyond your immediate capacities of assimilation and comprehension." By such means, a performer may claim that certain skills in manipulating sounds are the exclusive property of himself, his teacher, and (perhaps) his brotherhood. Furthermore, he may insist upon the didactic value of his work, as a means of calling public attention to the standards of "civility, humane behavior, abstinence from cruelty" embodied in the texts of Ferdousi and others. He may ask that his listeners submit to instruction: patrons of one teahouse in Meshhed did in fact describe a person who attends to a naqqal's words as his *murid* ("pupil"), a term normally used in the context of Sufic training. Justifications of the didactic value of a naqqal's work are applied with particular frequency to recitation of ghazavot, the narratives that recount the heroic deeds of 'Ali, although some persons attribute a greater didactic value to verses in praise of 'Ali (*madḥ-o manqābat*) which avoid the romanesque aspects of ghazavot. In similar fashion, the stories and fables known as *pandiyāt* (which often include sections of sung verse) are described by those naqqals who recite them as "exercising a good effect (*'amal*) on the intellect."[50]

Such an emphasis on didacticism colors the practice of many darvishes and naqqals, not merely the members of the Ni'matol-lahi order. The opposite point of view, the willingness to approach "begging," remains largely the province of the Khaksars, how-ever, and carries associations with a quite different repertoire—the verses, termed *rouže, moṣibat*, and *nouḥe*, that narrate and lament the martyrdom of the Shi'ite imams (particularly Ḥossein) and members of their families. Some darvishes and naqqals, along with many other persons, recite rouze and mosibat at devotional gatherings held in private homes, where listeners (particularly the older persons among them) tend to respond very emotionally, weeping profusely. In performances of nouhe, the group of dev-otees responds to the soloist's verses by repeating a short refrain line or by a beating of breasts at regular intervals of time. The singing of religious verses by Khaksar darvishes, standing or walk-ing along a street, often exhibits close affinities to the recitations given in private homes. The musical structures employed in the *shbi* (dramatic representations of events surrounding the martyr-dom of the imams) fall under the same general stylistic category.

Muslim thinkers of many persuasions have long attacked the recitation of rouze and mosibat (whether confined to the home or extending to the street, teahouse, mosque) as an exploitation, on the performer's part, of his listeners' emotional self-indulgence.[51] In general, these performers address a large public, although offi-cial disapproval has somewhat restricted public manifestations of the traditions, particularly shbi.[52] Spooner attributes much of the impact of *rouže-khvuni* to the participation of the devotees in a collective experience, although he also regards each individual's show of sympathy for Hossein as an attempt "to attract the attention of the Imams" who alone can partially bridge "the distance between man and God." In both respects, the traditions carried by the rouze-khvun and the shbi-khvun minister to needs which "official" religion refuses to acknowledge.[53]

Manners of presenting the more "didactic" repertoires in teahouses allow varying types of access to the public, determined in part by the reciter's usage of vernacular language. Each naqqal must react in one way or another to the existence of cheap printed paraphrases (and derivative versions) of the *Shāh-Nāme* stories, which are widely sold in towns and villages throughout Iran.[54] Some persons object that the elements of "fantasy" in these books emphasize entertainment in place of didacticism. On occasion, performers draw upon the style of the printed paraphrases as a model for the spoken narrative (in a more or less vernacular language) with which they introduce the recitations of Ferdousi's verse. The proportion of spoken paraphrase to sung verse varies considerably in the performances of different naqqals, according to each man's attitude toward concepts of "popularization." The same type of alternation between spoken prose and sung verse (and the same variety in a naqqal's use of printed versions with "fantastic" elements) marks the performance of ghazavot and pandiyat.

Propriety versus impropriety

Either of the preceding distinctions might be subsumed under a broader opposition between propriety and impropriety. Although naqqals and darvishes display considerable disagreement as to whether a particular type of performance is "proper," "acceptable in its place," or "improper," the question of propriety is invariably an important issue. The extreme position grants "propriety" only to those performances that establish themselves as "nonprofessional" (lacking remuneration) and "nonpublic" (avoiding efforts to attract attention). Accusations of "impropriety," which accrue with greater or lesser frequency to nearly all genres save recitation of the Qur'ān and the *azān*, frequently include the allegation that a given mode of performance fosters "fantasy, indolence, untruth," appealing only to idlers in unsavory surroundings (teahouses, street corners). Yet the opposite extreme in this polarity— embracing multiple connotations of "professional," "public," and "improper"—has been explicitly adopted by many groups of performers throughout Iranian history. According to Trimingham, "the distinction between *malāmati* and *qalandari* is that the former hides his devotion and the latter externalizes and even exploits it, going out of his way to incur blame." In this sense, the Qalandar is the predecessor of the contemporary Khaksar.[55]

The social and cultural focus upon "propriety" has generated an intensive concern with "melody types"—the most frequently discussed aspect of musical structure among Khorasani performers. Persian words used by my informants for "type" in this sense include *jur, nou', raqam, rāh,* and *ṭariqe* (literally "way" or "manner"), as well as the French loanwords *model* and *form.* Khorasani singers make distinctions among melody types in order to indicate "properties" (attributes deemed to be "proper") inherent in particular genres or characteristic of specific social groups. The following criticisms of one naqqal's manner of recitation, made by two different informants, illustrate the manner in which such discriminations are expressed in words. It is important to observe that the concept "melody type," in the usage of both informants, embraces features of singing style as well as rhythmic and tonal organization.

> *Informant A:* The man who recites on the radio is like me [because he can either read from a book or recite from memory]. But the way (*jur*) that I'd like to recite is not the way he does. The tune (*āhang*) for reciting the *Shāh-Nāme* is warlike (*razmi*). . . . I use three or four types (*jur*) of tune for reciting the entire *Shāh-Nāme.* He recites the *Shāh-Nāme* in the manner of his former occupation. . . . He didn't learn from a master (*ustād*). . . . Formerly he attracted a circle, and he uses the model of mo'areke-giri for the *Shāh-Nāme.*

> *Informant B:* The naqqal who recites on the radio is one who attracts crowds, causes people to weep, recites mosibat, and collects money from people. He entered the profession of naqqali on his own initiative, but he can't recite the *Shāh-Nāme*, because it is honorific (*tajlili*). One ought not to recite it in his way (*rāh*), as if it were a mosibat.

Informant B, like the naqqal whom he was criticizing, was a member of the Khaksar order. Informant A had learned to recite the *Shāh-Nāme* by studying for three years under an older professional but was not himself associated with a darvish order.

Although both men readily described themselves as professional performers, their remarks insist upon the need for distinguishing the "warlike" or "honorific" styles proper to the *Shāh-Nāme* from those used by "less educated" performers who "attract crowds" and "take money from people." Informant A further described the melodic practice applied indiscriminantly by the latter type of performer to both mosibat and the *Shāh-Nāme:* "There isn't just one type (*jur*) of tune for mosibat. It must be spoken until I kindle a reverberation (*mon'akes*) in your mind (*nazar*)."

Criticism of the melody types and vocal styles employed by *other* performers functions as a sort of disclaimer, whereby a naqqal asserts that he is *not* engaging in one or another sort of "undesirable" (improper) activity. His musical choices advance similar disclaimers. The manner in which a performer adopts particular melody types and singing styles while avoiding others suggests that he justifies his position within a complex social network by this means. When asked to name those men from whom he had acquired his repertoire and his techniques of recitation, each naqqal mentioned one or more of the following: (*a*) his father, invariably described as having recited "only in the home"; (*b*) his teacher (either a darvish or a "professional reciter"); (*c*) other performers in Meshhed or Bojnurd to whom he had listened; (*d*) other darvishes with whom he had come into contact (often while they were visiting Meshhed as pilgrims). There was remarkably little duplication or overlapping in the names cited in each of these respects by the eight naqqals whom I interviewed in Meshhed and Bojnurd. Although further information is needed on this point, it would appear that each performer lays claim to a distinctive confluence of "traditions." I was unable to locate two performers who admitted having learned techniques or material from the same source, although two naqqals expressed admiration for the darvish criticized by Informants A and B. Most comments made by one naqqal on another's work adopted a critical tone, similar to that of Informants A and B. Words of praise were generally couched in comparative terms: "X has a better voice than Y, but Y tells the story better than X."

The teacher may bestow his sanction upon a pupil in a somewhat ceremonial manner, as described by two naqqals who were members of the Khaksar and Ni'matollahi orders, respectively:

Informant B: He gave me permission to speak. Everything that I know, I must say honestly. . . . If someone tells me to pack up my books, I can tell him to get lost.

Informant C: After twelve years in his service, we went holding hands to the bazaar, the coffeehouse. . . . He introduced me as one of his sons (*farzandān*) and said, "Today I want to place him behind this table to speak." He sent forth a *ṣalavot* and gave me permission to begin.

Subsequent attachment to the teacher's practice, both in recitation and in critical judgments, provides a justification of one's own propriety. A performer may judge his contemporaries against standards attributed to his teacher or to the latter's epoch. Informant A supported his criticism of the confusion between the styles appropriate to the *Shāh-Nāme* and to mo'areke-giri by (erroneously) denying the very existence of the latter in better days: "Attracting a crowd is not good. It is injurious to Iranians. In the time of my master (*ustād*), these setups (*dastgāh-hā*) and these circles did not exist."[56]

The social circumstances of performance nonetheless make it impossible for a naqqal to justify himself solely by reference to his teacher's "authority." He insists upon his own mastery and attempts to circumvent potential challenges to his position. Proprietors of teahouses, as well as customers, employ the noun *ustād* (master) in comparative degrees: "X is *ustādtar* (more of a master) than Y"; "X is the *ustād* (superior) of Y." A performer quotes various proverbial expressions on his own behalf, praising himself by denying that he is doing so:

Informant A: I don't praise myself. Praise has no result; art must make itself known. After me, I don't think anyone else will recite with such power and such worth. No one will do this, because it's very difficult.

It is difficult (and dangerous) to display trust in one's pupils or listeners. Informant B observed that his teacher "looks into a pupil's eyes to decide whether he is capable of this work."

Reactions to radio broadcasts illustrate the naqqal's art of maintaining face by overt refusal of one or another existing practice. The objections raised by Informants A and B against the style of recitation broadcast by Radio Meshhed were extended by other naqqals to the very idea of presenting the *Shāh-Nāme* on the air (a practice initiated by the local radio station in 1969):

> *Informant C:* They invited me to recite [the *Shāh-Nāme*] on the radio, but I refused to go, because I must work as an individual.
>
> *Informant D:* [The radio broadcasts] are not good. "The proof of the musk is its own odor, not what the perfumer says about it."[57]

As a form of popularization through mechanical reproduction, the radio, like the printed paraphrases of *Shāh-Nāme* stories in vernacular language, represents a threat to the "authority" of both the performer and his repertoire. An analyst interested in the effects of technological change might interpret this conflict along the lines suggested by Walter Benjamin: "The authenticity (*Echtheit*) of a thing is the essence of all that is transmissible from its beginning, ranging from its substantive duration to its testimony to the history which it has experienced. Since the historical testimony rests on the authenticity, the former, too, is jeopardized when substantive duration ceases to matter. And what is really jeopardized when the historical testimony is affected is the authority of the object. . . . That which withers in the age of mechanical reproduction is the aura of the work of art."[58] The circumstances of public recitation in the teahouse, in which the proprietor and his customers evaluate a performer's style, allow the latter to control the references of his actions to "history"—through obvious means (choice of repertoire; reading from an ancient book or manuscript in his family's possession) as well as more subtle ones (the timing of his musical decisions).

Yet we have seen that the choice of "accessibility to the masses" over "doctrinal purity" distinguished the activities of some Khorasani performers in the eleventh and twelfth centuries. Over the past millenium, performers have attempted to exercise different types of authority against constant challenges. The naqqal who recited over the radio in the style of mo'areke-giri identified himself with a different set of circumstances, a different "aura," than those allowed by his critics, who insisted upon a greater distance between performer and listener. Following Ernest Gellner, we might speak of a continuum extending from the concept of "communal consensus" on the left to the idea of "organization, leadership, ancestry" on the right: " 'Left' and 'Right' are here in effect defined in terms of egalitarianism versus hierarchy and hereditary inequality."[59] Before examining the musical techniques with which a darvish increases or reduces the distance between himself and his listeners, I will discuss the working conditions of the bakhshi.

The Bakhshi

Like the naqqal, the Khorasani bakhshi earns a portion of his income through performance of several musico-poetic genres—in this case, Kurdish narratives and verses praising khans and sardars, Turkic narratives (*hekāyatler*) concerning famous pairs of lovers, Turkic and Kurdish verses (largely with a religious import) attributed to legendary poets (*āsheqlar*),[60] other songs and dance pieces—all of them accompanied with the *dutār*, a long-necked lute with two strings. The bakhshi has traditionally drawn on several possible sources of support: (*a*) the patronage of khans (leaders of tribal clans with fixed residences), over extended periods of time; (*b*) occasional "one-night stands" in the homes of interested persons; performances (*c*) in urban teahouses, (*d*) at village weddings, and (*e*) at picnic spots on the outskirts of towns and in certain villages where large groups of people gather for entertainment. In the latter two circumstances, he competes with other types of popular musicians who are termed *motreb* and *āsheq*.

At the beginning of this century, a number of bakhshis appear to have attached themselves to individual khans, for whom they performed more or less exclusively: a bakhshi active in Bojnurd in 1969 described an older man to whom he had listened in his youth as "one of the bakhshis of Faraj Qoli Khān." A second bakhshi in Bojnurd recounted his affiliation with Sayyed Rashid, an outlaw (apparently of Gypsy origin) who took a strong interest in the traditional bakhshi repertoire and occasionally retained one or two singers in his service. Yet the bakhshis of Sayyed Rashid eventually moved on to travel from village to village, as their services were needed. Proprietors of teahouses have also attempted to assert exclusive rights to a particular bakhshi's performances. A bakhshi in Bojnurd remarked that the owner of the teahouse where he sang nightly did not allow him to perform elsewhere and kept his dutar hanging on the wall as a symbol of this bond—all of which did not prevent him from singing at village weddings. Thus, for the past several decades, the bakhshi has worked both for "patrons" and in diverse "markets," urban and rural. The important collection of Khorasani Kurdish folklore made by Ivanov in 1918–20 includes a story describing a dutar player who was kidnapped by the Turkmen, then rescued by government troops and taken to Tehran, where he performed for the Shah until loneliness spurred his return to Khorasan after a refusal of the Shah's pleas that he remain at the court.[61]

The patronage of shahs and khans was no longer available to Khorasani bakhshis in 1969, although one man had traveled to Tehran for "folkloric" performances. Each of the bakhshis interviewed in Meshhed and Bojnurd had supplemented his income, at one time or another, with other types of work: as a gardener, cobbler, carpenter, barber, tinker, or ice-carrier.[62] In 1972, at least four bakhshis resided in Bojnurd, performing in teahouses or at picnic spots, and traveling to villages in the surrounding region. Although roughly two-thirds of the population of Bojnurd speak a Turkic dialect, many persons seemed unaware that nightly performances of Turkic narratives were offered in one teahouse. Nearly everyone who was questioned, on the other hand, knew at least one of the three or four teahouses where naqqals recited the *Shāh-Nāme* on a regular basis. As Ilhan Başgöz observed in Azerbaijan, performances of Turkic oral literature in urban teahouses may appeal more to villagers visiting the town than to permanent residents.[63] At any rate, the bakhshis of Bojnurd are clearly dependent upon their journeys to village weddings and circumcisions. This is even more the case in Meshhed, where I found only one bakhshi who controlled a large repertoire of both Turkic and Kurdish verse. During our conversations, this informant named over ninety villages to which he had traveled. His performances in the immediate region of Meshhed (where few persons understand Turkic languages) emphasized other portions of his repertoire, in place of the long narratives that he sang for villagers in Turkic areas.

A bakhshi enjoys the heaviest demand for his services at village weddings in the season from late autumn until the New Year (March 21). Two informants mentioned receiving fees ranging from 50 to 70 tomans ($6.50 to $9.10) for performances at village weddings. By way of comparison, members of the urban middle classes often hire ensembles of four or five persons to perform at weddings for 200 to 1000 tomans ($26 to $133). Reports of the rewards given by khans in whose honor a bakhshi had sung verses ranged from 20 tomans (from a minor Kurdish outlaw) to 200 (from a rebel in the Sarakhs region for whom one bakhshi composed verses in Persian). One informant remarked that he normally received 100 tomans for one evening of singing in a private home. He might hope to equal this sum by performing in public parks all day on Friday, but he could expect no more than 30 or 40 tomans on weekdays. He claimed that a bakhshi might collect 100 to 130 tomans in public parks every day of the week in the late 1950s. Bakhshis, like other musicians, remain silent throughout the religious months of Moharram and Safar (which occur in different seasons, following the Arabic lunar calendar); some informants indicated that they engaged in rouze-khvuni and darvishi during this period.

Like the naqqal, the present-day bakhshi acts only to a limited extent as a professional performer. His willingness to perform in public situations varies with changes in his circumstances; in 1969, for example, one landowner who had formerly served as one of the bakhshis of Sayyed Rashid considered public performance to lie beneath his current social standing. Of necessity, a bakhshi commands other skills with which he can support himself. He sometimes speaks of a father or an uncle who sang portions of the bakhshi repertoire "only in private, for the family and a few friends." He struggles against various concepts of "propriety" with which major portions of his repertoire are in conflict.

The Kurdish narratives and verses praising khans and sardars constitute a repertoire which has become "improper" from one point of view because of political change. Most of the protagonists of these narratives acted as outlaws or rebels against provincial or national authorities. The oldest sequence of verses in the current repertoire describes the participation of a group of Kurdish khans in the struggle between Mohammad Teqi Khān and Reẓā Shāh (then Reẓa Khān) in the early 1920s.[64] The most popular verses (accounting for eleven out of eighteen recorded

41

performances) are those associated with Sayyed Rashid, his son Khalil Sardār, and his companion Ḥabib Ṣādeqi: folklore has endowed Sayyed Rashid, who was killed by government troops in the early sixties, with the stature befitting a protector of the poor, an enemy of the rich.[65] His activity as a patron of bakhshis may have fostered the wide currency of the verses in his honor. One informant who had performed before the outlaw recounted Sayyed Rashid's preference for the refrain line *Shir-e meidān Rashid Sardār* in place of the more common *Shir-e meidān Rashid Khāna* (see ex. 5a below), since the epithet *khān* implies a fixed residence, a restraint upon the freedom of a *sardār*. The strong centralized power exercised by Reẓā Shāh during the thirties and eventually reestablished by his son in the sixties effectively checked the activities of rebels and outlaws. We may assume that the verses in the current repertoire were created as a function of the greater social instability characteristic of the twenties and fifties—periods of weak central authority. It is unlikely that new uprisings, stimulating the composition of new verses, will occur in the near future, and the frequency of performance of existing verses may gradually decline. One bakhshi (the same one who has given folkloric performances in Tehran) stated quite explicitly in 1969 that it was no longer "suitable" to sing the verses praising Sayyed Rashid, now that he had been killed by the government. These verses nonetheless remain extremely popular with other Khorasani performers, including singers who do not engage in public performance for profit. Verses once composed to honor or commemorate a particular khan may remain available for performance in other circumstances. A bakhshi living in Meshhed claimed to have composed verses for Nou Ruz Khān (who gave him a small reward), but he attributed the poem which he sang in 1969 to the latter's widow.[66]

The Turkic narratives of lovers have acquired an aura of "impropriety" for reasons quite different from the increasingly centralized control of outlaws. Performance of the Turkic hekayats, unlike the singing of Kurdish narrative verse, alternates between spoken prose and sung verse (which represents the words of characters in the story). A single hekayat may continue for two or three days and nights at a wedding, or several afternoons of reci-

tation in a teahouse. The length of time consumed by such narratives, along with the overtly "romantic" and "legendary" content of the hekayats, causes some religious leaders and educators
to charge that the tales encourage idleness and escapism. The fact
that a number of bakhshis are addicted to opium serves to cast
further doubts upon the "propriety" of the repertoire in some
circles. One bakhshi active in Bojnurd spoke of the "intoxication"
(*heif*), induced by opium, that enabled him to sustain a variable
level of excitement throughout a long narrative; he had served a
term in prison for his addiction.

The "impropriety" attached to the Turkic narratives recalls the
common charges that the verses and tales recited by naqqals and
darvishes serve merely to pass the time of the unemployed, filling
vacant minds with fantasy and amusement. The modernist view
of both "popular entertainment" and "popular religion" as symp-
toms of a culture of poverty, far removed from twentieth-century
ideals of social and economic well-being,[67] echoes in some respects
the criticisms leveled at "fantasy" by many Muslim scholars and
educators (including some darvishes). Both the bakhshi and the
naqqal confront a common set of problems in attempting to survive with a measure of dignity in a largely hostile environment.
We have seen that the three distinctions discussed above with
reference to the naqqal are equally pertinent to a description of
the bakhshi's working conditions. Three further distinctions are
also important in examining the role(s) of the bakhshi, with implications as well for my earlier analysis of the naqqal's activities.

Literacy versus illiteracy

For the most part (with exceptions to be noted below), a naqqal
or a bakhshi is distinguished from the general public by his literacy. The availability of printed or manuscript texts has long
been an essential factor in maintaining the oral traditions associated with both the naqqal and the bakhshi. In the case of the
bakhshi repertoire, the Turkic hekayats are widely diffused by
means of manuscripts and inexpensive prints,[68] whereas the Kurdish verses in praise of khans and sardars are transmitted solely
by ear. The existence of a printed or manuscript text serves in
fact as a major criterion in the "folk classification" of musical

styles, just as the fact of literacy to some extent defines the professions of the naqqal and the bakhshi. Statements of three bakhshis active in Bojnurd emphasized this point:

> *Informant E:* I learned the Turkic *qeṣṣe* [in this context, a synonym for *ḥekāyat*] from books. Anyone can discover a song and sing it, but books are necessary for singing Turkic verses.
>
> *Informant F:* Something that isn't written down, we don't call a story (*dāstān*); songs like "Khajei lore" and "Lālezār" we made ourselves. It isn't a story when we collect some verses about a girl.
>
> *Informant G:* [When asked if he could sing the hekayats of "Ṭāher Zohre" and "Karam Aṣli"] No, since I'm not literate. You have to sing those from books. You've got to have books, baby.

A bakhshi may not be literate, though he seldom recites from books or manuscripts in actual performance (unlike a naqqal, for whom a printed or manuscript version of the *Shāh-Nāme* is often an important "prop"). Among the persons interviewed, every bakhshi had nonetheless made use of printed or manuscript versions either for learning the Turkic hekayats or for maintaining them in his memory. A bakhshi in Meshhed, himself illiterate, mentioned that he relied on hearing the stories read to him by his nephew in order to refresh his memory. Informant E (quoted above) possessed a large number of notebooks in which he had copied many hekayats, along with other Turkic and Kurdish verses. These notebooks, which apparently combined materials learned in oral tradition with others acquired through reading, served primarily as memory aids. Naqqals and darvishes similarly made use of notebooks for copying down important segments of their repertoires. Bakhshis and naqqals alike counted manuscripts and notebooks among their most highly prized possessions and frequently described the provenance of a particular book or manuscript in some detail.

An important aspect of literacy among the bakhshis of Bojnurd involves the ability to deal with materials in different Turkic languages and dialects. The relationships of the various Turkic dialects spoken in Khorasan to Azerbaijani, on the one hand, and Turkmen, on the other, await investigation by linguists.[69] The bakhshis active in Bojnurd associate some of their books and manuscripts with each of the three regions (Khorasan itself, Azerbaijan, Central Asia). Statements of two informants raised the question of a performer's modifications of the written text; and it is clear that a substantial amount of alteration does occur in "reading." Informant F insisted that Khorasani bakhshis invariably sing verses printed in Azerbaijan "in a different dialect and to different tunes." Informant E, on the other hand, took pride in claiming that he did not change the language of Azerbaijani books to match the speech of Bojnurd: "There is no one else here in Bojnurd who can tell these stories as they are printed in the books; I sing what is printed. . . . [Prints and manuscripts] come from Azerbaijan, from the Turkmen, from Tajikistan." Speaking of a Turkmen manuscript containing the story of Gurogli, Informant E described its language as "very ancient": "It can't be read. It *can* be read, but only by one with more literacy than I." Informant E's large repertoire nonetheless includes verses in several Turkic dialects, and (despite his denials) he appears to be highly skilled in making adjustments and "translations" of one sort or another.

A naqqal or a bakhshi who possessed a number of books and manuscripts might nonetheless boast of his lack of dependence upon these aids. The naqqal quoted above as Informant A described himself as "a bookless person," adding that "there's no difference if I read from a book or recite from memory; I don't need a book." Several informants, in praising a particular bakhshi, noted his capacity to recite a story "from beginning to end," although most actual performances consist of segments or self-contained sections of the stories. A good bakhshi performs "from memory" (*az bār*); his mind is said to be "very full" (*kheili pur*) of verse and prose in the proper sequences.

Memorization versus originality

Fortified by his literacy and even more so by his memory, a bakhshi thus performs poetry that allegedly exists in fixed, written form, with a value that derives from its antiquity and from the fact of its preservation. When questioned about various sorts of material in their repertoires (including verses that they claimed to have composed themselves), bakhshis often replied that "ancient poems are the most important." The values of "antiquity" and "preservation by means of writing" extend to the Turkic and Kurdish verses ascribed to legendary 'asheqs as well as to the

Turkic hekayat. It is possible that the contrast between the Turkic hekayat (a closed repertoire) and the Kurdish songs praising khans and sardars (a repertoire which has acquired new verses in recent times) has lent a greater degree of prestige to the former. For whatever reason, the Kurdish verses bear the impress of Turkic models. The power of the Turkmen in the nineteenth and early twentieth centuries (a time of weak central authority in Persia) may have lent considerable prestige to Turkmen musical styles in northern Khorasan.[70] Khorasani Turks share the preference of their Turkmen neighbors for memorizing existing verses rather than creating new ones. The musical traditions carried by the Khorasani bakhshi differ from those of the Turkmen in at least one important respect, however: whereas scholars have frequently mentioned "the traditionally weak development of the dance" among the Turkmen,[71] the musical structures of the Khorasani bakhshi make frequent reference to dance types.

Like many bakhshis, Informant E was somewhat scornful of the activity of "making arrangements" (tanzim kardan) of Kurdish and Persian folksongs for broadcast over the radio. The extent to which bakhshis, in their verbal statements, stress the importance of memorizing ancient verses inhibits discussion of the many techniques of "arrangement" that a bakhshi must employ in performing existing texts. Nevertheless, a bakhshi's choices in the following respects cover a wider range of variants than do the relatively limited techniques (along similar lines) used in radio arrangements: (a) the prose context in which the poems are sung; the balance between verse and prose; (b) the length and position of dutar interludes; (c) the addition of "extra" syllables and refrain lines not included in the written text; (d) variant "readings" of the printed verses; (e) the possible repetition of certain lines two or three times, presumably for musical reasons. The greater value attached to "memorization" over "originality" or "arrangement" implies in this case an emphasis upon the bakhshi's gaining access to a repertoire that contains within itself many possibilities for individual differences in mode of performance. Thus, a bakhshi discusses "the balance between verse and prose" as an attribute of each narrative, without talking about the ways in which his own choices affect this balance.[72]

Learning versus ignorance

The Khorasani bakhshi controls a repertoire that includes many of the same dance pieces commonly performed by motrebs—musicians, dancers, clowns, and acrobats who, like the bakhshi, provide entertainment at weddings in both towns and villages. His mastery of the dutar nonetheless distinguishes the bakhshi from the motreb, who is more likely to play a different instrument (kemenche, gheichek, violin, tar, sorna, qushma, doire, or dohol). More significantly, the bakhshi's repertoire extends beyond the common stock of dance pieces to embrace many genres that are foreign to the motreb's world. It is these types of music-making (the Turkic and Kurdish narratives and religious verses) that make it possible for a bakhshi to present himself as a man of "learning." The rhythmic and melodic structures used by a bakhshi in performing Turkic and Kurdish verse make reference to the stereotyped patterns of dance music, though a process of "sublimation" whereby certain relatively predictable features of the dance patterns are interrupted, expanded, or contradicted.[73]

The concept of sublimation points toward the essential distinction between the skills acquired by a bakhshi and those picked up by a motreb. For the latter, skill as a "singer" is subordinate to control of the body in dancing, comic routines, and playing of instruments. In the troupes of about half a dozen motrebs that often perform at celebrations and public gatherings, each member generally has some competence in more than one type of activity: he may function in turn as instrumentalist (*sāzande* or *navāzande*), dancer (*rāqqās* or *bāzigar*), actor (*moqalled*), acrobat (*bāzigar*), athlete (*pahlavān* or *varzeshkār*), magician (*hoqqe-bāz* or *jādugar*). Interaction among the members of the group results in what is termed "playful clowning" (*bāzi*), marked by deliberate vulgarity and impropriety. A troupe of motrebs encourages the "audience" to participate in its joking behavior, setting aside for a time the restraints of rectitude and politeness. The term *jāheli* connotes a manner of speech, of facial gestures, of physical stance, and of etiquette that may be adopted by both performers and audiences in situations of amusement. In the words of one informant, "a *jāhel* is a man who knows nothing, who doesn't know

how it's done." The skills of a motreb are similarly defined by onlookers in negative terms: "He can't do anything; he lets his hair
grow long and wears women's clothes." In other words, a motreb
encourages a release of the tensions attached to "correct" behavior precisely by acting "ignorant."

A bakhshi's "learning," on the other hand, represents a claim
to personal control of special skills, achieved by dint of diligent
effort. Whereas motrebs have traditionally defended themselves
against Islamic opposition to music-making by banding together
in troupes and guilds, single performers have been obliged to attach themselves to patrons possessing a degree of power or prestige sufficient to afford protection.[74] Verbal justifications of one-
self as a man of learning may represent a similar adaptive strategy.
Like the naqqal, the bakhshi frequently stresses his personal efforts to acquire and to transmit the cultural heritage of "ancient"
times—a legitimate and necessary activity from an Islamic stand-
point. In conversations, some naqqals expressed respect for particular bakhshis for these reasons, although others dismissed the
Turkic romances as unworthy forms of poetry. As Chodzko observed, the Turkic verses ascribed to legendary 'asheqs deal explicitly with religious and ethical topics. It is not surprising that
the bakhshi's verbal descriptions of his own activities emphasize
his literacy (if any) and his "full" memory, rather than his "musi-
cianship" and performance techniques. Nevertheless, his musical
choices often seem calculated to differentiate his performances
from those offered by motrebs and from those broadcast over the
radio. Not every dutar player is called a bakhshi, although usage
of this term varies according to one's demands: some persons accept a performer with a small repertoire of dance pieces and popular songs as a bakhshi.

The "learned" or "elevated" styles cultivated by some darvishes,
naqqals, and bakhshis demand a measure of exclusion: not everyone can be literate, or control a large memory, or escape the economic constraints that block the attainment of "amateur" status.
As a result, a performer must distinguish his singing from the practices of "negative reference groups." He demonstrates neither
"learning" nor "propriety" if he is too easily understood. For this
reason, the specialized techniques developed by Iranian singers
have retained a broad range of options for creating idiosyncratic

variants which resist immediate assimilation into one or another concept of "genre."

The Usage of Rhythmic and Melodic Frameworks

As singers, the darvish, the naqqal, and the bakhshi must deal with the following problems, among others: (a) remembering existing texts; (b) creating new lines where appropriate; (c) adjusting musico-poetic genres to particular circumstances. Examination of the rhythmic and melodic frameworks employed for these purposes may begin with close attention to the extent to which each line in a given performance aligns itself with the most stable forms of rhythmic organization occurring in the performance. It may pay equal attention to the overall pattern of changes, the degree of variability in rhythmic placement that distinguishes the entire performance (as a "polyphony of lines," presented in succession but remembered to some extent in simultaneity)[75] in relation to other performances experienced by the same musicians and listeners. Although we may find that a given genre, or a particular set of circumstances, generally allows the performer a relatively high level of variation along these lines, the extent to which he exercises such options seems to be limited by the role he wishes to adopt with respect to his listeners.

In his penetrating survey of Arabic folk music, Amnon Shiloah examines the issue of "melodic patterns" in terms of a polarity between "simple melody with short repeated formulas performed in an antiphonal or responsorial way" and "relatively more sophisticated songs which considerably withdraw from the simplicity, the uniformity and the restriction in range and tone content of the former ones" and are "essentially soloistic." Shiloah speaks of an intermediate category, lying between these two extremes, in which, despite "the frequent use of simple repeated formulas . . . the melodies are more complex in form, melodic organization, range and tonality." It is in fact one of the strengths of Shiloah's discussion, like Artur Simon's similar typology of Egyptian folk music, that his categories are defined as ideal types, making possible an assessment of the *extent* to which any given performance approaches or departs from any or all of the distinctive qualities used to define one end of the continuum.[76] Shiloah believes that those songs fall-

ing to a greater or lesser degree in his first category foster "participation of the audience"; and it is perhaps reasonable to assume
that momentary departures, more complex variants of the "short
repeated formulas" may temporarily challenge (perhaps even lose)
the group of listeners. In other words, I am suggesting that the
notion of "audience participation" might embrace not only overt
actions (singing a response, clapping, shouting encouragement,
and so forth), but also the possibility of the group's renewing its
grasp of an "essential" pattern at those points of greater rhythmic
"simplicity" where a group could clap together or sing a unison
response.[77]

Shiloah observes that the restricted number of pitches in songs
of his first category makes possible a "rhythmical richness . . . expressed through more complicated formulas," although "simple
and straightforward [rhythmic] formulas are not excluded." He
further notes that "the links between the simpler tunes [of the
first category] and particular functions are very flexible and not
determinant." In these respects, the question of genre in Near
Eastern vocal practice affords a striking contrast to Nketia's generalized description of genre in West Africa: "An aspect of the
art of African music consists in varying the complexity of . . . tex-
ture as well as its intensity through the preselection of instrumental devices and the structural mold into which the sounds are
fitted. This variation, however, is largely confined to musical types
rather than to individual items or to performance. . . . Hence the
variety of instrumental sounds tends to be distributed in relation
to the formal types that are recognized."[78] In Khorasan, musico-
poetic genres cannot be defined with the degree of clarity and
precision attained by Nketia's study of Fon and Ashanti genres
(and types of ensembles) in relationship to changes in political institutions, particularly the patronage of kings.[79] Nor does the terminology that describes the roles of Khorasani musicians represent
distinct and mutually exclusive categories, as does that employed
by the Hausa of Zaria City.[80] The high level of variability in the
"individual items" performed by Khorasani darvishes, naqqals,
and bakhshis yields only a very flexible concept of "genre," which
changes as the performer attempts to define his own role on any
given occasion.

Khorasani performers employ several techniques for distributing sounds in time, in order to create difficulties for listeners *to a greater or lesser extent,* as a means of allowing different degrees of "comprehension" and/or "participation." In extreme cases, the performer's choices may almost insist upon what Gregory Bateson has called "camouflage (the opposite of communication)." In many instances his performance "first proposes a rule of symmetry and then subtly denies the rule by proposing a more complex combination of rules."[81]

Although the naqqal and the bakhshi act primarily as soloists, the repertoires of both include or refer to genres that elicit active musical responses from a group. Elicitation of a response generally involves emphasis upon "simple and straightforward" groupings of an equal pulse, with relatively harsh attacks. The broad spectrum of means for establishing, abandoning, and returning to a pulse extends over many variants which foster different levels of "comprehension." At one end of the continuum stand

(a) equal pulses played on a *dohol* (barrel drum) or *doire* (frame drum) in the dance pieces of the motreb repertoire;

(b) strong pulses maintained by regular beating of breasts (or flagellation of the back with chains) in *nouhe sine-zani* and *zenjir-zani.*

Both *a* and *b* typically move within "stable" rhythmic frameworks, with relatively constant groupings of pulses into measures and of measures into phrases. Both are commonly considered less "proper" and less "learned" than the variants grouped at the opposite end of the spectrum:

(c) lines and strophes in which a bakhshi effects a regular grouping of "percussive" attacks on the dutar, throwing into sharp relief those portions of the lines or strophes where the instrumental attacks are less sharp and/or less regular;

(d) solo recitation of religious verses in which a naqqal or a darvish consistently avoids placing the vocal attacks in successive lines at the same positions in time, perhaps establishing a greater regularity at the end of a section.

The verbal statements of Khorasani performers occasionally reflected an awareness of the range of variants lying between these two extremes (*a* and *b* as opposed to *c* and *d*). The naqqal quoted above as Jnformant B remarked that he could sing the songs of a particular motreb for his friends and acquaintances (but *not* for the "public"), adding, "If I sing such songs, it is without doire. Instead, everyone sits around in a circle and strikes two fingers against the palm of his hand." This particular substitute for the motreb's drumming lent a more intimate, less public aura to the naqqal's versions of popular songs—a style somewhat similar to that of the bakhshi, which this informant in fact described as "sweeter" than the singing style of a motreb. In this instance, the modification of *a* involved a lessening of the "harshness" (rather than the equal spacing) of the doire pulses.

A bakhshi may play dance pieces on the dutar, perhaps at the same time singing verses to the metric pattern of the dance. Listeners are rarely, if ever, immobile during performances of dance songs. Even if no one is dancing, listeners may clap either throughout the performance or only during the refrains. They may also join in singing some or all of the refrains. A dance song invariably includes sections that move away from the simplest version of the metric pattern, limiting the possibilities for a group response, by an increased inequality of pulse and/or by an expansion of the range (and number) of pitches. The bakhshi may himself clarify the musical structure at refrains or at terminations of lines by tapping a pulse on his dutar or by returning (with voice, dutar, or both) to the equal pulse or the regular grouping of pulses (or the narrower range of pitches) that he had temporarily abandoned. In the dance pieces performed by a bakhshi, handclapping, tapping on the belly of the dutar, and percussive attacks on the strings serve as modifications of the drumbeats that characterize the motreb's versions.

Example 1 illustrates one type of alternation between departures from a dance pattern and returns to a "regular" group of refrain lines. It is taken from the sorna and dohol accompaniment to a comic skit performed at a village wedding by a group of motrebs who work both in and around the city of Meshhed. The entire performance alternated between seven statements of the refrain (with a fair amount of variation) and seven "departures" or solos, played by the sorna over a series of ungrouped pulses on the dohol. During the solo lines, a motreb who had dressed as a woman danced alone in a sexually provocative manner, making faces and gestures which elicited laughter from the audience of

Ex. 1

men and boys. When another motreb bumped into the "woman's" rear end, the instrumentalists moved to the refrains, and more persons (including some spectators) joined in the dancing and handclapping. The juxtaposition of duple and triple meters (6/8 against 3/4) in the refrains of Example 1 occurs frequently in Iranian folk and popular music.

Example 2, taken from a commercial recording by the singer Setar Zade (with his own dutar accompaniment), is a dance song that alternates verses in Kurdish with refrains in the Turkic dialect of Bojnurd and Quchan. In this case, the refrain remains constant after each of the three verses, of which only the second is given in the transcription. Throughout the performance, a group provides handclapping on every third eighth-note. The verses link together three lines of eight syllables each (covering four dotted-quarter-note pulses in the transcription), which share a common rhyme, and the same tristich also occurs as a unit of text in other songs (such as ex. 3a below). In example 2, however, each line of the tristich is followed by an "extension" of seven or eight additional syllables (marked in the transcription and in table 1 by brackets).[82] The dutar interlude that introduces each verse presents two melodic phrases, the first of which is subsequently employed for each line of the tristich, the second for the extensions. Table 1 indicates the variable number of syllables in each line, along with changes in the total range and the cadence points of the two melodic phrases. The superscripts outline the highest and lowest scale degrees included in each phrase; the cadence of a phrase invariably occurs on the lowest of these tones. While the

TABLE 1

	Number of Syllables	Number of Pulses	Phrases of Tune
Interlude		$4 + 4$	$A^{5/2} + B^{5/1}$
		$4 + 4 + (2)$	$A^{5/2} + B^{5/1} + (X)$
Tristich	$8 + [7]$	$4 + 4$	$A^{7/4} + B^{7/1}$
	$8 + [8]$	$4 + 4 + (4)$	$A^{7/2} + B^{4/1} + (X)$
	$8 + [7]$	$4 + 4$	$A^{7/4} + B^{7/1}$
Refrain	$8 + 8$	$4 + 4$	$A^{7/3} + B^{5/1}$
	$7 + 7$	$4 + 4$	$A^{7/3} + B^{4/1}$
	9	4	$B^{4/1}$
	$10 + 3 + 7$	$4 + 4$	$A^{7/2} + B^{4/1}$

Ex. 2

verses expand the range of both melodic phrases to encompass a minor seventh, the refrain gradually renews the initial emphasis upon lower cadence points in the first phrase and a smaller total range in the second. This aspect of pitch organization is consistent with the contrast between the occasional extended durations in the verses and the greater equality of pulse in both refrains and interludes.

The ordering of pitches in example 2 closely resembles that of example 1; the same scale is presented in similar segments in both cases, as indicated in the accompanying diagrams of the essential melodic contour. In example 1, however, the relationship between the two tetrachords (in both the refrain and the solo sections) is not fitted within a symmetrical alternation between two melodic phrases of four pulses each, as in example 2.

Example 3a sung by a bakhshi in Bojnurd to his own dutar accompaniment, presents a variant of the same tristich heard in example 2 preceded and followed by a different group of refrain

lines, this time in Kurdish. The performer went on to sing a second tristich and returned to the same refrain lines; these sections are not included in the transcription. As in example 2, the tristichs and the refrains are distinguished by contrasting rhyme schemes. Example 3b illustrates the manner in which the same performer employed a similar melody type for singing verses from the Turkic hekayat of *Köroghli*, which he read from a book printed in Tabriz. The entire performance from which example 3b is extracted included twenty-four quatrains, sung to two different melody types and placed within six sections of prose narration. Typically, a group of four or five quatrains share a common final line, which functions as a short refrain. In both performances (exx. 3a and 3b), the singer inserted dutar interludes at various points and emphasized the terminations of some vocal lines by tapping on the dutar.

In example 3a (a dance song), the tapping within the central portion of each line functions as a substitute for handclapping, establishing a series of four equal pulses beneath each eight-syllable line. The tapping on the fourth pulse (and the eighth syllable) of each line generally sets up cross-rhythms against the earlier triple subdivision of each pulse. The cross-rhythms are always omitted in the final line of the refrain, in favor of "extra" syllables (again marked by brackets in the transcription and in table 2) that extend the line with two or four additional pulses. The terminations of lines in example 3a are thus marked by either a cross-rhythm tapped on the dutar or by one or two groups of five "extra" syllables. Table 2 indicates the relationship between the "extra" syllables in the tristich and the refrain; the variable groupings of pulses; and the phrase structure of the melodic line. Comparison

Ex. 3a

of the diagrams taken from examples 2 and 3a reveals the central position in the latter of a single melodic phrase, surrounded by contrasting melodic shapes that terminate (phrase B) or initiate (phrase X) the principal phrase and that coincide with the "extra" syllables on either side of the eight-syllable lines.

In example 3b, the same melody type (with the same initial, central, and terminal segments) is treated more flexibly, partly in order to accommodate the eleven-syllable lines of the Turkic qua-

TABLE 2

	Number of Syllables	Number of Pulses	Phrases of Tune
Interlude		(4) + 4 + 4	(X) + A + A
Refrain	[1] + 8	(4) + 4	(X) + A
	8	4	A
	8 + [5 + 5]	4 + (4)	A + (A + B)
Interlude		4 + 4	A + A
		(1) + 4 + 3	(X) + A + A
		2 + 4	A + B
Tristich	[1] + 8	(3) + 4	(X) + A
	8	4	A
	8	4	A
Refrain	8	·4	A
	8	4	A
	8 + [5]	4 + (4)	A + (B)
	[1] + 8 + [5]	(2) + 4 + (2)	(X) + A + (B)

Ex. 3b

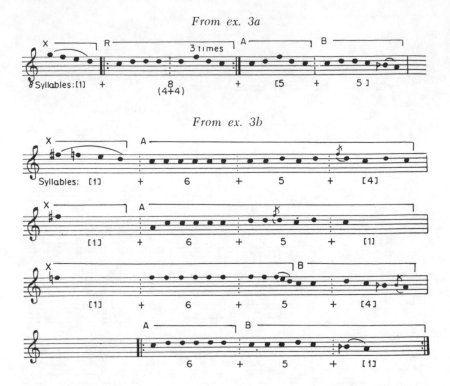

From ex. 3a

From ex. 3b

train. Repetitions of the final three syllables in the first and third lines of the quatrain act as "extensions" in much the same sense as did the "extra" syllables in examples 2 and 3a; for this reason, the repetitions of these segments are also marked by brackets in the transcription. The same phenomenon may be observed in the first lines of examples 4b, 4c, 5a, 5b, 5c, and 5d. The variable treatment of repeated segments of text represents one of the bakhshi's options in manipulation of both text and rhythmic-melodic framework. The rhythmic framework of example 3b rests on an equal pulse only at the terminations of lines (marked by tapping on the dutar in all but the first line).

Furthermore, in contrast to the unvaried reiterations of the central melodic phrase in example 3a, each new line in example 3b shifts the alignment of the three segments of the melody type against the eleven syllables; the repetition of the fourth line alone fails to change the rhythmic (and tonal) positions of the eleven syllables. The accompanying diagrams indicate the relationship

Ex. 4a

between pitches, melodic segments, and prosody in the dance song (ex. 3a) and the narrative verse (ex. 3b).

Examples 4a, 4b, and 4c illustrate the manner in which a single performer may manipulate the same text in different rhythmic and melodic frameworks. The text itself is at least fifty years old, since it was included in Ivanov's collection of Khorasani Kurdish poetry.[83] Although all three dance songs were recorded out of context, they typify the performances given by this bakhshi on Friday afternoons in the parks outside Bojnurd. Example 4a presents the tristich in a relatively straightforward manner: each eight-syllable line is followed by a single extra syllable, with the whole unit distributed over one measure of six pulses. The dance pattern of two measures (twelve pulses) is established in the dutar introduction and remains constant. Singing is normally confined to the first measure of the pattern, the sole exception being the interpolation *beshkan* ("clap!") after the first line. Following the tristich, the refrain presents seven more lines in the same manner; only the first of these is included in the transcription.

Example 4b employs a strophic structure in which the five lines extend over 9, 4, 4, 4, and 6 measures respectively. "Extra" syllables invariably break each line into segments of four syllables each. The final segment of each line is the most stable, rhythmically and tonally. The accompanying diagram again shows the relationship between prosodic and melodic structure.

Ex. 4b

Ex. 4c

In example 4c, the bakhshi does not play dutar while he is singing, matching the practice of the bakhshi who performed examples 3a and 3b. Just as the continual presence of the dutar in
examples 4a and 4b maintained a constant meter, so does its absence permit the vocal lines of example 4c to temporarily abandon
the dance pattern, which is quickly regained as the melody descends to cadence on the principal tones of the dutar introduction.
Extra syllables break the descending melody of each line into
three principal segments (marked in the diagram by brackets).
Within each line, and from one line to the next, each segment
represents a transposition of the preceding, focusing upon lower
tones within the range. Comparison of the diagrams drawn from
examples 4b and 4c indicates a contrast between the stability of
pitches in the bracketed material of the former and the transposition techniques that characterize the latter.

In the performances represented by examples 4b and 4c, the
rhythmic and melodic framework seen in the transcriptions (which
include only the first strophe of each performance) was retained
with relatively minor variations for the singing of additional text.
Having established a musical framework for the presentation of
a conventional tristich in the initial strophe, the singer apparently
proceeded to link together various lines chosen for their sonorous
values, abandoning the arrangement of tristich plus refrain.[84] After
two strophes on the model of example 4b, the performer added
nineteen additional ten-syllable lines, of which the following are
representative:

Kachki dilbārei	[a le lei lei]	to dar Shirvānei
[lei] Dele ma ber	[kechike]	chāve veri [lo]
Kachki Aghāzi	[a le lei lei]	badan kaghāzei
Badan kaghāzi	[kavutei]	tu makkä nāzei

From ex. 4b

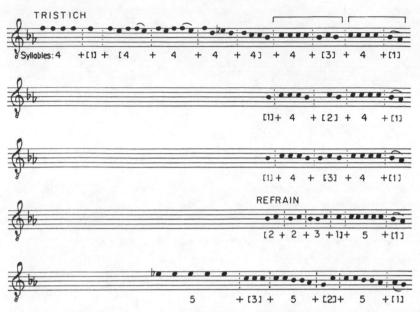

From ex. 4c

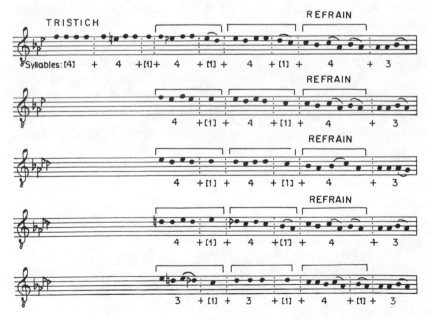

Kachki Kelātāi   [lei]   zülfi ta sattä
Zülfi kho shakä   [melvori]   berma riza [lo]

Each group of five syllables appears to function as a unit, which can be shifted from the final to the initial position within the line under certain circumstances. The third line quoted above also occurs in one of Ivanov's texts:

> Kachke Kumishi;—shiräfurushi; ·
> kachke Oghoji;—bädän koghazi;
> kachke Madani;—nozäk bädäni;
> kachke Sabzewor;—dar zire kursi.[85]

Each line in Ivanov's text describes the girls of a different town. My informant employed only one of these lines, in a framework that replaced the duple groupings (5 + 5 syllables) of Ivanov's text with quadruple groupings (5 + 5 + 5 + 5) in which some or all of the syllables in the second group might be repeated in the third.

A similar process of reordering conventional lines and half-lines into new strophes seems to characterize the Kurdish verses in praise of Sayyed Rashid and his companions. The recordings of "Sayyed Rashid" verses available to me include eleven performances by nine different singers, totaling 318 lines.[86] Although many of the same lines occur in several performances, groupings of lines into tristichs and strophes are generally unique to each singer (judging from the available corpus). I noticed only one strophe that was included in performances of "Sayyed Rashid" by two different singers. On the other hand, some versions of "Sayyed Rashid" draw on conventional tristichs that occur in other types of song; in the recordings of 1969, many of the tristichs in Ivanov's collection turn up both in the "narrative" verses praising particular khans and in dance pieces or love songs.

Example 5 presents excerpts from four performances of "Sayyed Rashid" verses by four different singers. Example 5a was sung by the same bakhshi who performed the three dance songs of example 4. As in example 4c, he played dutar only before and after (never during) the vocal lines. Example 5a is the second of the five strophes included in this performer's version of "Sayyed Rashid." Unlike the other strophes (not given in the transcription), it is constructed around a relatively constant measure of 2 + 2 + 3 eighth-note pulses. The threefold repetition of the last four syl-

Ex. 5a

[Ai] Shir-e mei-dan [a - - - i] Ra - shid Kha -

na, ____ Mâr-de mei - dan __ kha-lil ja - nâ.

lables of the first line falls neatly within the $2 + 2 + 3$ meter.

The organization of pitches in examples 4a, 4b, 4c, and 5a (performed at a single session) rests on rather similar divisions of a series of conjunct fourths into tetrachords that are balanced against one another. The specific orderings of these balances and imbalances in time, however, take radically different forms in all four cases. The chains of fourths and fifths function as "consonant" points of reference, calling attention to transpositions and transformations of small melodic shapes and to the timing of the more variable pitches that fill in the framing fourths.

In the transcription, examples 5b, 5c, and 5d are vertically aligned to permit comparison of the manner in which three different singers employed the $2 + 2 + 3$ meter in singing verses about Sayyed Rashid. In all three cases, the four lines of the strophe comprise a tristich followed by a single refrain line. Example 5b was sung by a Kurdish motreb to his own kemenche accompaniment; the singer is one of nearly two dozen motrebs residing in the village of Khānloq, north of Shirvān; example 5c was sung by a bakhshi residing in the village of Honāme (further north of Shirvān) to his own dutar accompaniment; example 5d was sung by a gypsy living in a tent outside Meshhed, without instrumental accompaniment. In the transcription (which does not include the instrumental parts), the first line of each performance is placed beneath Arabic numerals, representing the eighth-note density referent; the second line of each performance comes next, and so on. This arrangement indicates that all three versions share a common rhythmic framework, although each employs a different melody type. It seems likely that the rather rigid framework assists the singer as he groups together existing lines and formulas into a strophic structure.

Exx. 5b, 5c, and 5d

The text of example 5d, unlike the other "Sayyed Rashid" verses known to me, includes formulas that also occur in the fragments of Khorasani Kurdish narrative poetry published by Ivanov:

Ivanov:	*Example 5d:*
Haspe Jaju hin joni-y-a;	Asbe Khalil [lei] hin joniya
khurjini wi Turkmoni-y-a;	Shāle sare [lei] tormoniya
khawar hot nomerod chuya.[87]	Berne kutā [lei] almāniya
	Marde meidān Khalil, ai!
(The horse of Jaju Khan is so young,	(The horse of Khalil Khan is so young,
the saddle is of Turkoman make;	The scarf on his head is of Turkmen make,
news came that a calamity befell him.)	His short Bren gun is of German make,
	A man of the battlefield, Khalil, ai!)

The types of correspondences that extend throughout these two tristichs occur less frequently than do single lines and half-lines that might be called "formulaic" in Lord's sense—"because they follow the basic patterns of rhythm and syntax and have at least one word in the same position in the line in common with other lines or half-lines."[88] Following the notation of Parry and Lord, the "system" of formulaic expressions to which the first line of example 5d belongs includes the following:

Haspe
$\left\{ \begin{array}{l} \text{Jāju} \\ \text{Khalil} \\ \text{Rashid} \end{array} \right\}$
$\left\{ \begin{array}{l} \text{hin joniya} \\ \text{malworiya} \\ \text{-khān kechika} \\ \text{yorqa tara} \\ \text{süiru bashai} \\ \text{vabenbuza} \end{array} \right.$

In studying the texts of Khorasani Kurdish song, it is also useful to define systems in a broader sense, indicating possible *shifts* in the positions of important words within a line. The first lines of examples 5a, 5b, and 5c belong to the system shown in table 3. Each of the thirteen lines quoted is the first line of a different strophe. The lines are arranged to show increasing degrees of difference in the sequences of syllables that occur in this position. Each of the thirteen lines begins with the name of the protagonist (covering two, three, or four syllables), then proceeds to descriptive epithets or verbs. Unlike the Yugoslav narratives discussed by Lord, the Khorasani verses need not (and generally do not) present a coherent narrative.[89] The bakhshi's techniques apparently function to convert conventional phrases into musical materials that may be distributed at particular points within a strophe, without necessarily following a narrative line.

TABLE 3

Line	1	2	3	Syllable 4	5	6	7	8	Singer
1	Ha-	bib	char-	re	qa-	ra-	bāgh-	ei	A (Ex. 5a)
2	Va-	li	Khān-	e	qa-	ra-	mān-	i	A
3	Seyd	Ra-	shid-	e	kha-	re-	mān-	i	B, C (Ex. 5c)
4	Seyd	Ra-	shid	Khān	dā-	ya	yān-	ei	C
5	Say-	yed	chu-	ya	gho-	lā-	mān-	i	D
6	Say-	yed	che	nāv-	e	jan-	gal-	a	E
7	Say-	yed	var	kad	takht-	e	far-	a	E
8	Ra-	shid	var	kad	la	san-	gar-	a	F
9	Ra-	shid	Khān-	i	va	san-	gar-	a	G (Ex. 5b)
10	Ra-	shid	jān	[lei]	pei-	gham-	bar-	a	A
11	Ra-	shid	Khān-	e	zha	Che-	nār-	ān	A
12	Va-	li	Khān-	e	zha	māl-	dār-	ān	A
13	Kha-	lil	Khān-	e	zha	jān-	dār-	ān	D

We have seen that Khorasani singers do not make use of books and manuscripts in learning to sing the Kurdish verses in praise of khans and sardars. Performances of the Turkic hekayats (where written versions play an essential role in transmission of the repertoire) reveal similar processes of reordering the (written) lines within strophic structures, although particular strophes retain a stronger identity. A performance of the hekayat "Ṭāher Mirzā Zohra" by an illiterate bakhshi living in Meshhed contained sixteen quatrains (72 lines): eight of these, in a highly varied form, were included among the sixty-five quatrains (358 lines) of the same narrative as sung by a (literate) bakhshi in Bojnurd. Here, it is reasonable to infer that both performers stood at a considerable distance from a common source of the texts. The melody types and singing styles of the two bakhshis seem to derive from very different traditions. The first performer, for example, invariably sang the verses over a constant dutar accompaniment (with a constant

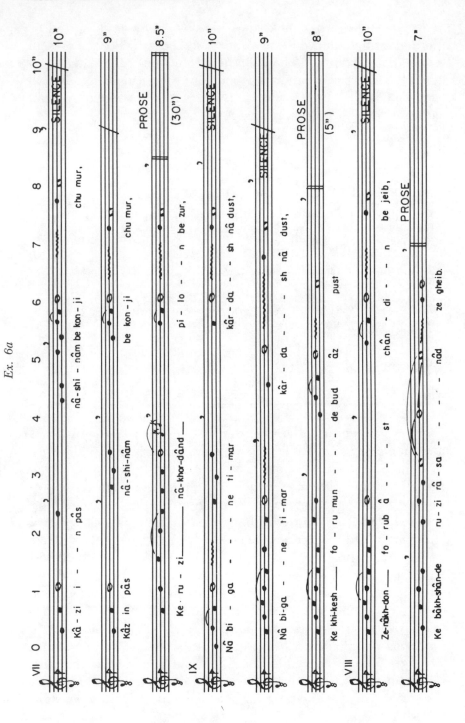

Ex. 6a

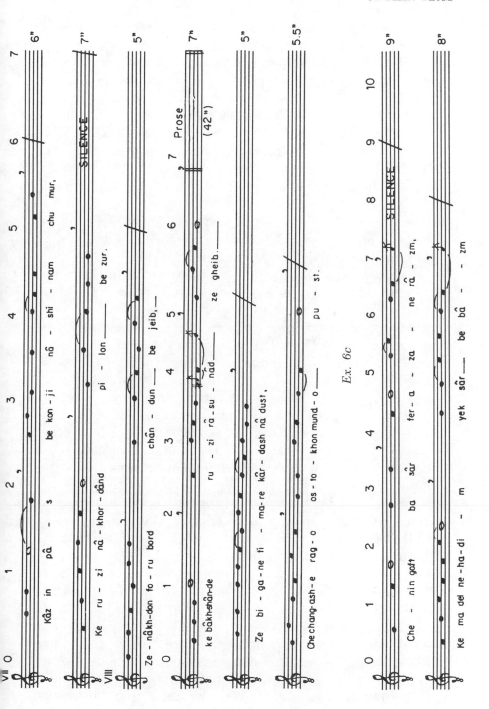

Ex. 6c

pulse), while the second bakhshi alternated solo vocal lines with dutar interludes (as in ex. 3b above).

A final set of examples illustrates the manner in which darvishes and naqqals also adopt strikingly different manners of performing written texts. In comparison with the Turkic hekayats, the texts of classical Persian poetry recited in teahouses are subject to much less variation, and printed sources are more easily accessible to performers. Example 6a presents three lines from Sa'di's *Bustān* as recited by the naqqal quoted above as Informant A. Example 6b gives the same three lines as recited by the darvish (a member of the Khaksar order) whose manner of recitation Informant A criticized so severely. Finally, example 6c is a single line of Ferdousi's *Shāh-Nāme*, taken from the recitation of one episode by a member of the Shah Ni'matollahi order.

The performances from which examples 6a and 6b are extracted were described by the singers as *pandiyāt*, fables carrying a moral burden. In both cases, the singers inserted Sa'di's verses within a context of prose narration, generally reciting only one or two lines before continuing the narrative. Informant A recited only eight lines of Sa'di's poem in all, while the performer of example 6b included all twenty lines of the original text. In the transcriptions, each excerpt is aligned beneath numbers that represent not a density referent, but real time in seconds. Each half-line begins on a new staff and continues up to the diagonal slash (which becomes the starting-point of the next line). The length of each half-line in seconds is also indicated in the right-hand margin. Since the notation of pitches distinguishes only between relatively shorter and longer durations, I have added commas at certain points to indicate the termination of a sound. Finally, the symbol ∿ in example 6a stands for a type of vocal tremolo commonly employed by Informant A. Roman numerals denote the lines of Sa'di's poem.[90]

In example 6a, the first half of lines VII and IX is repeated. Each half-line cadences on the second degree of the scale, until the last half of line VIII falls to the tonic. The entire performance included only one other cadence on the tonic, at the end of the final line. By this means, the singer maintains a large number of phrases in a state of suspension. Despite the absence of an equal pulse, the terminations of half-lines exhibit a remarkably consistent spacing of tones, compared to the greater rhythmic diversity at the beginning of each half-line (or hemistich). The final hemistich in each line is generally marked by a shorter total duration.

None of these generalizations applies to example 6b. The durations of the hemistichs are much shorter, and very few syllables are given extended durations. Example 6b lacks the "musical rhyme" effected in example 6a by the similar termination of each hemistich. The two hemistichs of each line often stand in an *ouvert/clos* arrangement, where the first hemistich cadences on the second or third degree of the scale and the second descends to the tonic. The melodic framework is handled in a very flexible manner: the first hemistich descends in one way or another from the fifth degree of the scale (perhaps going as far as the tonic), while the second hemistich emphasizes a descent from the third degree to the tonic. The greater predictability of the sequence of pitches in example 6a, on the other hand, focuses more attention upon the timing and duration of each pitch.

Those features that distinguish example 6a from example 6b constitute the basis of the "honorific" style that the naqqal who recited the former found wanting in the performances of the Khaksar darvish who recited the latter. The performer of example 6a employed the same techniques (and the same melody type) in his recitation of the *Shāh-Nāme*. A darvish of the Shah Ni'matollahi order also used a similar melody type in his own performances of the *Shāh-Nāme* (ex. 6c). The length of each hemistich is approximately the same in examples 6a and 6c. The latter, however, uses silence in place of the prolongation of tones (with or without tremolo) that distinguishes the former. The many slight pauses and the rather abrupt terminations of the lines create a style of deliberate understatement. As in example 6a (but not ex. 6b), the final melodic shape in each hemistich serves as a musical equivalent for the rhyme.

The "honorific" style of examples 6a and 6c rests on various means of sustaining a line in time—with an average phrase length, in this case, of about nine seconds' duration. Example 7, an excerpt from a performance of sine-zani by residents of a village outside Meshhed, illustrates the very different rhythmic and melodic qualities of religious verses involving the alternation between a soloist and a group. The soloist's opening line lacks a clear grouping of equal pulses, but it gradually condenses into a response of two measures' duration with a very definite pulse. At the soloist's third entry, the members of the group begin to strike their breasts on the sixth eighth-note pulse of each measure—a procedure that continues throughout the remainder of the performance (not shown in the transcription). The soloist gradually extends the durations of his lines to five and finally to sixteen measures, always accompanied by a regular beating of breasts. In addition to this rhythmic regularity, example 7 is distinguished from examples 6a and 6c by a greater concentration on the lowest areas of the range, although the range of the soloist's line does move upward in the phrases with longer durations. Comparison of examples 6 and 7 suggests that the ways of avoiding both regular occurrence of the tonic and exact rhythmic parallelism between lines in the former may be interpreted as inhibiting the type of group response that occurs in the latter.

Ex. 7

Summary and Concluding Observations

On the basis of the preceding discussion, I suggest the following conclusions:

(1) The music-making of the darvish, the naqqal, and the bakhshi does not constitute an "ingenuous" or "naïve" art that adheres to existing models without reflection, subject to the "preventive censorship" of a community. Diversity in the relationships between musicians and audiences is perhaps the most striking characteristic of music-making in Khorasani cities. The coexistence of many conflicting values and traditions fosters a strong "style-consciousness" in performers and listeners alike. Acting as a soloist, each performer is obliged to choose forms of behavior (including organization of sounds and verbalization about music) so as best to "convey an impression to others which it is in his interests to convey."[91] Pursuit of his interests requires competitive behavior that takes into account both the activities of other performers and the demands of different (actual and potential) patrons. A varied spectrum of both activities and demands offers the performer a wide range of options, but the strong level of competition indicates that performers do not regard these options as unlimited. We do not know at what points and in what respects the scarcity of available support leads to a tightening of the constraints perceived by performers.

(2) "Music-making" is not a distinct field of activity in Iranian society; rather, the darvish, the naqqal, and the bakhshi control techniques for organizing sounds and methods for "reading" texts. We have no reason to assume, however, that the process of competition among performers directly mirrors or symbolizes other types of social action in Iran, despite the claims of Chodzko and others that the behavior of performers reflects fundamental dispositions of society at large.[92] The work of performers *is* itself a type of social action. This is not to deny that performers and listeners must *to some extent* draw upon modes of interaction learned in "nonmusical" as well as in "musical" contexts, or that techniques of singing and reading may focus and strengthen dispositions for competitive behavior also applied to different circumstances. But we must investigate, in particular contexts, the specific similarities and differences between the actions of performers as such and

other actions by similar and different agents, not assume their existence in advance. Furthermore, we must bear in mind the possibility that performers may attempt, for various reasons, to criticize (rather than "express") particular modes of action or configurations of values. I have suggested that a set of six distinctions defines some of the alternatives within which performers may elaborate specific positions. Since music is not an isolated field of activity, these distinctions must be considered useless if they do not eventually help us understand relationships between organization of sounds or "reading" and other forms of human behavior in Iranian society. Consequently, evaluation of my own or any other musicological theory requires broader studies of social interaction.

(3) We have seen that a performer learns to control both a repertoire of existing texts and diverse conventions for presenting them. His control of poetry depends upon the existence (and use) of printed and manuscript texts rather than memory, although he must memorize texts (both written and unwritten) to some extent. His control of melody and rhythm depends upon memory rather than notation, although he must retain a high degree of stability in some respects as a means of lending significance to subtle variations.[93] Neither the text nor the rhythmic and melodic means of presentation remains entirely fixed. On one level, the manner in which a performer transfers a particular text through several rhythmic and melodic frameworks, and the extent to which consistent features of his frameworks accommodate a number of texts, demonstrate his degree of proficiency. Yet the competence of the most mediocre performer also extends to other levels, as he isolates and reorders particular relationships among words, lines, tristichs or quatrains, and various temporal orderings of attacks, pitches, and timbres.

It is therefore difficult to reduce the formal variety encountered in Khorasani musics to a limited number of "models."[94] Nor does it seem feasible to derive a set of rules that might generate new pieces acceptable to carriers of "the tradition," since almost any two singers will disagree on what is "acceptable." Analysis of the social context of music-making in Khorasan suggests that a performer may have good reasons for avoiding excessive symmetry or predictability, and that he may at times define rules that in some respects remain specific to a single performance (or even to a portion of a single performance).

(4) The relative merits of "reading silently" versus "reading aloud" (within however wide a range of musical options) have been debated by many Near Eastern religious thinkers; one need only recall the strong impression made upon Saint Augustine by Saint Ambrose's practice of reading silently.[95] In general, Islam has most often revealed a powerful bias in favor of reading aloud, as indicated by the origins, and practices of teaching and understanding the Qur'an.[96] The manner in which Khorasani performers deal with existing texts, particularly those techniques that stress "learning" and "propriety," are largely in accord with Islamic ethical precepts, and the practices of performers offer parallels to Gellner's continuum extending from "communal consensus" to "organization, leadership, hierarchy" (cited above). The tensions within Islamic thought and practice that occasion shifts in either direction of the continuum affect musicians with particular force. On the one hand, "reading aloud" is one of the most meritorious activities (in which each member of the community should participate), while on the other the appeal of organized sound to large groups of people runs grave dangers (especially if not tightly controlled by a hierarchy). Members of darvish orders have played important roles as mediators of the tensions inherent in this dichotomy.

(5) Finally, we may ask to what extent the darvish, the naqqal, and the bakhshi not only work within but depend upon urban institutions and circumstances. Many scholars have claimed that "the city is necessary for Islam, since it is only there that the virtuous life as Islam conceives it can be fully lived."[97] Although many Khorasani Muslims could easily imagine a "virtuous life" without any darvishes, naqqals, or bakhshis, the performances of the latter often aspire to particular virtues that might be termed "Islamic" in some respects, although they also have roots in Iranian and Turkic traditions that predate Islam.[98] Yet this is not to say that such "Islamic" virtues can be practiced only in cities.

Nevertheless, the cities appear to provide a locus where the performer may learn to synthesize aspects of diverse practices, during brief visits or prolonged periods of residence. Both of the naqqals and three of the four bakhshis interviewed in Bojnurd had immigrated to the city from their native villages. Instruction in recitation of Persian religious poetry is probably best found in cities, as is the support provided by a darvish order. On the other hand, it was possible to learn the bakhshi repertoire from rural practitioners thirty or forty years ago; at the present time, it is uncertain whether anyone desires to learn this repertoire in either towns or villages.

Like many urban specialists, performers active in Meshhed and Bojnurd extend their services to surrounding villages. In the case of the bakhshi, each individual partly depends upon his travels to villages. Some darvishes, naqqals, and rouze-khvuns find an adequate market for their recitations in the cities, but other specialists in religious recitation (especially rouze-khvuns) travel to villages during the months of Moḥarram and Ṣafar. These facts indicate that we cannot regard such performers as an exclusively "urban" phenomenon.

NOTES

1. For the concept of a "musical consensus," see Mantle Hood, *The Ethnomusicologist* (New York: McGraw-Hill, 1971), pp. 300–301.

2. I have adopted the term *intermediaries* as used by McKim Marriott, "Changing Channels of Cultural Transmission in Indian Civilization," in *Intermediate Societies, Social Mobility, and Communication,* ed. Verne F. Ray (Seattle: University of Washington Press, 1959), p. 66.

3. The author's fieldwork in Meshhed and Bojnurd, from January through August, 1969, was supported by a generous grant from the Midwest Universities Consortium for International Activities. For a more detailed account of the research project, see my dissertation, "Musics in Contact: The Cultivation of Oral Repertoires in Meshed, Iran" (University of Illinois, 1972). I revisited both cities for one month in the summer of 1972. Maurice Wong, a research assistant provided by the University of Illinois Graduate College Research Board, made drafts of several of the transcriptions (exx. 1–7), which have been revised by the author.

4. In Azerbaijan and Anatolia, the term *'āshiq* denotes a type of performer similar in many respects to the Khorasani *bakhshi.*

5. Alexander Chodzko, *Specimens of the Popular Poetry of Persia* (London: W. H. Allen, 1842), p. 7.

6. Ibid., pp. 401–2.

7. Ibid., pp. 379–91.

8. The phrase "Turco-Iranian world" is borrowed from Xavier de Planhol, *Les fondements géographiques de l'histoire de l'Islam* (Paris: Flammarion, 1968), p. 196.

9. Ernest Gellner, "Post-Traditional Forms in Islam: The Turf and Trade, and Votes and Peanuts," in *Post-Traditional Societies*, ed. S. N. Eisenstadt (New York: Norton, 1973), p. 192.

10. Ibid.

11. See Claude Cahen's review of *Les fondements*, by de Planhol, in *Journal of the Economic and Social History of the Orient* 12 (1969), 218–22. Cahen argues against "considering economic and social processes as primarily [determined by] religious [constraints]" throughout the area of diffusion of Medieval Islam.

12. Edward G. Browne, *A Literary History of Persia*, vol. 2 (London: T. Fisher Unwin, 1906), p. 373.

13. Ibid., p. 133.

14. Jan Rypka, "Poets and Prose Writers of the Late Saljuq and Mongol Periods," in *The Cambridge History of Iran*, vol. 5 (Cambridge: Cambridge University Press, 1968), p. 551.

15. C. E. Bosworth, "The Development of Persian Culture under the Early Ghazvanids," *Iran* 6 (1968), 40.

16. Ibid.

17. C. E. Bosworth, "The Political and Dynastic History of the Iranian World (A.D. 1000–1217)," in *The Cambridge History of Iran*, vol. 5, p. 10.

18. Richard N. Frye, "The Sāmānids," in *The Cambridge History of Iran*, vol. 4 (Cambridge: Cambridge University Press, 1975), p. 155.

19. Alessio Bombaci, "The Turkic Literatures: Introductory Notes on the History and Style," in *Philologiae Turcicae Fundamenta*, vol. 2 (Wiesbaden: Franz Steiner, 1964), p. xviii. Bombaci believes that the word *rāh* in this passage may refer to a musical mode.

20. Bosworth, "Development of Persian Culture," p. 40.

21. Jan Rypka, *Iranische Literaturgeschichte* (Leipzig: Otto Harrassowitz, 1959), p. 156; Bosworth, "Development of Persian Culture," p. 40.

22. Jiri Cejpek, "Die iranische Volksdichtung," in Rypka, *Iranische Literaturgeschichte*, p. 465; Gilbert Lazard, "The Rise of the New Persian Language," in *The Cambridge History of Iran*, vol. 4 (Cambridge: Cambridge University Press, 1975), p. 615.

23. Pertev Naili Boratav, "L'épopée d'Er-Tostuk et le conte populaire," in *Volksepen der uralischen und altaischen Völker*, ed. Wolfgang Veenker (Wiesbaden: Otto Harrassowitz, 1968), p. 75; Boratav, "Littérature orale," in *Philologiae Turcicae Fundamenta*, vol. 2, pp. 11–13.

24. Pertev Naili Boratav, "Ḥikāya: The Narrative Genres of Turkish Literature and Folklore," in *Encyclopedia of Islam*, new ed., vol. 3 (Leiden: E. J. Brill, 1971), p. 374.

25. Alessandro Bausani, "Religion in the Saljuq Period," in *The Cambridge History of Iran*, vol. 5, pp. 293–94.

26. Nasrollah Falsafi, "Tārikh-e qahve va qahve-khāne dar Irān," *Sokhan* 5:4 (1954), 261.

27. Vladimir Minorsky, "Iran: Opposition, Martyrdom, and Revolt," in *Unity and Diversity in Muslim Civilization*, ed. Gustave E. Von Grunebaum (Chicago: University of Chicago Press, 1955), p. 200.

28. Ibid., p. 187. See also Dwight M. Donaldson, *The Shi'ite Religion: A History of Islam in Persia and Irak* (London: Luzac, 1933), p. 277.

29. Fazlur Rahman, *Islam* (New York: Anchor Books, 1968), pp. 158–59; Bosworth, "Political and Dynastic History," p. 6.

30. See e.g. Mantle Hood's distinction between *ingenuous* and *cultivated* musics in "The Reliability of Oral Tradition," *Journal of the American Musicological Society* 12 (1959), 201: "The term 'ingenuous music' refers to an artless and relatively naive expression lacking in its development the idea of *conscious* improvement, therefore *unstudied*. 'Cultivated music,' on the other hand, refers to an expression which has evolved through a conscious effort to improve and refine the various attributes of its disciplines." In "Thoughts on Improvisation: A Comparative Approach," *Musical Quarterly* 60 (1974), 11, Bruno Nettl suggests "a division of the world's musical cultures and of their subsystems—genres, periods, composers—into two groups. One of these would be the music which is carefully thought out, perhaps even worked over with a conscious view to introducing innovation from piece to piece and even from phrase to phrase; the other, that which is spontaneous but model-bound, rapidly created, and simply conceived." Unlike Hood, Nettl does not imply that a process of evolution leads from "model-bound forms" to those stressing "innovation."

31. This point is discussed by Clifford Geertz, *Peddlers and Princes: Social Change and Economic Modernization in Two Indonesian Towns* (Chicago: University of Chicago Press, 1963), p. 145. For Weber's dichotomy, see his *Economy and Society*, trans. G. Roth and C. Wittrich (New York: Bedminster Press, 1948), vol. 3, pp. 1375–80.

32. Roman Jakobson and Petr Bogatyrev, "Die Folklore als eine besondere Form des Schaffens," reprinted in Jakobson, *Selected Writings*, vol. 4 (The Hague: Mouton, 1966), pp. 10–13.

33. Bruno Nettl, "Historical Aspects of Ethnomusicology," *American Anthropologist* 60 (1958), 524.

34. Albert B. Lord, *The Singer of Tales* (Cambridge: Harvard University Press, 1960), pp. 279–80.

35. Ibid., pp. 4–5, 130.

36. In some respects, the approach to analysis of Khorasani music-making suggested here resembles Leo Treitler's concept of "transmission through reconstruction" that "cuts across the categories of 'oral' and 'written' as well [as those of reproduction and invention]"; see his " 'Centonate' Chant: *Übles Flickwerk* or *E pluribus unus?*," *Journal of the American Musicological Society* 28 (1975), 11 n. My concern with the performer's musical choices as he adjusts and modifies rhythmic and melodic frameworks in the act of presenting (and/or manipulating) existing texts is close to that of Bruce Rosenberg, *The Art of the American Folk Preacher* (New York: Oxford University Press, 1970). Rosenberg modifies the Parry-Lord theory of oral composition so as to take into account the ways in which black preachers in the U.S. make adjustments "between stress for sound's sake and for the sake of meaning," a technique that "in several ways . . . exploits literacy" (p. 96–98).

37. Jakobson and Bogatyrev, "Die Folklore," pp. 7–9.

38. Ibid., pp. 13–14.

39. Y. M. Sokolov observes that "those of the religious verses which were of an epic cast . . . were not separated from the *byliny*" but "went under the general designation of 'ancient songs,' and were not always the exclusive property of the professional beggar singers" (*Russian Folklore* [New York: Macmillan, 1950], p. 371). Similarly, the repertoires of Khorasani darvishes include classical Persian poetry (such as passages from Ferdousi's *Shāh-Nāme* or Sa'di's *Bustān*), which are also sung by more prestigious performers

(including nonprofessionals), as well as old and new religious verses created and transmitted primarily or entirely through oral tradition.

40. See further Meyer Schapiro, "On the Relation of Patron and Artist: Comments on a Proposed Model for the Scientist," *American Journal of Sociology* 70 (1964), 364–66.

41. This point was eloquently stated by Mozart in a letter of December 28, 1782: "To win applause, one must write things which are either so intelligible that a coachman could sing them, or so incomprehensible that they give pleasure precisely because no rational human being can understand them" (*Briefe und Aufzeichnungen*, ed. W. A. Bauer and O. E. Deutsch, vol. 3 [Kassel: Bärenreiter, 1963], p. 246).

42. R. Grämlich, *Die schiitischen Derwischorden Persiens, I. Die Affiliationen*, Deutschen Morgenländischen Gesellschaft, Abhandlungen für die Kunde des Morgenlandes, vol. 36 (Wiesbaden, 1965), pp. 89–90.

43. For earlier descriptions of these types of performances in Meshhed, see Edmond O'Donovan, *The Merv Oasis* (London: Smith, Elder and Co., 1882), vol. 1, p. 490, and G. Stratil-Sauer, *Meschhed: Eine Stadt baut am Vaterland Iran* (Leipzig: Ernst Staneck, 1937), p. 20 and photograph facing p. 96.

44. W. Ivanow, "Some Persian Darwish Songs," *Journal of the Asiatic Society of Bengal* n.s. 23 (1927), 238. According to Ivanow, darvishes of the Khaksar order consider begging "a sort of collection of their dues (*haqq-i talab*)" since they "are guarding the world against calamity" (p. 237). One naqqal, himself a Khaksar, told me that "if the bowl of a darvish fills up with money, he gives it all to the poor." A bakhshi in Bojnurd expressed his belief that reciters on the streets who collected *sahm-e imām* ("the imam's portion") generally kept the entire sum for themselves. Other persons denied that a reciter would dare to ask for sahm-e imam, "which is given only to religious leaders."

45. Some of those interviewed described their teachers or themselves as janitors, waiters, rug weavers, itinerant merchants. Epithets referring to spiritual stature included *haqq-shenās* (one who knows the truth), *pāk-dāman* (one who is chaste), *sarparast* (guardian), among many others.

46. The Gunābādi branch of the Shah Ni'matollahi, unlike the Khaksar order, includes members of the upper classes (well-to-do merchants, government officials, military officers). See Grämlich, *Derwischorden Persiens*, p. 64, and W. McE. Miller, "Shi'ah Mysticism: The Sufis of Gunābād," *Muslim World* 13 (1923), 347.

47. Compare Ivanow, "Some Persian Darwish Songs," p. 238.

48. J. Spencer Trimingham, *The Sufi Orders in Islam* (Oxford: Oxford University Press, 1971), p. 264.

49. The darvish orders in Meshhed do not permit outsiders to attend sessions of *zekr*, "rhythmical repetitive invocation of God's names" practiced as "a spiritual exercise designed to render God's presence throughout one's being" (Trimingham, *Sufi Orders*, p. 302). The need for private performances of zekr is a consequence of the diffusion of Sufic practices across a wide range of public performances: "In the course of time, when Sufism was brought to the level of the average man, the very *dhikr* of the divine names was so vulgarized . . . as to become despiritualized" (ibid., p. 194). For examples of "vulgarized" zekrs, see Ivanow, "Some Persian Darwish Songs," pp. 241–42.

50. Some pandiyat were described by informants as *qeṣṣe,* and the distinction between qesse and *afsāne* drawn by one naqqal clearly indicates the didactic intent of the former: "Qesse is something that happened. It is related to advice, instructions about life. Afsane was made up out of someone's head. It is something manufactured." The cross-reference among genres that is so important in Khorasani musical life is illustrated by this informant's performance of a "qesse in the guise (*ṣurat*) of an afsane."

51. Arthur de Gobineau provided a classic account of the impact exercised by a rouze-khvun on his listeners in *Les religions et les philosophies dans l'Asie centrale,* 3d ed. (Paris: Ernest Leroux, 1900), pp. 374–75.

52. Reẓā Shāh's opposition to rouze-khvuni and related practices is briefly discussed in Joseph M. Upton, *The History of Modern Iran: An Interpretation* (Cambridge: Harvard University Press, 1960), pp. 111–12. One patron of a teahouse in Meshhed spoke as follows of the *shbi:* "From the point of view of Islam, the shbi is not correct (*saḥiḥ*). From the point of view of the police, it is forbidden. People perform it in open areas, away from the police." Although I am not aware of performances of shbi in urban areas in 1969, several were presented in Khorasani villages, either by residents or by traveling groups of performers.

53. See B. J. Spooner, "The Function of Religion in Persian Society," *Iran* 1 (1963), 86–87, 91, 94–95, and Jalāl Āl-e Ahmad's criticisms of Spooner's essay in *Arziyābi shetāb-zade* (Tehran, n.d.), pp. 191–96.

54. See Cejpek, "Iranische Volksdichtung," pp. 466–67, 519.

55. Trimingham, *Sufi Orders,* p. 267. See also Grämlich's discussion of the Khaksar as "Vertreter des Geistes des Qalandartums" (*Derwischorden Persiens,* p. 76).

56. In fact, the phenomenon of mo'areke-giri is mentioned by Kashifi at the beginning of the sixteenth century; see Cejpek, "Iranische Volksdichtung," p. 509. Engelbert Kaempfer's account of several types of public recitation in seventeenth-century Iranian cities is easily accessible in Frank Harrison, *Time, Place and Music* (Amsterdam: Frits Knuf, 1973), pp. 146–47. Grämlich discusses the historical context of mo'areke-giri with reference to the Khaksar order (*Derwischorden Persiens,* p. 80).

57. As often happens, Informant D made his point by quoting a familiar proverb, translated here after S. Haïm, *Persian-English Proverbs* (Tehran: Beroukhim, 1956), p. 377.

58. Walter Benjamin, "The Work of Art in the Age of Mechanical Reproduction," in *Illuminations,* trans. Harry Zohn (New York: Harcourt, Brace & World, 1968), p. 221.

59. Gellner, "Post-Traditional Forms," p. 193.

60. For a brief discussion of this repertoire, see Stephen Blum, "The Concept of the '*Asheq* in Northern Khorasan," *Asian Music* 4:1 (1972), 34–42.

61. W. Ivanov, "Notes on Khorasani Kurdish," *Journal of the Asiatic Society of Bengal* n.s. 23 (1927), 216–17.

62. Cejpek describes similar occupations as typical of professional (Persian) storytellers in Iran ("Iranische Volksdichtung," p. 509).

63. Ilhan Başgöz, "Turkish *Ḥikāye*-Telling Tradition in Azerbaijan, Iran," *Journal of American Folklore* 88 (1970), 393. Like their counterparts in Khorasan, the Azerbaijani 'ashiqs whom Başgöz interviewed perform in teahouses, in private homes, and at village weddings (p. 395).

64. The struggle between Moḥammad Teqi Khān and Reẓā Khān is de-

scribed in Richard Cottam, *Nationalism in Iran* (Pittsburgh: University of Pittsburgh Press, 1964), pp. 108–9, and at greater length in Ramaẓān 'Ali Shākri, *Joghrāfiyā-ye tārikhi-ye Quchān* (Meshhed: Chāpkhāne-ye Khorāsān, 1967), pp. 73–75.

65. In this respect, Sayyed Rashid resembles the Turkic hero Köroghli; see e.g. Victor Zhirmunsky, "Epic Songs and Singers in Central Asia," in Nora K. Chadwick and Victor Zhirmunsky, *Oral Epics of Central Asia* (Cambridge: Cambridge University Press, 1969), p. 301.

66. Ivanov noted that "cycles of [Khorasani Kurdish] songs deploring the death of some hero are usually attributed to the sister of the deceased,— not to any other of his relations, or friends" ("Khorasani Kurdish," pp. 171–72).

67. See e.g. the excerpt from Moḥammad Mas'ud's *Gol-hā'i ke dar jahanam miruyad*, 2d ed. (Tehran, 1942), reprinted in Hassan Kamshad, *A Modern Persian Prose Reader* (Cambridge: Cambridge University Press, 1968), pp. 41–47.

68. See Zhirmunsky, "Epic Songs and Singers," pp. 316–17.

69. Gerhard Doerfer speaks of having discovered "a new Oghuz (Southwestern) Turkish language, Khorasani, which may number as many as 800,000 speakers"; he considers this language "closer to Turkmen than to Azerbaijani." See his "Irano-Altaistica: Turkish and Mongolian Languages of Persia and Afghanistan," in *Current Trends in Linguistics,* vol. 6 (The Hague: Mouton, 1970), p. 234.

70. See Lawrence Krader, *Peoples of Central Asia,* 3d ed. (Bloomington: Indiana University Press, 1971), p. 97.

71. Mark Slobin, "Central Asian Peoples of the USSR," to appear in *Grove's Dictionary of Music & Musicians,* 6th ed.

72. Thus, Informant E criticized the Turkmen story *Gol-o Sanubar* "because the lovers aren't together enough of the time" and cannot address verses to one another at frequent intervals. On the other hand, he described the Persian story *Najjema* as having "too many verses, too little narrative (*qeṣṣe*)"; consequently, "they don't ask for it at weddings."

73. The term *sublimation* has been used in much the same sense by Alexander Ringer, who points to a "sublimation of the widest possible variety of musical practices" in Beethoven's works; see his "Beethoven and the London Pianoforte School," *Musical Quarterly* 56 (1970), 757.

74. Nasser Pakdaman, "La situation du musicien dans la société persane," in *Normes et valeurs dans l'Islam contemporain,* ed. J.-P. Charnay (Paris: Payot, 1966), p. 327.

75. The phrase "polyphony of lines" is adapted from Roman Jakobson, "Grammatical Parallelism and Its Russian Facet," *Language* 62 (1966), 422–24.

76. Amnon Shiloah, "Arab Folk Music," to appear in *Grove's Dictionary of Music & Musicians,* 6th ed.; Artur Simon, *Studien zur ägyptischen Volksmusik* (Hamburg: Karl Dietrich Wagner, 1972), vol. 1, pp. 23–25.

77. This hypothesis suggests that Khorasani singers make use of a principle that Bruno Nettl observes in the dastgah traditions of Tehran: a performer must "move from familiar to less familiar, and finally to the familiar" ("Aspects of Form in the Instrumental Performance of the Persian *Āvāz*," *Ethnomusicology* 18 [1974], 412).

78. J. H. Kwabene Nketia, "African Music," in *Peoples and Cultures of*

Africa, ed. Elliott P. Skinner (New York: Doubleday/Natural History Press, 1973), p. 588.

79. J. H. Kwabene Nketia, "History and the Organization of Music in West Africa," in *Essays on Music and History in Africa,* ed. Klaus P. Wachsmann (Evanston, Ill.: Northwestern University Press, 1971), pp. 12–19.

80. See David W. Ames, "A Socio-Cultural View of Hausa Musical Activity," in *The Traditional Artist in African Societies,* ed. Warren d'Azevedo (Bloomington: Indiana University Press, 1973), pp. 135–41.

81. Gregory Bateson, "Cybernetic Explanation" (1967), reprinted in his *Steps to an Ecology of Mind* (New York: Ballantine Books, 1972), p. 410; idem, "Redundancy and Coding" (1968), reprinted in *Steps,* p. 414.

82. I have adopted the term *extension* as used by Boris Kremenliev, "Extension and Its Effect in Bulgarian Folk Song," *Selected Reports* (Institute of Ethnomusicology, UCLA), vol. 1 (1966), p. 1: "The extensions in Bulgarian folk music are of two basic types: those that result from syllables or words, including exclamations, that are not part of the text, and those resulting from unexpected pauses within, or at the end of, the melody." Unlike Kremenliev, I have also treated repetition of various segments of the text as a third type of "extension."

83. Ivanov, "Khorasani Kurdish," p. 211.

84. In his studies of folksong in Kurdestan, Dieter Christensen describes the difference between these two ways of handling text as "rigid" and "open" forms, respectively; see e.g. "On Variability in Kurdish Dance Songs," *Asian Music* 6 (1975), 3–4. The manner in which singers of Kurdish texts link together groups of syllables, sometimes with scant regard for "semantic" considerations, recalls the "two factors making for obscurity in Turkish folk song texts," as described by Picken in a penetrating book review, *Journal of the International Folk Music Council* 20 (1968), 75: "One [factor] is that, in order to facilitate polysyllabic rhyme, both internal and terminal, certain neutral words are commonly used as rhyming 'leads,' to be followed by more meaningful rhyming words. . . . The second factor making for obscurity is the tenuousness of the semantic link between stanzas in many songs."

85. Ivanov, "Khorasani Kurdish," p. 212.

86. These performances include recordings made by Bruno Nettl in 1966, by Robert Peck in 1969, and by myself in 1969. Peck's recordings (including ex. 5c) are archived in the Museum für Völkerkunde, Musikethnologische Abteilung, Berlin. Nettl's recordings (including ex. 5b) are Collection 8 in the University of Illinois Archives of Ethnomusicology, and my own are Collections 61 and 109 in the same institution.

87. Ivanov, "Khorasani Kurdish," pp. 185–86.

88. Lord, *Singer of Tales,* p. 47.

89. In "The Popular Verse of the Bakhtiari of S.W. Persia," *Bulletin of the School of Oriental and African Studies* 16 (1954) 548, D. L. R. Lorimer similarly observed that "the Bakhtiari poet makes no attempt to set out the events of a story in a continuous intelligible narrative. . . . Names of persons are mentioned without any indication of their relationship, and without even making it clear to what side or party they belong. The listener must bring with him an intimate knowledge of tribal history and geneology." Lorimer points to musical as well as social reasons for the "obscure and allusive" manner of presentation: "The Bakhtiari poet is often more concerned

with ringing changes on sound, than in recording a series of events or pursuing a definite line of thought."

90. For the complete text, see *Kolliyyāt-e Saʿdi,* ed. Moḥammad ʿAli Forughi (Tehran: Enteshārāt-e Jāvidān, n.d.), p. 280.

91. Erving Goffman, *The Presentation of Self in Everyday Life* (New York: Anchor Books, 1959), p. 4.

92. In his generalized description of "the Bardic style of the Orient," Alan Lomax claims that "solo performance is . . . dominant, but various levels of accompaniment support and reinforce the authority of the soloist-leader" ("Song Structure and Social Structure," *Ethnology* 1 [1962], 442). Lomax interprets "complex, shifting, and sometimes meterless rhythm" as maintaining a high level of redundancy in the process whereby "typical" vocal timbres symbolize submission to authority (*Folk Song Style and Culture* [Washington, D.C.: American Association for the Advancement of Science, 1968], pp. 134–35). Unlike Nketia (cited earlier), Lomax takes scant heed of the manner in which "preselected" timbres and pitches are "fitted into a structural mold," with greater or lesser degrees of predictability. His descriptions of the general timbre of a style, considered as an expression of various patterns of social behavior, fail to examine the extent to which rhythmic frameworks control the selection and distribution of timbres and pitches.

93. Hans Hickmann, quoting the story of King Thamus and the inventor Theuth from Plato's *Phaedrus,* suggests that Near Eastern musicians perhaps did not develop systems of notation because of a realization that essential features are lost without the effort required by memorization ("Die Musik des arabisch-islamischen Bereichs," in *Handbuch der Orientalistik,* part 1, supp. vol. 4 [Leiden: E. J. Brill, 1970], p. 47). Cf. Si Hamza Boubakeur, "Psalmodie coranique," in *Encyclopédie des musiques sacrées,* vol. 1 (Paris: Éditions Labergerie, 1968), pp. 389–90.

94. The less specialized repertoires of Persian "folksong" in Khorasan present a limited number of melody types and rhythmic frameworks; see Stephen Blum, "Persian Folksong in Meshhed (Iran), 1969," *Yearbook of the International Folk Music Council* 6 (1974), 86–114.

95. *Confessions,* book 6, chap. 3.

96. F. Buhl, "al-Ḳurʾān," in *The Shorter Encyclopedia of Islam* (Leiden: E. J. Brill, 1953), pp. 273–86.

97. This view is discussed by A. H. Hourani, "The Islamic City in the Light of Recent Research," in *The Islamic City: A Colloquium* (Oxford: Bruno Cassirer, 1970), pp. 12–20. For a generalized discussion of "the urban landscape of Islam," see Xavier de Planhol, *Le monde islamique: Essai de géographie religieuse* (Paris: Presses Universitaires de France, 1957), pp. 5–45.

98. In addition to the references cited above in nn. 15, 18, 19, 21, and 22, see Mary Boyce, "The Parthian *Gōsān* and Iranian Minstrel Tradition," *Journal of the Royal Asiatic Society,* 1957, pp. 10–45.

Go to My Town, Cape Coast!
The Social History of Ghanaian Highlife

DAVID COPLAN

One of the most important sectors of ethnomusicological research is that of inquiry into the dynamic interrelation of musical and social subsystems within the larger process of human cultural life. In the field of African music, a number of eminent ethnomusicologists have sought to understand how the constitutive elements of musical form and content "enter into active relation with the system of life values that governs human affairs."[1] Their pursuit of this knowledge however, has been conditioned by special historical and archivistic considerations. Research has centered on whatever might be considered uniquely "African" in human musical culture, focusing on the interaction of music and society in the specific interests of "discovering" and preserving traditions of African musical life whose survival appears endangered. The urgency that has informed this perspective should not be minimized—and its value is unquestioned—but it now appears equally crucial for ethnomusicologists to address themselves to more acculturated systems of musical expression, for example, those that have emerged from the rapidly expanding world of urban Africa. It is precisely here, in the sociohistorical and musical development of such syncretic forms, that the relation of musical systems to the other structures of human society may be most visible. In considering musical style as an instrument of sympathetic communication and aesthetic sociability, we should be able to learn a great

David Coplan is a doctoral candidate in anthropology at Indiana University, Bloomington.

deal from situations of musical change concerning the ways in which artistic behavior and its consequences operate as a variable in sociocultural life.[2]

Theoretical considerations of this sort, however, can be pursued only against a background of secure conceptual definition and ethnographic and historical description. It is the intention of this paper to summarize the present state of our knowledge of the social and musical history of one such syncretic form, Ghanaian highlife, in the interests of developing such a background and of suggesting some fruitful directions that future theoretical and analytical inquiry might take.

Let us first clarify the conceptual dimensions of our subject matter. In simplest terms, highlife is a musical hybrid resulting from the acculturative impact of Europe on West Africa during the colonial period. More specifically, we must recognize highlife as not merely the result of mechanical or passive acculturation but as a creative, incorporative response to the political and economic impact and cultural challenge of the West. Highlife is a syncretic form in that it modifies and integrates both Western and indigenous musical elements into an organic, qualitatively new style that retains expressive continuity with the traditional music system. As a syncretic, expressive subsystem, highlife transmits Western influences and values into a rapidly emerging urban sociocultural system.[3]

The situation may be seen as analogous to the developmental process characteristic of pidgin languages, in which if "the concept of mixture is limited to the notion of a base language larded with borrowings, it is too crude to account for the complex process of semantic transformation and syntactic fusion that is likely to occur if one thinks of language primarily in terms of its users."[4] We must always remember to view music in terms of the needs of its participants, and not merely in terms of its constitutive elements. With these considerations in mind, let us turn from the conceptual to the sociohistorical dimensions of this development.

The vaguely defined intermixture of musical subtypes on which English-speaking West Africans have bestowed the name *highlife* was the first terminologically discrete category of syncretic music to attain both national and international significance and distribution on the Guinea coast. As such it served as both a symptom and a symbol of acculturative change taking place throughout West Africa. That a seminal development of this kind should have taken place in what was until 1957 the Royal Colony of the Gold Coast, more specifically in the growing cities of what is now the southwestern coast of the Republic of Ghana, is a result of certain sociohistorical conditions of which we have as yet only the sketchiest impression. What information we do have can be best presented in terms of a set of contrasts or oppositions.

Prior to 1945 the cultural domination of the Europeans in the French West African territories extended to the composition of local dance bands, so that Westernized African musicians were few and poorly skilled. The British, by contrast, began early to train indigenous musicians in missions and native military regiments. British-style brass bands began to develop out of native military-fort bands as early as 1750.[5] Colonial policies provided another kind of enduring influence on modern West African music when the British imported a brigade of West Indians who later formed the Cape Coast West Indian Rifles Band during the early 1800s.[6] By the 1830s, freed Brazilian slaves had returned to the Guinea coast in considerable numbers, and by 1840 they occupied a "Brazilian Quarter" in Accra.[7] John Beecham noted in 1841 that the native band at Cape Coast Castle, in addition to the usual British military music, had in its repertoire several current popular melodies, which were played by ear.[8]

While the cultural and aesthetic value of their contribution is highly questionable, the musical role of Christian missionaries, who set lyrics in indigenous languages to traditional church melodies and provided training in Western musical techniques as well as Western instruments, is highly significant. In 1920, a Presbyterian seminary tunebook was published with familiar European songs and English church hymns set to lyrics in Twi. Also, many popular Ghanaian recreational songs first arose in church during this period.[9] Robert Sprigge points out the frequent presence of phrases and progressions in highlife that are reminiscent of hymn music, and he argues that apart from their African rhythmic setting, many highlife melodies could be used without difficulty in a Scottish Presbyterian church.[10] Some bands in the present day, such as Yamoah's Band, are well aware of these influences and achieve highly comic effects by employing hymnlike melodic progressions in songs with decidedly irreligious lyrics. Church music in general stands as a continuing thread of influence, closely interwoven in the fabric of syncretic musical development.

Church educators guided Akan singing in the direction of diatonic intervals, focusing harmonization on the tonic, dominant, and subdominant; and they replaced the complex multilinear polyphony of traditional ensembles with the rigid four-part organization and the bland melodic preferences of British suburban clerical taste, ignoring the tonal requirements of spoken Twi. The ballast of indigenous rhythm remained, however, and secular Ghanaian musicians were able to blend church melodies and the more diatonic scale with their traditional vocal phrasing and preference for thirds and sixths. It is a characteristic of pidgin languages that elements of their parent languages are simplified in the process of hybridization. It can be argued that highlife is a musical pidgin in which both rhythmic and melodic elements of African traditional music are simplified. Nevertheless, its development must be seen as a creative selection and integration of cultural materials on the part of Ghanaian musicians in response to a new situation—not as the result of the uncritical but imperfect assimilation of traits from politically dominant intruders.

The social history of the Fanti area of the Gold Coast differed from that of other British West African colonies in several important respects. This area was not only the first in Africa to support a permanent colonial installation (the Portuguese fort of São Jorge del Mina, begun in 1482), but it was also the first to develop a purely indigenous Westernized social and economic elite, who identified with and assimilated Western cultural values, and to varying degrees became hostile to their own native political, social, and cultural systems. The colonial elite of Nigeria did not reach such heights of economic and sociopolitical superiority over the leaders of the traditional system until much later. The elite of Sierra Leone had no local ethnic roots, but was composed of a conservative and more thoroughly Westernized class of freed slaves who, unlike the Akan elite of Ghana, had no specific tradition of indigenous music on which to draw.

The Fanti area was one of great ethnic mixture, owing to the rapidly expanding economic activity around the ports of Sekondi-Takoradi, Cape Coast, and Winneba. As a result, the social aspirations of the rising elite interacted with a variety of formative influences from abroad, as well as with elements of traditional Akan musical styles. A number of incipiently syncretic forms arose, and these later influenced or became part of the mainstreams of dance-band and guitar-band highlife.

The two instrumental traditions of dance-band and guitar-band highlife have developed to some degree in a parallel fashion; but despite their continuous mutual interaction, each has achieved and maintained an identity as an autonomous system.

Let us consider first the development of dance-band highlife. By the second decade of the twentieth century the rising Christianized elite possessed quantities of wealth and leisure time previously unknown in Fantiland. The proper enjoyment of this new status demanded entertainment on a grand scale, which meant, of course, in the style of the Europeans. African musicians, provided with Western instruments and playing skills by the churches and the military, began to hire themselves out as professionals, playing Western popular dances like the waltz and the quickstep for the large social affairs of British officials and their native counterparts. By World War I, large orchestras like the Excelsior Orchestra were playing such music in large ballrooms for Africans in evening dress. The exorbitant price of admission kept the less fortunate members of this newly urbanized and socially stratified society outside. In the 1920s it became customary for such orchestras to include a few Akan melodies, orchestrated in Western four-part harmony, in each evening's entertainment. Thus it was that African music entered through a Western door, rather than vice versa. Western-trained Africans began to select indigenous elements from their own musical idioms, with which they "Africanized" European popular music for the benefit of black elite audiences.

It was also common at this time for large numbers of people from the lower strata of Gold Coast society to crowd around the dance halls and gaze in with a mixture of fascination and disapproval at these distinctly un-African goings-on. It was these onlookers, joined by the musicians themselves, who both in envy and derision coined the term *highlife* for the music that was played.[11] The musicians, poorly paid semiprofessionals of relatively low status who had themselves benefited only slightly from the new state of affairs that occasioned their employment, adopted the term officially and soon began to introduce Western orchestrations of traditional melodies as "highlifes." Despite subsequent attempts to eradicate it, the name (and the attitudes it connoted) persisted, and the term *highlife* retained its appeal throughout its subsequent history.

Before reviewing the important developments that followed World War I, we should retrace our steps a bit and consider the parallel development of the other major instrumental tradition, guitar-band or "palm-wine" highlife. Following World War I, the new elite rapidly began to serve as a reference group for more traditional, nonliterate Africans as the new urban socioeconomic reality became progressively less comprehensible to the latter and less responsive to mediation by traditional values and systems of social control. At the same time that the brass bands and dance orchestras were bringing African melody back into their repertoires, a complexly interactive variety of outside influences was transforming the recreational music of the Fanti area into new syncretic forms.

It is well known that recreational music in Africa is more amenable to innovation and alteration than is music that is more directly associated with traditional religious and political systems, and that its discrete forms are more transient. Additionally, in the area under study there were instrumental, rhythmic, and melodic similarities between Akan folk styles and the many foreign styles that acted upon them. Among the important indigenous forms involved in this interaction were the singing groups of the Fanti fishermen, who utilized a large, box-shaped sansa or "hand piano" called *apremprensemma* (known in the West Indies by the name *mirimbula*) as well as hand drums. Other related styles included Fanti *adenkum* female singing groups and Fanti *nuyentoku* groups, some of which used the traditional Akan lute, *seprewa*, on whose melodies many later highlife tunes were based.

A new music grew out of the interaction between these forms and the folksongs and shanties of both white and black sailors, the latter including West Indians, Afro-Americans, and (in particular) Krus from Liberia.[12] Akan youngsters who were used to the music of the seprewa found little difficulty in picking up the guitar instead, and they readily learned the two-finger style of the Kru sailors. Kwame Asare, popularly known as Sam, claims to have learned the basis of the two-finger style known as *dagomba* from a Kru sailor. Robert Sprigge contends that it was the technical problem of working out Akan melodies in two-finger style upon the new instrument that accounts for the particular form of "Yaa Amponsah" (still considered the prototype of the standard or "mainline" highlife rhythm and melody) and other early highlife melodies.[13] A. A. Mensah notes that on the early 78 rpm highlife recording "Owea Kwaduampon" (Decca WA 643) the guitar introduction is entirely in the style of the Akan seprewa.[14] The African-derived rhythms of the West Indian sailors' music could also be congenially blended with indigenous recreational rhythms, eventually producing the characteristic highlife beats that are so similar to the rhythms of the calypso.

As a result of this interaction a number of syncretic proto-highlife styles began to develop, notably Fanti *osibisaba* music and the Akan acoustic-guitar bands that also employed voices, claves, drums, and apremprensemma. Harmonization was after the fashion of the Christian hymn.[15] Some bands and soloists used primarily sailors' instruments like the harmonica, concertina, and accordion; and Sam is known to have recorded songs on accordion and concertina in England probably no later than 1928.[16]

At the same time that foreigners were streaming in, the 1920s saw Ghanaians and their fellow West Africans being sent to work by the British in Nigeria, Sierra Leone, the Congo, and the Cameroons. In this way, carpenters from the coastal tribes of the Gold Coast returned from the Cameroons with a type of syncretic singing in pidgin English called *gombe,* in which the rhythm was said to be the characteristic beat of hammer on anvil. The melodies of this form also reveal the influence of the European hymn. Gombe may have been related to the development of similar forms later called *gumbeh* in Sierra Leone and *kumbeh* in Nigeria.[17]

New musical influences were felt also in the Akan hinterland, where brass bands as well as guitar bands were popular, and an important form called *konkomba* highlife developed.[18] This was a choral type of highlife in which the dancers' fancy Westernized attire (shorts with colored handkerchiefs tied around the waist, and peaked caps) reminds one of the Kalela dancers of Rhodesia described by Mitchell.[19] Military and brass bands derived their melodies and rhythms from osibisaba music, which was played with sailors' instruments, and whose name served as a generic term for many syncretic blends prior to the introduction of the term *highlife*.

A consideration of the development of syncretic music in the Ga area of the Ghanaian coast may help give the generalization of these historical processes some comparative substance. Although the port of Accra was subject to similar patterns of ethnic heterogeneity and rapid socioeconomic change, the Ga people had no traditional stringed instrument like the seprewa and no traditional singing bands like those of the Fanti. In addition, their traditional scale is pentatonic, and polyphonic intervals of fourths and fifths are favored. Thus it happened that the tones of Ga melodies and their harmonic preferences were much further removed from the musical traditions of the West than were the nearly diatonic Akan seven-note scale and the absolute pitches of the neutral thirds and sixths they preferred as polyphonic intervals. The Gas, despite the popularity of gombe, which featured only voices and drums, received only the dance-band form of highlife, which was brought initially to entertain the middle class in the new colonial capital at Accra. New recreational dance forms such as *ashiko* took the place of guitar highlife, and older informants cite ashiko as an early name for highlife. Dance music was provided during the twenties by such pacesetters as Teacher Lampley's Accra Rhythm Orchestra, and the Jazz Kings. The first Ga guitar band to achieve widespread popularity, Wulomei, did not appear until 1972.

The series of dramatic musical innovations grouped under the rubric *highlife* gained increasing popularity and distribution because they provided affective expression, and therefore mediation, of the social and interpersonal conflicts inherent in the colonial order and its attendant processes of enforced modernization. These processes included wage labor, migration and urbanization, bureaucratization, the spread of the money economy, the rise of African nationalism, and both horizontal and vertical social stratification and mobility. As Clifford Geertz has demonstrated for modern Indonesia, this background of social conflict "is not simply indicative of a loss of cultural consensus, but rather is indicative of a search, not yet entirely successful, for new, more generalized, and flexible patterns of belief and value."[20] Artistic creativity, Hallowell states, "fulfills man's need to supply himself with mediative factors in his cultural mode of adaptation, whereby a world of common meanings has been created in human societies."[21] For the new elite and the urban poor, indigenous music could no longer be entirely relied on for such fulfillment.

Because of these mediative processes and the ways in which they came to operate in response to social change, the influence of Western music and the development of highlife brought about a different perspective on the position of music and musicians in Ghanaian society. The relative specialization of composition and performance in highlife, as opposed to traditional Ghanaian music, made the role of highlife musician, like that of other social actors in the newly urbanized setting, highly differentiated and socially specialized in comparison with his traditional counterpart. Village or court musicians operate as highly respected social functionaries, fully integrated into the structure of social relations existing in the communities in which they perform. Highlife musicians, by contrast, are constantly on the move, working for cash.

In the twenties and thirties, the big dance bands were a good place for school-leavers to find work.[22] Pay was seldom high enough for the bandsmen to become fully professional, a state of affairs that has continued until recently; and even today only a minority are able to support a family solely through music. As a result, the professional lives of highlife musicians continue to be characterized by a high degree of fragmentation, interpersonal conflict, and instability—this in spite of efforts of bandleaders to substitute formal rules and group officers on the one hand, or dictatorial managerial policies on the other, for more traditional structures of social organization and control.

This situation is by no means characteristic of Ghana alone. Naomi Ware reports that Sierra Leonese bands, like Ghanaian ones, tend to change membership and break up with bewildering frequency.[23] Rycroft notes that the many small African dance bands of Johannesburg, South Africa, seem constantly to be changing their names and personnel despite the steady and enthusiastic demands for their services.[24] As in many countries, the high cost of modern equipment, without which few bands can attract an adequate following, often ties musicians to the constrictive demands and shoddy contractual practices of wealthy promoters. These musical entrepreneurs are constantly luring musicians away from other promoters and from the more "traditional" highlife bands. Players from the latter are especially vulnerable, as such groups often disdain promoters in favor of a manager-bandleader, who seldom provides financial security for his "band boys."

Thus the position of the urban Ghanaian musicians has gradually become comparable to that of the popular musician in Western countries, as low social status accompanied by an unsavory reputation are characteristic of social attitudes toward both. Perhaps the situation will change as innovative musicians in Ghana, like such personalities as Miles Davis in America, also come to be recognized as skilled professionals and "artists."

Although I have oversimplified the situation in the interests of elucidating some general trends, it does appear evident that the social organization of highlife bands reflects in its processes and conflicts the forces at work in urban West African society as a whole. Despite their transience and role specialization, guitar-band musicians have never operated, indeed could not have operated, as isolated professionals. They have retained their identification with and awareness of the everyday concerns of their audiences. Since they themselves share in these concerns, the highlife musician as artistic social actor has emerged as a mediator between values of continuity and change, and between the collective and individual striving for expression in Ghanaian society.[25]

The two main instrumental traditions of highlife have continued to function to some degree as independent musical systems. Both responded to (and to a degree created) aspirations, identity, and socially adaptive needs among their respective audiences. In this way Ghanaian social and ideological life began to organize itself along what Collins calls a "highlife-bush continuum."[26] The poles of this continuum symbolically opposed not only the urban to the rural environment, but also the high status and modern social aspirations of the elite to the low status and traditional cultural values that the newly urbanized laborers found it difficult and not always profitable to actively maintain.

Comparable symbolic processes appear to have taken shape

elsewhere. A form of syncretic music that attained popularity in Tanzania was known as "tarubu" music. *Tarubu* in Swahili means "civilized."[27] The symbolic conceptualization of social conflicts and rapid changes in values in terms of such a continuum has been cited for a number of rapidly modernizing societies, notably among the Javanese urban proletarians studied by James Peacock.[28] The effect of this conceptualization upon the social behavior of Ghanaians is evident in the character of the differential development of dance-band and guitar-band highlife.

In order to see the nature of this effect more clearly, let us briefly review the major musical and social developments in each tradition. John S. Roberts notes that African traditional popular music can be divided into two styles that reflect contrasting sociocultural purposes.[29] The first is a style intended for communal dancing, in which lyrics tend to be simple and de-emphasized. The second is a "listening" style that features relatively lengthy texts full of introspection, nostalgia, social commentary, and narrative elaboration. Dance-band and guitar-band highlife respectively represent these two styles in syncretic Ghanaian popular music. Recreational dance is traditionally accompanied by a drum ensemble in West Africa, and dance-band highlife has essentially superimposed entirely Western melodic instruments over African or Afro-Caribbean rhythms for the purpose of creating lively dance music. By contrast, "listening"-style songs have traditionally been accompanied by idiophones, chordophones, and linguaphones; dancing has tended to be incidental to the songs' fundamentally expressive purpose. The guitar has been introduced into this style to create guitar-band highlife. Guitar-band performances have characteristically featured rapt audience attention to musical narrations full of philosophical and social observations on everyday life and values.

Such distinctions are by no means rigid. Not only have the guitar and percussion ensembles of "highlife *adowa*" traditionally been danced to, but in recent years whole nightclub audiences have danced to guitar bands, while dance bands may feature elaborate and highly topical lyrics. Nevertheless, Roberts's stylistic contrast does serve to orient our understanding of the developmental trends in highlife music as a whole during the first half of this century.

The events of World War I, and the increased contact with black merchant seamen from the Commonwealth and North America, intensified the ongoing process of musical acculturation. In addition, the increasing availability of disc recordings, radio, and sheet music had the effect of bringing Ghanaian popular music into more immediate contact with current Western trends, as well as providing highlife with widespread distribution throughout the hinterland of British West Africa.

Western ballroom music and ragtime had an influence on dance-band highlife during the interwar years, and styles like the fox-trot, quickstep, and Europeanized rumba were popular. Later on, in the 1930s and 1940s, swing bands like that of American Jimmie Lunceford were imitated by the large colonial highlife orchestras. Up until World War II, dance-band "highlifes" continued to consist mainly of Akan melodies, played in 2/4 time and given a Western feel through "correct" four-part harmonization, such pieces being inserted into an evening of Western dance music. Some syncretic dances, such as *timo* and Nigerian *ashiko,* also became popular in Accra ballrooms at this time. While the rhythmic flavor of highlife continued to benefit from the growing popularity of calypso and other West Indies forms, a steady Westernization and modernization of instrumentation occurred, so that Latin instruments like congas, bongos, and maracas were substituted for bass and side drums; and tubas and violins gave way completely to trumpets and saxophones. The importance of the Western ballroom orchestra as a model is reflected in the prestigious-sounding names of the leading orchestras, such as the Accra City Orchestra, the Royal Babies, and the Juabeng Royal Orchestra.

World War II was an important catalyst for both social and musical change in West Africa. A new crop of innovative musicians, trained in church, school, and the "street bands" of their boyhood, returned after the war from abroad with new musical influences, in particular those of the West Indies and North America.[30] E. T. Mensah, the "King of Highlife," was the first to orchestrate both traditional themes and indigenous rhythms for dance band, and in the process organized his famous Tempos Band after a new model, that of the jazz combos and Latin dance-bands of the war era. Mensah's band was smaller than prewar orchestras; and the music reflected the influence of contemporary

107

swing, cha-cha, and calypso more than that of the fox-trot or quickstep.[31] The instrumentation consisted of trumpet, trombone, saxophone, Latin percussion, electric guitar, and string bass. The music was characterized by the perhaps unavoidable absence of polymetric effects and by an incomplete assimilation of harmonic skills that led the horns to play in unison, following a single melodic sequence rather than a chord progression, and to some degree isolated from the rhythmic background.[32]

Band names of this period, such as the All Stars, Star Gazers, and Hot Shots, reflected the change in musical models. As the gradual shift was made from purely English lyrics to lyrics set in the vernacular, the dance-band tradition of highlife continued to be tied to the tastes and social needs of the elite, who were beginning to inherit power from the British with the rise of African nationalism in Ghana. The lyrics were unlike those heard in the low-status guitar bands in that they contained little social criticism, but rather concentrated on romantic love and other Western ideals.

Throughout its development, guitar-band highlife maintained greater continuity of musical structure with indigenous recreational music than did dance-band highlife. Rather than identifying with the ideals of the Westernized elite by trying to bring African elements into "civilized" Western musical tradition, guitar highlife developed from the needs of the ethnically heterogeneous Ghanaian urban working class to express emotional response to the conflicts inherent in the new social environment. On the level of cultural meaning, there was much less contrast between an urban laborer and a villager than between such a worker and a member of the urban elite.[33] The very name *highlife* in this connection connoted the performers' disapproval as much as their envy of the elite's high-living ways; and the lyrics of guitar-band songs included much adverse comment on the social, political, and economic wrongdoings of people in high places.

This tradition of social commentary has continued up through recent times, and it has been responded to by the Nkrumah administration in its efforts to get the name *highlife*, with its critical connotations, changed officially to the more "African-sounding" term *osibisaba music*. The new name never caught on, in any case, and when Nkrumah fell, the famous African Brothers Band issued the hit song "Ebi Tie Ye" (Some Sit Well), which deliberately criticized governmental corruption and the injustices of social stratification. Perhaps because there is no indigenous term for "elite," *ebi tie ye* has passed into popular language as a means of signifying Ghana's new social hierarchy.[34]

More commonly, song lyrics have dealt with the typical contemporary social problems of individuals in painfully familiar situations; and they represented an attempt to conceptualize and formulate moral positions on the urban situation in terms of the value system of traditional Ghanaian culture. Amid a social environment radically more complex than the traditional tribal milieus, urban Ghanaian workers clung noticeably to the values and symbols that had guided them or their forebears through life in rural society.[35] This tenacity is evident in the songs of social-problem lyrical content. The prevalence of topical songs and lengthy personal narratives set to highlife demonstrate the functional and structural continuity of guitar-band highlife with the time-honored tradition of music as a means of social commentary, communication, and control.

At the same time that some highlife songs were decrying the false attractions of urban life and criticizing those working-class or elite Ghanaians who had abandoned the constraints and moral guidance of traditional values, other songs, like the African Brothers' "Obiba Broke," attempted to explain to its audience the nature of social forces that draw young people to the city. Songs such as E.K.'s "'se Woko na Anny e Yie a San Bra" refer openly to kissing and affirm the value of Western-style romantic love.[36] Concurrently, highlife brought urban attractions into the villages through radio, phonograph, and live performance. Not confined to the larger towns as were the dance bands, guitar bands trekked throughout the hinterland, criticizing and explaining the forces that were changing people's lives, while at the same time taking part in and symbolically representing the process of modernization itself.

Thus guitar highlife and the "concert party" (a popular form of Ghanaian musical drama that came to be associated with highlife from 1952 onward) provided therapy for tensions stemming from modernization by drawing people into empathy with its action. Thus it facilitated participation in modernism by making it easier for those who were involuntarily involved with it.[37] The polyglot nature of highlife lyrics, which might feature several languages in a single song, reflected the role of highlife as a lingua franca of socialization and as a medium for the expressive release from social tensions. The identification of highlife with the rise of Ghanaian national consciousness has been demonstrated on a high level: although the king of Ashanti is always accompanied by traditional drummers on state visits, Nkrumah preferred the accompaniment of highlife—from E.K.'s Band—when he visited Liberia in 1953.[38]

The Nkrumah government was well aware of the importance of highlife as a social force and vehicle of political communication. Beginning in 1959, the government began to co-opt the social function of highlife by sponsoring its own bands, with each department competing to produce the best bands. Nonstate bands who strove to retain their independent sociopolitical perspective often provoked Nkrumah's personal displeasure and censorship, and in general they found it difficult to keep personnel.

Guitar-band highlife was able to perform a mediating function to some degree by virtue of its close musical connection to indigenous forms. In their inception, as we have seen, guitar bands developed out of indigenous ensembles that had been influenced by church harmonies and the sailors' songs of fellow Africans. Highlife later recombined with indigenous forms to provide recreational music for young people's associations; and in turn it gave birth to such traditional styles as *kolomashie, oge,* and more recently *kpanlogo.*

In some cases older, purely indigenous forms were able to blend with highlife, and such styles as highlife adowa developed, in which traditional Akan dances were performed to the accompaniment of so-called traditional highlife acoustic guitar and drums. In many parts of Ghana today and in particular the North, highlife itself is played on purely indigenous instruments. In terms of instrumentation, the major changes in guitar-band highlife have been the addition of the trap-drum set and the electric guitar. Latin American congas also early replaced indigenous drums.

With the rise of rock 'n' roll as the most popular form of dance music in the West, the instrumental and social tradition of dance-band highlife has declined, and there is very little new dance-band highlife being produced in Ghana today. This is due as much to its loss of social relevance and symbolic significance since independence for the elite as it is to the hegemony of the electric guitar in other styles.

The youth of Ghana, with their "Afro" culture, also tend to deny the sociopolitical relevance of highlife, and consider it old-fashioned and "colo" (colonial). Contemporary trends in African cultural revitalization and pan-African nationalism have, however, generated an important exception to this last statement, one that bears closer examination.

In 1972 the internationally respected Ghanian musician and arranger Saka Acquaye, long known as an innovator in modern African syncretic forms, teamed up with a group of traditionally oriented Ga musicians and dancers led by Nii Ashitey to form Wulomei, perhaps the most popular band in Ghana in the summer of 1974. *Wulomei* means "priests" in Ga, and the young male and female performers dress in a slightly modernized form of the white cloths and black-and-white beads of Ga ritual officiants. The instruments include traditional Ga drums and idiophones of various types matched with bamboo recorders and apremprensemma from the Akan. An acoustic guitar with a single pickup replaces the usual solid-body electric guitar. The other Western instrument employed, a pair of Latin congas, is "Africanized" by the addition of black paint and raffia fringe decoration. The music is derived from traditional Ga melodies, guitar-band highlife, gombe, and the kpanlogo music of Ga young-people's associations. Although all lyrics are in Ga, there is some dancing taken from the traditional styles of other groups; and one of the six dancers is an Ewe tribeswoman. Lyric content leans strongly in the direction of social criticism and relations between the sexes. Despite the self-aggrandizing emphasis on Ga language and ethnic identity throughout all phases of the performance, Wulomei is popular with Akan young people, and audiences are always ethnically mixed. We may tentatively suggest some reasons why this is so.

Like much of Ga neotraditional music, that of Wulomei has been strongly influenced by the traditions of the Akan. In addition to the use of the guitar, unique for neotraditional Ga forms, the songs are sung in a more-or-less completely diatonic version of the Akan seven-tone scale. Like the melodies of kpanlogo, the songs of

111

Wulomei show the influence of church harmonies, Akan highlife melodic progressions, and a preference for intervals of thirds and sixths. The guitar is played by a Fanti musician in the Akan "traditional" highlife style. Musically, the Wulomei are modern Akans in neotraditional Ga clothing, with even a little Ewe thrown in. The music appeals across ethnic boundaries to all kinds of young Ghanaians, but the neotraditional mise-en-scène, complete with fetish dancing, raffia skirts, and a good deal of sexual suggestion, has a special appeal to an unurbanized generation seeking to return to values drawn from many indigenous traditions, as these young people are seeking models for a modern society based on social justice and free of the ethnic chauvinism inherent in their traditional value system.

In this way the creation of a multi-ethnic symbolic complex in the guise of Ga cultural revitalization serves the cause of national and pan-African social consciousness, while at the same time providing ethical models for a new, made-in-Ghana society by taking advantage of the socially critical tradition of highlife song. Wulomei thus contributes to the resolution of the conflict "between traditional cultural identities and contemporary nationalist ideologies" that Geertz shows to be characteristic of the politics of so many young states.[39] It will not be long before neotraditional bands of this kind begin bringing the new highlife message to other West African countries, just as other great Ghanaian bands have done before them.

At the same time, more conventional guitar-band highlife continues to be featured in the first part of concerts otherwise devoted to the performance of extremely popular forms of Afro-American and contemporary African music such as soul and afro-beat. More importantly, highlife is now intimately tied to the performance of Ghanaian concert party, which in its symbolically dramatic treatment of topical issues and contemporary social problems continues to provide the kind of expressive mediation between traditional and modern values that is required by those caught up in the modernization process. Because it has always stood at the cutting edge of change, highlife, with its social content and symbolic meanings, may provide a uniquely revealing source of understanding for scholars interested in the problems of urban Africa. In this case, the study of a musical art form in relation to the social forces that gave it birth (and which it in turn helped to direct) may serve as a better key to Ghana's social change than would the study of more diffuse and inaccessible aspects of Ghanaian social behavior.

NOTES

1. Jan Mukarovsky, *Aesthetic Function, Norm, and Value as Social Facts* (Ann Arbor: University of Michigan Press, 1970), p. 88.
2. K. Peter Etzkorn, "On the Sphere of Social Validity in African Art: Sociological Reflections on Ethnographic Data," in *The Traditional Artist in African Societies*, ed. Warren L. d'Azevedo (Bloomington: Indiana University Press, 1973), pp. 347, 350.
3. E. J. Collins, "Highlife: A Study in Syncretic Neofolk Music" (unpublished paper, 1972), pp. 8, 26. My sincerest thanks must go to Mr. Collins for making available to me a wealth of information and insight without which this paper would not have been possible.
4. Elizabeth Tonkin, "Some Coastal Pidgins of West Africa," in *Social Anthropology and Language*, ed. Edwin Ardener (London: Travistok, 1971), p. 130.
5. E. J. Collins, *E. T. Mensah, The King of Highlife* (Accra: Ghana Publishing, forthcoming), p. 3.
6. Ibid.
7. Collins, "Highlife," p. 27.
8. John Beecham, *Ashantee and the Gold Coast* (London: John Mason, 1841), p. 112.
9. Attah Anan Mensah, "The Impact of Western Music on the Musical Traditions of Ghana," *Composer* 19 (1966), 19–22.
10. Robert Sprigge, "The Ghanaian Highlife: Notation and Sources," *Music in Ghana* 2 (1961), 70–94.
11. E. J. Collins, personal communication, 1974.
12. Ibid.
13. Sprigge, "Ghanaian Highlife," p. 89.
14. Mensah, "Impact of Western Music," p. 21.
15. Ibid.
16. Collins, personal communication, 1974.
17. Bruce King, "Introducing the Highlife," *Jazz Monthly*, July, 1966, pp. 3–8.
18. Collins, "Highlife," p. 12.
19. J. Clyde Mitchell, *The Kalela Dance* (Manchester: Manchester University Press, 1956).
20. Clifford Geertz, *The Interpretation of Cultures* (New York: Basic Books, 1973), p. 150.
21. A. I. Hallowell, "Myth, Culture, and Personality," *American Anthropologist* 49 (1947), 544–56.
22. Collins, *E. T. Mensah*.
23. Naomi Ware Hooker, "Popular Musicians in Freetown," *African Urban Notes* 5:4 (1970), 11–18.
24. David Rycroft, "African Music in Johannesburg: African and Non-

African Features," *Journal of the International Folk Music Council* 11 (1959), 25–30.

25. Warren L. d'Azevedo, "Introduction," in *The Traditional Artist in African Societies,* ed. Warren L. d'Azevedo (Bloomington: Indiana University Press, 1973), p. 17.

26. Collins, "Highlife," p. 22.

27. Ibid.

28. James Peacock, *Rites of Modernization* (Chicago: University of Chicago Press, 1968).

29. John S. Roberts, *Black Music of Two Worlds* (New York: Praeger, 1972).

30. J. H. K. Nketia, "Modern Trends in Ghana Music," *African Music* 1:4 (1957), 13–17.

31. Collins, "Highlife," p. 13.

32. King, "Introducing the Highlife," p. 4.

33. Geertz, *Interpretation of Cultures,* p. 165.

34. Collins, "Highlife," p. 16.

35. Geertz, *Interpretation of Cultures,* p. 165.

36. Collins, "Highlife," pp. 16–17.

37. Peacock, *Rites of Modernization,* p. 238.

38. J. H. K. Nketia, "The Gramophone and Contemporary Music in the Gold Coast," *Proceedings of the Fourth Annual Conference of the West African Institute of Social and Economic Research* (Ibadan, 1955), pp. 189–200.

39. Geertz, *Interpretation of Cultures,* p. 243 ff.

Music in Madras:
The Urbanization of a Cultural Tradition

KATHLEEN L'ARMAND AND ADRIAN L'ARMAND

There was little musical activity in Madras for the first two hundred years after the city's founding in 1640.[1] Rather, music flourished in the temples and courts of South India, then the centers of Carnatic, or classical South Indian music. Carnatic music is now almost entirely centralized in Madras. In this investigation we have attempted to identify the type and extent of change of the musical tradition in this new urban setting. Adopting the terminology of the Redfield-Singer hypothesis on the cultural role of cities, we could say that this is a study of the secondary urbanization of a "Great Tradition" in culture.

The Redfield-Singer theory may be schematized thus:[2]

PROCESS	PRODUCT	CITY TYPE	AGENTS
	Little Traditions		
Primary Urbanization		Orthogenetic (Entirely within the culture)	"Literari" as transmitters of traditional culture
	Great Tradition		
Secondary Urbanization	Modern Urban Culture	Heterogenetic (Metropolitan)	"Intelligentsia" as mediators of indigenous/foreign cultures

Kathleen L'Armand is Chairwoman, Social Science, Widener College, Chester, Pennsylvania. Adrian L'Armand teaches at the Settlement Music School, Philadelphia, Pennsylvania.

115

Milton Singer, co-author of this theory, visited Madras in 1954–55, 1960–61, and 1964. His interest was in the study of a Great Tradition and its literari in a metropolitan center. Singer lists three methods of "localizing a Great Tradition within a limited area: through a study of its sacred geography, of its professional representatives and their social organization and of its cultural performances (including religious rites and ceremonies)." He undertook his study using primarily the second and third methods, those of examining cultural performers and performances.[3]

Singer identified and studied five types of cultural performance: folk, ritual, popular, devotional, classical, and modern urban (film and drama). Within the classical field he gives the fullest treatment to dance, but also describes classical music. He characterizes music and dance performances as having both modern and traditional components. He concludes, however, that classical music and dance in present-day Madras are "essentially urban developments of the last one hundred years, although they have more ancient precedents."[4]

We propose testing the same overall hypothesis regarding change, while examining the Carnatic music tradition in greater detail. Areas in which we will be looking for change over time, including a few also examined by Singer, are some that relate to musicians (number, specialization, sex, place of origin, and training); and some that relate to performance (occasions, type of music played, and patronage system). Whether or not a given amount of change in a cultural system justifies describing it as modern (rather than as a variant of the older system) is of course a matter of judgment. We consider the descriptive function of this study to be more important than any conclusions.

In examining the question of continuity and change in the cultural traditions surrounding music, we will first describe Carnatic music and musicians in modern-day Madras. We will then describe music in South India of the seventeenth, eighteenth, and early nineteenth centuries, moving to a consideration of changes in Carnatic music as it gradually became localized in Madras after 1850. Finally, we will look for evidence of more recent changes in the musical tradition, covering the period 1938–67.

Method

We have of course used different sources, as available, for the several historical periods treated.

The main source for the description of music and musicians in present-day Madras has been the Madras daily newspaper *Hindu,* which prints announcements of public concerts[5] and a complete schedule of the programming of All India Radio Madras. In both of these sections, the names of principal performers and usually of accompanists are included in the announcement of performance. From this source we compiled information on all Carnatic-music concerts for a twelve-month period (August, 1966, to July, 1967) and on all Carnatic-music radio broadcasts for a three-month period (August, September, and October, 1966). The listing of musicians obtained by this method could not be exhaustive, of course, but we assumed that most professional musicians would appear at some time during this period. To check the completeness of the list of musicians, we compared the number obtained by this sampling method (784) with the number registered as eligible to play for A.I.R. Madras during the same period (782).[6] Indeed, in categorizing as a professional musician anyone who appeared in a concert or performed over the radio, we chose to err on the side of including too many rather than too few people on the list.[7]

South Indian names often contain a great deal of information, in the following order:

(1) Place-name or initial	(2) Father's initial	(3) Given name	(4) Caste name
Example: Srirangam	R.	Ranganatha	Iyer

The place-name given is that of one's "native place." It need not refer to actual place of residence, but is the place considered to be the family home. The place-name is sometimes omitted and sometimes abbreviated to an initial. Then follows the initial of the father's given name. Married women substitute the initial of the husband's name for that of the father and have recently begun to use instead their own given name followed by that of their husband, for example Vasantha Ranganathan. The sex of the musician can of course be determined from the given name. Caste names were used in the 1966–67 sample by about one-fourth of the musicians. The groups in Tamil Nadu traditionally associated with music, whose members account for most of our sample, are Brahmins, Devadasis, and those of the barber caste.

The most common Tamil Brahmin caste names are Iyer and Iyengar. Sastri, although it is actually an honorific title, is also used in place of a caste name for Brahmins. Names for non-Brahmin castes have generally followed along the lines of hereditary occupations. The caste name Pillai is a special case. It was originally used by a community of agriculturalists (Vellalars) but is now used by a number of non-Brahmin castes. When members of the Devadasi (formerly temple dancers and musicians) and barber (also nagaswaram and tavil players) groups use a caste name at all, they will use Pillai. It is highly unlikely that musicians using this caste name would belong to other non-Brahmin castes.

In order to get more information on the castes of musicians who do not use the caste name, we presented our lists with requests for caste identification to five well-established professional Carnatic musicians. These informants, who wish to remain anonymous, themselves represented both Brahmin and non-Brahmin castes and all important specializations in performance. There were no instances of disagreement in identification. We were thus able to add caste identification to an additional one-third of the 1966–67 sample.

Naturally, we had more difficulty locating sources when we tried to get a picture of the musical tradition in South India before the twentieth century. Even with music of recent centuries—seventeenth and thereafter—we find that the sources available are largely of an anecdotal nature.[8] Of references used, the only two that might be called primary sources on early music are the observations of the Abbé Dubois, written between 1792 and 1816,[9] and the manuscript translated by Dr. V. Raghavan dealing with music in Madras about 1800.[10] The *Castes and Tribes* series, which is basically a nineteenth-century work including some earlier material, has been a useful source on music as a hereditary occupation, providing a large number of observations that can be checked against one another.[11]

In treating changes in the musical tradition as Madras gradually became the center of Carnatic music, we have had to rely largely on interviews in Madras, both our own[12] and those reported by Singer[13] and included in the accounts of Sambamoorthy[14] and Rangaramanuja.[15]

In documenting more recent changes in music in Madras, we have again used the *Hindu*. The same kinds of information on concerts and radio broadcasts collected in 1966–67 were gathered for similar time periods in 1938–39 and 1948–49. Since the *Hindu* began publication in 1878, the obvious next step in this investigation is to collect comparable data from an earlier period.[16]

The original contribution of our research lies, we feel, in the description of music in Madras from 1938 to 1967 based on the newspaper accounts of concerts and radio broadcasts. The sections on the history of Carnatic music should be regarded mainly as background to these descriptions; we have tried to use the sources prudently, although neither of us has been trained as a historian.

Music in Madras: 1966–67

Concerts

In a concert of Carnatic music there is usually one principal performer, melodic and rhythm accompanists, and a tambura or drone.[17] The principal performer may sing or play any of the melodic instruments. Table 1 shows a distribution of public con-

TABLE 1. CONCERTS IN MADRAS (1966–67) CLASSIFIED BY TYPE OF PERFORMANCE

Type of Performance	Concerts	
	Number	Percentage
Vocal	310	63
Harikatha	54	11
Veena	42	9
Violin	30	6
Flute	21	4
Nagaswaram	17	4
Gottuvadyam	1	. . .
Other	14a	3
Total	489	100

NOTE: There were four concerts of Hindusthani music in Madras during this period.

aViolin, veena, flute trio (6); viola (2); clarinet (6)

119

certs in Madras during the twelve-month period from August, 1966, to July, 1967, classified according to type. As shown in table 1, the vocal concert is far more popular than the instrumental concert; vocal and harikatha performances together account for 74 percent of all concerts during the year. Harikatha is a subset of vocal performance in which the principal performer narrates and acts out a story, of religious theme, interspersed with songs. Among the instrumental concerts, no one type of performance—of veena, violin, flute, nagaswaram, or other—is a clear favorite.

For melodic accompaniment, a violin is generally used for both vocal and instrumental concerts. Exceptions are veena concerts, in which either another veena or a violin may accompany; and nagaswaram and clarinet concerts, in which two like-instruments always play together. At times two singers or instrumentalists are featured. If there are two singers, there will be violin accompaniment as well. If there are two instrumentalists of equal importance, the concert will be announced as a duet performance, and there will be no additional melodic accompaniment.

For rhythm accompaniment, a drum is always used. Mridangam provides the principal rhythm accompaniment for all concerts except nagaswaram, where a tavil substitutes. Other percussion is often used in addition to mridangam.

A concert generally lasts from three to four hours, and the musical performance is almost nonstop. The concert will begin roughly at the appointed time, with few people in the audience. The first piece is generally a *varṇam*, a technical piece roughly equivalent to a western étude. It is used so that the performers can warm up. Following this brisk opening, the principal musician chooses a piece that pays homage to Shri Ganapathi, and in this traditional way requests the lord's blessings for the concert. This invocation will be in the form of a *kiruti*, which is one form of composed music. It is preceded and followed by highly structured improvisation in the form of *ālāpaṇai* (an exposition of the *rākam* or raga) and *kalpaṇai cuvāram* (a rhythmic presentation of the rākam under the control of units of time, *tāḷam* or tala). By the completion of the kalpaṇai cuvāram, approximately half an hour of the concert is finished and most of the audience have arrived. The pace of the concert is maintained by now presenting a few short kiruti(s) with brief ālāpaṇai and kalpaṇai cuvāram.

From this point, when both the artists and the audience have become comfortable, the concert is more intense. The artist will choose kiruti(s) in contrasting rākam(s) and tāḷam(s), pacing himself and the audience toward the high point of the concert, which is the *rākam-tānam-pallavi*. This format consists of ālāpaṇai or rākam exposition, *tānam* (a free rhythmic presentation of the rākam), a composed piece in the *pallavi* form, and as a finale a *rākamālikai* (kalpaṇai cuvāram in the same rākam as that of the ālāpaṇai and pallavi and then in additional rākam[s]). After the rākam-tānam-pallavi, the concert winds down with the presentation of short pieces, often including dance forms such as *tillānā(s)* and *jāvaḷi(s)*. Requests are often sent up from the audience. The

TABLE 2. DISTRIBUTION OF MUSICIANS (1966–67) BY SPECIALIZATION

Specialization	Number	Percentage
Vocal		
Vocal	418	53
Harikatha	11	1
Total	429	55
Melodic instruments		
Violin[a]	96	12
Veena[b]	43	5
Nagaswaram[c]	35	4
Flute[d]	24	3
Clarinet[e]	7	1
Gottuvadyam[f]	4	(<1)
Mukhavina[g]	1	(<1)
Viola[h]	1	(<1)
Total	211	27
Rhythm instruments		
Mridangam[i]	83	11
Ghatam[j]	23	3
Kanjira[k]	23	3
Tavil[l]	9	1
Morsing[m]	6	(<1)
Total	144	18
Grand Total	784	100

[a]Western violin, tuned differently and played in a different position. [b]fretted and stringed, played by plucking. [c]double reed, loud nasal tone. [d]made of bamboo, without keys. [e]Western clarinet. [f]veena without frets. [g]double-reed instrument with a soft tone. [h]Western viola in Carnatic tuning. [i]two-headed drum. [j]large mud pot. [k]similar to tambourine. [l]two-headed drum, played with a stick and one hand. [m]jew's- or jaw's-harp.

concert finishes with a short auspicious composition called a *maṅkalam*.[18]

Specialization

Table 2 shows a distribution of musicians by specialization. Three subgroups are shown: vocal, melodic instruments, and rhythm instruments. Within subgroups, instruments are ordered from more to less common. In the few instances where a musician has appeared on more than one instrument, he is counted only for the major instrument. As would be expected from the popularity of vocal concerts, singers comprise by far the largest group of musicians (55%). Players on the usual accompanying instruments, violin (12%) and mridangam (11%), account for the next largest groups.

Sex ratio

Considering all musicians, men predominate in the Carnatic field with a 75 : 25 ratio (see table 3). Most of the women are singers, 40 percent of vocalists being women. The only other group with a large percentage of women (44%) is veena players. It is very unusual for a woman to choose any specialty but singing, harikatha, violin, or veena. The two female flute-players in our sample are sisters taught by their father. The one female mridangam-player performs with an all-female ensemble that has been playing in Madras for more than twenty-five years.

Native place

Musicians using the place-name made up about one-third of the sample. Only two named Madras (or the Tamil name, *Ceṉṉai*) as native place, reflecting identification with origins outside the city. There were nineteen towns listed as native place by more than two musicians. Five of them were sites of courts of the seventeenth century or after: Chittur, Mysore, Palghat, Trivandrum, and Vellore. Nine were towns noted for important temples: Cuddalore, Kanchipuram, Kumbakonam, Mannargudi, Mayavaram, Nagercoil, Srirangam, Tiruvarur, and Trichinopoly. Three towns (Madurai, Tanjore, and Ramnad) were noted for both temples and courts. Of the two remaining, Salem is a modern industrial town, and Karaikkudi is the center of a class of merchants, the Nattu-

TABLE 3. DISTRIBUTION OF MUSICIANS (1966–67) BY SPECIALIZATION AND SEX

Specialization	Males		Females	
	Number	Percentage	Number	Percentage
Vocal	251	60	167	40
Harikatha	9	82	2	18
Violin	88	92	8	8
Veena	24	56	19	44
Flute	22	92	2	8
Mridangam	82	99	1	1
All others	109	100	0	0
All musicians	585	75	199	25

kottai Chettis, who are noted for their participation in temple management.

Caste

Of the 784 musicians in the sample, 176 (22%) used the caste name. The castes of an additional 253 musicians (33%) were obtained from several informants (as described above), making a total of 429 (55%) identified as to caste.[19] A distribution of these musicians by caste and specialization is found in table 4. The great majority of musicians listed are either Brahmins (66%) or Pillais (24%). As mentioned earlier, Brahmins have a traditional association with Carnatic music, as have the former temple dance-musicians and barber-musicians using the caste name Pillai. Of the 10 percent of the sample in the "other" category, the best general description is that they are high-status non-Brahmin castes.[20]

When the caste distribution of musicians specializing in each type of music is examined, some patterns appear.

Instruments played exclusively by non-Brahmins are the nagaswaram, tavil, and clarinet. Of these, the nagaswaram and tavil belong to the temple-music tradition, with the players traditionally being men of the barber caste. The Western clarinet was brought into South Indian music in the late nineteenth century in the dance-accompaniment group.

There is no specialization reserved exclusively for Brahmins. All of the identified harikatha players are Brahmins, but this is just a chance occurrence for this period—non-Brahmins do perform in harikatha. The veena is the only instrument that we would come close to calling a Brahmin instrument, with 90 percent of

123

TABLE 4. DISTRIBUTION OF MUSICIANS (1966–67) BY SPECIALIZATION AND CASTE

Specialization	Brahmin		Pillai		Other	
	Number	Percentage	Number	Percentage	Number	Percentage
Vocal						
Vocal	134	76	24	14	18	10
Harikatha	4	100	0	...	0	...
Melodic instruments						
Violin	48	70	14	21	6	9
Veena	16	90	1	5	1	5
Nagaswaram	0	...	21	88	3	12
Flute	11	58	7	37	1	5
Clarinet	0	...	3	50	3	50
Gottuvadyam	2	67	1	33	0	...
Viola	1	100	0	...	0	...
Rhythm instruments						
Mridangam	40	63	15	24	8	15
Ghatam	13	87	2	13	0	...
Kanjira	11	52	6	29	4	19
Tavil	0	...	7	100	0	...
Morsing	3	75	1	25	0	...
All musicians	283	66	102	24	44[a]	10

[a]Naidu (10), Mudiliar (9), Chettiar (7), Nair (6), Sarma (4), Pandaram (2), Naicker (1), Reddi (1), Asari (1), Muslim (1), Panikker (1), Christian (1).

identified players Brahmins. Brahmins predominate most strongly in the vocal field (76%), but for every instrument that they play at all they account for more than half of the musicians. This is the case even for the flute and the rhythm instruments mridangam, kanjira, and morsing, all of which are historically associated with the non-Brahmin dance-music tradition.

Music in the Temples and Courts of South India: Seventeenth, Eighteenth, and Early Nineteenth Centuries

Musical traditions

There are a number of musical traditions in South India. The types of music now forming the concert repertoire have several origins differing as to the occasion for performance, voice or in-strumental-group performance, musical form, and practitioners. Three distinct traditions are temple music, temple dance-accompaniment, and private devotional music.

The *periya mēḷam* or nagaswaram party[21] provided an accompaniment to daily temple ritual as well as to processions and festive occasions within and outside the temple. The main instrument, the nagaswaram, was accompanied by a reed drone—the ottu—and by drum.[22] There does not appear to have been a type of musical composition used by nagaswaram players. They specialized in exposition of rākam appropriate to the hour of the day. Players in the nagaswaram group were drawn from males of the barber caste, or at times from the Devadasi group described below.[23]

Dancing also was a part of daily and festive ritual in the great temples of Tamil Nadu. The *ciṉṉa mēḷam* consisted of accompanists to the dancer: a singer and flute, mukhavina, and drum,[24] probably mridangam.

The compositions for dance music reached their highest point in the seventeenth century with the composer of *patam(s)* Keshetrayya.[25] Patam(s) are written on the theme of the lover/beloved relationship;[26] usually they admit of dual interpretation, with the beloved being either the lord or a human. Other forms of dance music, such as *jāvaḷi(s)*, *tillānā(s)*, and *patavarnam(s)*, are more obviously rhythmical in nature and allow the dancer to show her footwork. Jāvaḷi(s) are often decidedly erotic in nature.[27] These latter types are mainly compositions of the nineteenth century.

The dancers and musicians were drawn from a group called Devadasis (servers of god). Girls in South India who were dedicated to the god rather than allowed to marry were called Devadasis. In Tamil country these girls were attached to temples and trained in dance and music. Although girls of various castes were thus dedicated, once they entered the service of the temple they and their descendants formed a quasi-caste group.[28]

Singing of songs in praise of the lord became a form of private worship after the rise of the late-medieval bhakti movement. The most glorious expressions of this music, in the musical form called kiruti(s), were composed in the late eighteenth and early nineteenth centuries by Tyagaraja (1767–1847), Muttuswami Dikshitar (1775–1835), and Syama Sastri (1762–1827).

The medium of expression for this music was singing and veena playing. Performers were Brahmins. The Abbé Dubois gives a typical description: "You may often hear Brahmins singing and accompanying themselves on a sort of lute which is known as a

veena. . . . It has always been a favorite among the better classes.
. . . It is generally taught by Brahmins, and as their lessons are
very expensive, and they persuade their pupils that a great many
are necessary in order to attain proficiency; it is obvious that only
the very rich can afford themselves this pleasure."[29]

These songs are traditionally held to have been composed and
performed only for praising the god, in private or house worship.
Yet at least from the time of Tyagaraja there are numerous references to their performance in a court setting, with at least a secondary purpose of artistry rather than devotion.

Princely patronage

After the fall of the Vijayanagar Empire in 1565, South India
was divided and redivided into smaller kingdoms with shifting
allegiances to one another and, later, to the East India Company
and the Crown. The most important and long-lived of these courts
were at Tanjore, Trivandrum, and Mysore. Sambamoorthy lists
fourteen places as "principal seats of music of South India during
the last three centuries . . . with the exception of Madras, the
Maharajahs, Rajahs or Zamindars of all other places mentioned
were all patrons of music."[30]

Musicians from all three of the earlier-mentioned groups benefited from princely patronage—nagaswaram parties and groups of
dancers and dance musicians were at times attached to a court
rather than a temple—but it is the relationship between royal patrons and Brahmin musicians that is cited as the cause of the great
flowering of Carnatic music during and just after the time of
Tyagaraja.

The administration of this system of patronage is unclear, as
rulers were as apt to boast of their musicians as of their other
assets. The largest number of musicians reported at a court is 360,
each adorning one day of the year, in the court of Serfojee of
Tanjore (1798–1833), "whose stipendiary life was most favourable
for the cultivation of taste and luxury."[31] All accomplished musicians at a court were entitled to the use of the term *āstāna vitvān*
or *camastāna vitvān*, meaning "palace master (musician)." These
musicians appear to have been supported most handsomely by
their patrons. For example, a salary of 50 rupees per month was
paid in 1824 to the camastāna vitvān of the Rajah of Ettiya-

puram.[32] Other musicians were not attached to a court but would travel to one or several courts to exhibit their skill.[33]

A salient feature of Carnatic music as practiced in the courts seems to have been competition. In this regard, a distinction was made between "competitions" among several musicians of the same or different courts and "contests" between two master musicians. "Defeat in a musical competition is a small affair but defeat in a musical contest means the loss of one's reputation . . . there have been instances when musicians defeated in contests gave up their musical careers for good."[34]

By the middle of the nineteenth century most of the southern princely states had been actually or effectively taken over by the Company or the Crown.[35] This did not mean a sudden collapse of the princely patronage system, especially in the larger and wealthier states (Mysore, Tanjore, and Travancore, the last of which remained a princely state until after Indian independence); but the shift from the courts to Madras that began on a large scale about 1850 was definitely completed by 1920.

Changes in Carnatic Music As It Became Centered in Madras after 1850

This section is organized by topic rather than by time periods, but an approximate chronological order is maintained.

Early merchant patronage

The earliest patrons of music in Madras were probably the wealthy merchants, who administered a system of patronage not unlike that of the rajahs before them and, in the beginning, contemporary to them. V. Raghavan has translated a Sanskrit manuscript of about 1800 that was composed for some merchant patrons of music in Madras about that time. According to this description, these merchants served as trustees of city temples, many of which were built and endowed by them, and patronized the "musicians, scholars, and courtezans" attached to the Madras temples. They also sponsored public concerts.[36]

Musicians reportedly began settling in Madras in the early nineteenth century. One of the first was Veena Kuppier, a Brahmin, a disciple of Tyagaraja, and a composer and performer. He lived in Mutthialpet. His son, T. Tyagayyar, also a musician, settled in Georgetown, as did Thachur Singanacharlu (1834–92), another well-known musician, who moved to Madras in the later nineteenth century.[37]

Dance and dance music as concert arts

With the Indian Renaissance movement of the early twentieth century, a number of efforts were made to "purify" Indian culture through social reform. One of these was the so-called anti-nautch movement, the aim of which was to eliminate the practice of Devadasi dedication. It is usual to attribute the declining fortunes of the temple dance-tradition to the influence of this movement,[38] but it seems equally reasonable to look to the reduced treasuries of the temples and courts that provided patronage for the art. In any case, temple dancing and dedication of Devadasis were prohibited only after Indian independence, by the Madras state legislature in 1947.[39]

From the early 1930s, however, there was a revival of the forms of temple dance as a concert art, with performers being both the hereditary temple/court dancers and girls of non-Devadasi families who had begun to learn dancing at that time.[40]

This development and, later, the 1947 legislative prohibition separated temple dance-music from its functional and institutional base. Former families of temple dancers and musicians, if they stayed in music, became concert artists and teachers.

New instruments

The violin was brought into Carnatic music, at least in the first recorded instance, by Balaswamy Dikshitar. He received his first lessons from the English bandmaster at Fort Saint George in Madras and then was made camastāna vitvān at Ettiyapuram in 1824 on the strength of his ability in playing the instrument.[41] The violin seems to have rapidly become important as an accompaniment to singers, as there are many references to players in the latter part of the nineteenth century. It is difficult to tell whether the violin replaced the veena as an accompaniment to the singer or whether the singer had at one time sung unaccompanied. There is a reference to a contest held in 1872 where one vocalist had a veena accompaniment and another a violin.[42] If the veena was the usual accompaniment, the violin soon usurped that position entirely.

The clarinet was first used in 1860 by Mahadeva Nattuvanar, who used it in the cinna melam, the dance-accompaniment group.[43] The instrument, when used, took the place of the mukhavina or flute.[44] No references to the clarinet's being used outside the cinna melam as a concert instrument occur until after 1920.

A number of instruments borrowed not from the West but from the folk tradition were used in classical music after 1850; they include the ghatam and morsing.[45]

Sabhas

In the 1890s was founded the first of the Madras sangita sabhas, voluntary associations sponsoring concerts. Four sabhas were established during this period.[46] The most influential of the Madras sabhas, the Music Academy, was founded in 1927, following the All-India Music Conference accompanying the Congress party meeting held in Madras that year.[47]

At first the Madras sabhas were founded by Brahmins. The largest number still are recognized as Brahmin organizations, but now there are several non-Brahmin sabhas. The sabhas were, when founded, regarded by their members as instruments of a "revival" of classical music and, later, of dance. Originally they presented only music concerts, but since the 1930s they have also sponsored dance performances. In 1948 there were about thirteen sabhas in Madras, in 1955 about twenty, and in 1966 about thirty-five.[48]

Performance format

Public concerts in sabhas since 1920 are reported to differ in several respects from earlier court, temple, or festive performances.

The change that has occasioned the most criticism is that of program arrangement. Modern concerts run from three to four hours, and they include many pieces performed with varying degrees of improvisation in the form of ālāpanai and kalpanai cuvāram. Accounts of pre-1920 concerts describe somewhat longer performances (four to six hours) but add that this time could be entirely taken up by elaboration on a single rākam.[49] This com-

parison seems to describe a shift in emphasis from elaborate improvisation on few rākam(s) to brief improvisation on many
rākam(s). In radio, where performance-time is rigidly fixed and
runs from fifteen minutes up to an hour and fifteen minutes, this
tendency is much more pronounced.

We have been unable to find the precise date of the first appearance of a microphone in a Madras concert hall (it was in the
1930s), but there is no denying the impact it has made on Carnatic music. The microphone has been held responsible for several
changes in the music itself: (a) Weak-voiced people can now become singers; (b) singers may lower the pitch to an easier-to-sing
but less audible range;[50] and (c) the veena, which has a soft tone,
now serves as a concert instrument. The favorable effects of the
microphone on the sabhas' financial stability have been various:
larger audiences can now be accommodated in the concert halls,
and the halls themselves can be erected cheaply with thatching,
and their acoustical properties can be overlooked.

In terms of musical forms, concert music now includes representatives from all three musical traditions. The "Brahmin" tradition of vocal/instrumental performance of the kiruti was, from its
background in private and court performance, the first to become
a concert art. As pointed out earlier, many Devadasi musicians
from the dance-accompaniment tradition became concert artists.
Singers and instrumentalists could present musical concerts (without a dancer) easily, as the dance forms, especially patam(s), are
amenable to concert performance. Later, musicians from this tradition widened their repertoire to include nondance forms.[51] Nagaswaram moved very late from exclusively temple/ceremonial use
to additional use in concerts. Rangaramanuja relates the first performance of kiruti(s) by nagaswaram players, and their first re-
cital appearance;[52] he does not mention the date, but the musicians involved appear on our list of musicians active in 1938.

Teaching and scholarship

The system of teaching music and dancing before 1920 had
been that of individual instruction, with students devoting all
their time to music or dance and usually living in the teacher's
house. This was called the gurukala system. Two of its effects were
to confine music to castes where music was a tradition and to pre-

vent girls from learning music unless they had relatives who were musicians.

A part of the organized "revival" of music and dance was the founding of formal schools for group instruction. Among the first music/dance schools founded in Madras are the Central College of Carnatic Music (1927) and Kalakshetra (1936). Later, music was introduced as a subject in the secondary and university curricula. The system of formal group-instruction has supplemented rather than supplanted the gurukala system.

The universities and the Music Academy, as well as the Indian government through various commissions and ministries, have contributed to the development of nontraditional scholarship on music. The Madras Music Academy, for example, publishes a yearly journal of articles on music, has sponsored a series of translations, and stages yearly music festivals that include daily technical discussions as well as performance.

Women in music

Women not of the Devadasi caste have only in this century begun to practice as professional musicians. The Abbé Dubois observed, around 1800, that "the courtesans of India are the only women who enjoy the privilege of learning to read, to dance, and to sing. A well-bred and respectable woman would for this reason blush to acquire any of these accomplishments." His editor noted a century later that reading and singing were at that time being taught to non-Devadasi girls, although dancing was not.[53] The first professional music performance by a non-Devadasi woman took place in 1910. The performer was Saraswathi Bai, a Brahmin, who was to become a celebrated harikatha artist.[54] The city of Madras seems to have provided a favorable climate for the entry of women into music. Sambamoorthy points out that "almost all the lady singers of eminence that South India has produced during the last century and the present century lived in Madras."[55]

In Madras city, girls who had no relatives from whom they could learn music could go to one of the music schools opened after 1920; later, they could study music in school or college. We have not been able to get information on the composition of the student body in early music schools, but we have observed that at present the student body of such institutions is overwhelmingly female.[56] Of course, not all of these students want to become professional musicians. Girls are very frequently sent to learn music as a desirable social accomplishment.[57]

Girls who do not learn music at an institution may learn at home; in a complete reversal of the gurukala system the teacher now comes to the pupil's house. Thus a new musical profession has been created, that of music teacher. The teachers are nearly all male.

Male students, by contrast, usually adopt a modified form of the gurukala system in which they pay a private instructor for lessons, become closely attached to his house, and fulfill such ceremonial duties as carrying his instrument at concerts.

Films

The film industry in its early days in Madras was a patron of music, but at present Carnatic musicians seldom enter the field. From 1935 to about 1945 the recording techniques for the films were such that the actors had to sing their songs while on the set during shooting. This meant that such famous Carnatic musicians as M. S. Subbulakshmi acted in films, as did many others in the classical field. Carnatic musicians could also work as background musicians, as the background music used in early Tamil films was much closer to Carnatic music than that used today. In the 1940s, when dubbing-in or "playback" replaced the recording of songs on the set, few Carnatic musicians became playback singers. For the last twenty-five years, because film music has evolved a style quite distinct from that of Carnatic music, classical musicians have not been greatly in demand in the film field. Those classical musicians who do work in the films can rarely pursue a concert career as well, because the times of work in films are so unpredictable as to preclude the scheduling of outside commitments.[58]

Radio

B. V. Keskar, minister of information and broadcasting from 1952 to 1957, reported of his work: "The object is to encourage the revival of our traditional music, classical and folk. Both were in a state of decay and somnolence. It is obvious that music, which formerly flourished on account of royal and princely patronage, will not revive and flourish unless the State can extend to them the same or extended patronage."[59] Keskar's first act upon taking office was to eliminate the playing of film music on A.I.R. More than half of all broadcast music during his tenure was Indian classical. The ban on film music was soon lifted, and there is not so much classical music played on A.I.R. at present, although it still accounts for a large share of the programming.

Potential performers are chosen by means of audition before a panel of judges, and are then graded into five categories. Categories are identified by the time allotted a performer: fifteen, thirty, forty-five, sixty, or seventy-five minutes. The pay scale in 1967 ranged from 35 to 150 rupees for a performance. As noted earlier, the 1967 list of musicians registered with A.I.R. Madras contained 782 names. It appears to be a policy with A.I.R., to judge from their programming, to use a wide variety of artists infrequently rather than feature fewer well-established artists. More than a third of the 1966–67 list of musicians was composed of performers who had no public concerts for one year and who appeared only once, for a half-hour or less, during a three-month period of radio broadcasting. A former national director suggests that the policy of A.I.R. is thus to encourage amateur performance.[60]

Weddings and other functions

Carnatic music was often a part of the festivities at marriages and the many other occasions that crowd the Indian life-cycle and calendar. The music played on such occasions was classical, of the type played at court and in modern concert performance. In the past thirty years Carnatic music has been in large part replaced at such celebrations, generally by film music played through loudspeakers. As this patronage provided the means of livelihood of the ordinary classical musician, its loss is perhaps the most important. Only the nagaswaram, which has retained its ceremonial function in the temple, has also kept its traditional position as an essential feature at weddings.

Recent Changes: 1938–67

The source of information for this section is concert and radio announcements printed in the *Hindu*. We collected concert announcements for three one-year periods, August to July in 1938–39, 1948–49, and 1966–67. We noted radio programming for three-month periods (August through October) in 1938, 1948, and 1966.

Concerts

As is shown in table 5, there were, for the successive one-year periods, 102, 207, and 489 concerts. The percent increases are appreciably greater than the corresponding population growth in Madras city during the same periods.[61] The increase in concerts

TABLE 5. CONCERTS IN MADRAS CLASSIFIED BY TYPE OF PERFORMANCE

Type of performance	1938–39		1948–49		1966–67	
	Number	Percentage	Number	Percentage	Number	Percentage
Vocal	66	65	170	84	310	64
Harikatha	16	15	11	5	54	11
Violin	2	2	7	3	30	6
Veena	8	8	5	2	42	9
Flute	6	6	11	5	21	4
Gottuvadyam	2	2	2	1	1	...
Nagaswaram	2	2	1	...	17	3
Other	...	...	...	...	14a	3
Total	102	100	207	100	489	100

NOTE: Concerts of Hindusthani music in Madras are not included in this listing. In 1938 there was one such concert; in 1948, eight; and in 1966, four.

aSee Table 1 for a listing of these concerts.

is somewhat smaller, proportionately, than the increase in number of sabhas.[62] This discrepancy is probably attributable to the fact that sabhas sponsor more dance and drama performances now than in previous years. Balancing this trend is the fact that concerts are at present scheduled on week-nights and in the afternoons in addition to the weekend evenings customary in 1938–39 and 1948–49.

Since many comparisons of the three time-periods will appear below, a methodological note is in order. In analyzing change over time, we have compared various distributions for each of the three time-periods, using the chi-square test to determine whether observed differences are statistically significant or could reasonably be attributed to chance factors. For example, in examining the relative popularity of vocal and instrumental concerts, we note a change over time, but no trend. Vocal concerts enjoyed a period of greater relative popularity (84% of all concerts) in 1948–49 than in either 1938–39 or 1966–67 (64% in both years). The distributions of vocal and all other concerts, when compared over time, differ significantly ($\chi^2 = 24.2$, $df = 2$, $p < .01$). Veena and harikatha, in contrast, dropped in popularity between 1939 and 1949 but resumed their former position by 1966–67. Percent differences in other categories are too small for meaningful analysis.

Specialization

The total list of musicians collected numbered 1,054 for 1938–39, 691 for 1948–49, and 784 for 1966–67 (see table 6). The very large number of musicians' names collected for 1938–39 reflects the fact that Madras was at that time the only All India Radio

TABLE 6. DISTRIBUTION OF MUSICIANS BY SPECIALIZATION

| Specialization | 1938–39 | | 1948–49 | | 1966–67 | |
	Number	Percentage	Number	Percentage	Number	Percentage
Vocal						
Vocal	703	67	422	61	418	53
Harikatha	39	4	7	1	11	1
Total	742	70	429	62	429	55
Melodic instruments						
Violin	73	7	84	12	96	12
Veena	74	7	55	8	43	6
Nagaswaram	51	5	11	2	35	4
Flute	54	5	16	2	24	3
Clarinet	3	(<1)	7	1	7	1
Gottuvadyam	12	1	4	(<1)	4	(<1)
Mukhavina	...	...	...	...	1	(<1)
Viola	...	...	...	...	1	(<1)
Jalatharangam	13	1	...	...	...	...
Total	280	27	177	26	211	27
Rhythm instruments						
Mridangam	23	2	59	9	83	11
Ghatam	2	(<1)	5	1	23	3
Kanjira	3	(<1)	16	2	23	3
Tavil	1	(<1)	1	(<1)	9	1
Morsing	...	...	2	(<1)	6	(<1)
Konugol	3	(<1)	2	(<1)	...	...
Total	32	3	85	12	144	18
Grand total	1054	100	691	100	784	100

station in the South, and many musicians traveled to Madras to perform.

Players on melodic instruments comprise about one-quarter of the total number of musicians for all three time-periods. Over time, however, the proportion of vocalists has gone down, while that of rhythm players has increased. This difference is statistically significant ($\chi^2 = 124.1$, $df = 4$, $p < .01$), but the increase may be at least partially apparent rather than real. Announcements of performances in 1938–39 and 1948–49 omitted the names of rhythm players more often than did 1966–67 announcements. Thus there may have been some anonymous and uncounted drummers in the earlier years. Evidence for a true rather than a spurious increase is the fact that individual rhythm-players had many more concerts in the two earlier time-periods, suggesting a smaller group of available musicians. It should also be noted that 1966–67 saw a large rise in listings of players of ghatam, kanjira, and morsing—all rhythm instruments played in addition to mridangam.

Two types of performance are found in earlier years but not at present: jalatharangam (a set of bowls of different sizes filled with water and played with two sticks) and konugol (a method of keeping the rhythm by reciting syllables).

Sex distribution

Considering all musicians, the proportion of women rose slightly (21%, 27%, 25%) though significantly ($\chi^2 = 9.8$, $df = 2$, $p < .01$) from 1938 to 1968. These changes were effected by increased numbers of women in vocal, harikatha, violin, and veena, not by women beginning to play new instruments. In each of the three periods there were only three women outside these fields. Therefore the more meaningful comparison is between male and female musicians in those fields that women ordinarily enter. The percentage of musicians in this subgroup increases from 25 in 1938–39 to 33 in 1948–49 to 35 in 1966–67. The male/female ratio differs significantly over the three time periods ($\chi^2 = 19.0$, $df = 2$, $p < .01$).

It is of course not startling to note that the participation of women in Carnatic music is increasing. As pointed out earlier, women from nonmusical families may now study music, and non-Devadasi women may perform. We propose the hypothesis, however, that the proportion of women who are active professionals has remained constant over the last thirty years, while the increase in the number of women musicians is accounted for by amateurs and less important musicians. To test this hypothesis we divided our subsample of vocal and harikatha performers, and violin and veena players into three categories: (*a*) Probable amateurs (no concerts in one year, 15-20–minute radio performance): this group accounted for 7 percent of the total in each of the time periods. (*b*) Less important musicians (no concerts in one year, 30-minute radio performance only once in three months): this group accounted for 21 percent of the total in 1938–39, 48 percent of the total in 1948–49, and 29 percent in 1966–67. (*c*) Active musicians (all others): this group was 72 percent of the total in 1938–39, 45 percent in 1948–49, and 64 percent in 1966–67. The proportions of male and female musicians in each category were then compared separately for each of the three time-periods. These comparisons are shown in table 7. The hypothesis was supported as presented. The sex distribution in the active-musicians category, as predicted, remains constant over the years. Females are *not* overrepresented

TABLE 7. VOCAL, HARIKATHA, VEENA, AND VIOLIN PERFORMERS CLASSIFIED BY SEX AND IMPORTANCE

Sex	Probable amateurs Number	Percentage	Less important musicians Number	Percentage	Active musicians Number	Percentage
			1938–39			
Males	45	71	139	74	485	76
Females	18	29	47	26	155	24
Total	63	100	186	100	640	100
			1948–49			
Males	26	60	167	61	189	75
Females	17	40	105	39	63	25
Total	43	100	272	100	252	100
			1966–67			
Males	15	41	84	51	273	75
Females	22	59	79	49	95	25
Total	37	100	163	100	368	100

NOTE: Results of significance tests comparing male and female distributions across the three categories of importance are:

1938–39: $\chi^2 = .43$, $df = 2$, not significant
1948–49: $\chi^2 = 11.99$, $df = 2$, $p < .01$
1966–67: $\chi^2 = 29.68$, $df = 2$, $p < .01$

137

in the lower categories in 1938–39, but are overrepresented in these categories in 1948–49 and 1966–67, more so in the latter time-period.

Native place

The percentage of musicians using the place-name rose from 26 to 27 to 32 over the three time-periods sampled. The towns commonly named in the earlier years did not differ from those named in 1966–67 (listed above).

Caste

The percentage of musicians using the caste name declined from 34 in 1938–39 to 24 in 1948–49 to 22 in 1966–67. This is a statistically significant difference ($\chi^2 = 39.1$, $df = 2$, $p < .01$).

To the caste identifications made from names we added those made by informants. For 1938–39 the informants were able to identify very few musicians, so we identified castes only on the basis of caste name (34%). For the 1948–49 sample, informants were able to name the caste of 12 percent; when this was added to the 24 percent using the caste name, a total of 36 percent of the sample for this period is identified. For the 1966–67 sample, 22 percent of musicians used the caste name and an additional 33 percent were identified by informants, making a total of 55 percent caste identifications. It is upon these musicians identified as to caste that table 8 is based.[63]

Caste distributions did not change significantly between 1938 and 1967. There were no differences of appreciable magnitude

TABLE 8. DISTRIBUTION OF MUSICIANS BY CASTE

| Caste | 1938–39 | | 1948–49 | | 1966–67 | |
	Number	Percentage	Number	Percentage	Number	Percentage
Brahmin	249	69	174	70	283	66
Pillai	63	17	50	20	102	24
Other	51[a]	14	26[b]	10	44[c]	10
Total	363	100	250	100	429	100

NOTE: $\chi^2 = 7.18$, $df = 4$, not significant.
[a]Naidu (15), Mudiliar (11), Chettiar (6), Sarma (6), Oduvar (4), Naicker (3), Nair (2), Christian (2), Reddi (1), Muslim (1).
[b]Naidu (8), Chettiar (4), Naicker (3), Mudiliar (2), Nair (2), Sarma (2), Asari (1), Christian (1), Reddi (1), Pandaram (1).
[c]Naidu (10), Mudiliar (9), Chettiar (7), Nair (6), Sarma (4), Pandaram (2), Naicker (1), Reddi (1), Asari (1), Muslim (1), Panikker (1), Christian (1).

between the 1966–67 caste distributions within musical specialties and those of earlier years; therefore caste distribution by specialty is not included in table 8. As pointed out earlier, the flute and most rhythm instruments were originally used in the non-Brahmin temple dance-tradition but now are played more by Brahmins than by non-Brahmins. This change did not come about in the last thirty years. Although we have not given the minute attention to sources necessary to thoroughly document this point, we have noticed that in accounts of pre-1900 performances, rhythm players have non-Brahmin names.[64] Brahmins must have entered the rhythm field, we would speculate, between 1900 and 1930. There has been no corresponding rush on the part of nonhereditary performers to learn the nagaswaram. Nor have many non-Brahmins taken to the veena. The violin has been played since its introduction into Carnatic music by both Brahmins and non-Brahmins.[65] Vocal music is part of the devotional/court and temple dance-music traditions, so it is to be expected that both groups are represented in modern concert art; it is interesting to note that Brahmins predominate heavily.

Summary and Conclusions

After considering these many aspects of Carnatic musical tradition, we would now be likely to agree with Singer's judgment that classical music in Madras is an essentially modern, essentially urban development. The system of patronage has shifted from the temples and courts to the merchants of the growing city of Madras, to the organized sabha and impersonal All India Radio patronage of today. The Carnatic concert now includes musical forms and performers from three musical traditions: temple music, dance accompaniment, and private devotional/court music. The elements of ritual observance, private devotion, and direct public competition that variously characterized past occasions for performance are largely absent in the concert music of today.

Even if only like-forms of music are compared, the question of whether a Carnatic music performance would sound the same today as it did around 1850 cannot be answered with accuracy. The compositions rendered could have the same titles, but as these pieces were passed down largely by oral tradition, we cannot be sure that they would sound like earlier versions. Documented changes in style of performance that would tend to make a difference musically include changes in length of performance and customs relating to improvisation, as well as the use of new instruments, heavier use of rhythm instruments, and the use of the microphone.

Among professional musicians, music has largely remained the province of hereditary musician castes and of Brahmins. Within these communities, however, performers now may adopt the repertoire and instruments traditionally identified with another group.

Women who are not Devadasis can now learn Carnatic music and perform publicly, although most of the recent increased representation of women appears to be on the amateur level. Music schools and the custom of lessons at the pupil's house, new forms of instruction that would tend to make music available to those from nonmusical families, are used mainly by women. Men, who form the large majority among active professional musicians, still learn music in a modified form of the gurukala system.

The period from 1938 to 1967 does not seem to have been a revolutionary one for Carnatic music. The volume of concerts increased, but no new favorites in the type of concert appeared. Rhythm players became more prominent. The proportion of women in music increased, but this entry was at the lower levels. Similar groups of musicians were active professionally for the three time-periods. From historical accounts, the period from about 1900 to 1930 would probably be a more fruitful one in which to look for large-scale changes in the practitioners and performances of Carnatic music.

NOTES

1. Some of the research presented here was earlier reported in a paper, "Music in Madras: The Organization of an Urban Cultural Tradition," at a meeting of the Association for Asian Studies, New York, March 27–30, 1972. Some of the empirical data contained in the present paper differ from those in the 1972 paper: the sample of musicians for this paper is based on a twelve-month concert record for a given year, while that for the earlier paper was based on a three-month concert record.

In using Indian-language words the Tamil form is chosen for terms that have equivalents in several Indian languages. The current Tamil transliteration system of the U.S. Library of Congress is used. We have treated as derived forms (in common English spelling and not italicized) geographical names, proper names, names of castes, musical instruments, and some commonly used musical terms.

In the transliterated Tamil words, vowels are pronounced long if there is a macron above the letter. The letter *a* is pronounced as the vowel in *but*, *i* in *pit*, *u* as in *pull*, *ā*, *ī*, and *ū* as in *call*, *routine*, and *tune*; *e* and *o* as in *hey* and *go*, *ai* and *au* as in *time* and *cow*. Sub-dotted consonants are retroflexed. The letter *ṉ* is alveolar, and *ḻ* is a voiced, retroflexed, frictionless continuant. A *k* between vowels is pronounced as either *h* or *g*.

2. Robert Redfield and Milton Singer, "The Cultural Role of Cities," *Economic Development and Cultural Change* 3: 1 (1954), 53–73.

3. Milton Singer, *When a Great Tradition Modernizes: An Anthropological Approach to Indian Civilization* (New York: Praeger, 1972), p. 62.

4. Ibid., p. 185.

5. Most of the concerts listed in the *Hindu* are sponsored by voluntary organizations known as sabhas. Sabha concerts are nearly always announced in the newspaper. Admission is charged for these concerts. Concerts at temples, where the performers are not paid and admission is free, are announced customarily, though not always. Privately sponsored concerts, such as those given at wedding receptions, are of course not announced.

6. The number of musicians registered at A.I.R. Madras was obtained by letter (1967) from the station director.

7. We considered cutting the list by eliminating those whom we judged probable amateurs—musicians who had no concerts in the twelve-month period and who could be placed in the lowest A.I.R. grade by a performance time of fifteen to twenty minutes. This method of classification was applicable only to singers and players of melodic instruments, as players of rhythm instruments always act as accompanists, and their radio-performance time is determined by that of the soloist. The "probable amateur" category accounted for a small percentage of this group: 7% in 1966–67 (comparable samples for 1938–39 and 1948–49 showed 6% and 8% respectively). We decided against eliminating these performers from the sample, as we considered both the small numbers involved and the possibility that we could be dealing with younger professionals as well as amateurs.

8. We have used the historical accounts of P. Sambamoorthy (e.g. those cited in nn. 14, 18, 21, and 32) as a source of description of the place of music in the temples and courts of seventeenth-, eighteenth-, and early nineteenth-century South India. His *Great Musicians* (Madras: Indian Music Publishing House, 1959) was also helpful. Sambamoorthy has assembled a large and extremely valuable collection of reference material, but his books, written for students, do not cite sources.

9. Abbé J. Dubois, *Hindu Manners, Customs, and Ceremonies*, 3d ed., trans. and ed. H. Beauchamp (Oxford: Clarendon Press, 1906 [first published, 1816]).

10. V. Raghavan, "Some Musicians and Their Patrons about 1800 in Madras City," *Journal of the Music Academy, Madras* 16 (1945), 127–36.

11. E. Thurston, *Castes and Tribes of South India*, 7 vols. (Madras: Government Press, 1909). These volumes are not indexed. We have gathered references in them to music into two unpublished papers that are available upon request: Kathleen L'Armand, "The Musicians of Village Hinduism: Music as a Traditional Occupation in South India, Following the Description

of Thurston" (1967), and Adrian L'Armand, "The Caste Structure of Performing Artists in Hindu Ritual: Nineteenth Century South India" (1968).

12. Adrian L'Armand studied Carnatic music in Madras from 1962 to 1966 and from 1969 to 1970. Kathleen L'Armand spent the years 1963–65 and 1969–70 in Madras. The interviews were informal in nature.

13. Singer, in *Great Tradition*, reports extensive interviews with harikatha singer Saraswati Bai, dance critic K. V. Ramachandran, dance teacher Chokkalingam Pillai, and dancer Balasaraswati.

14. P. Sambamoorthy, *History of Indian Music* (Madras: Indian Music Publishing House, 1960), p. 24. Sambamoorthy comments that he used interviews of families and descendants of musicians as a source. Unfortunately, he does not note specific instances when such interviews provided information contained in his books. The people whom he interviewed provided personal observations dating as far back as the 1870s (he was born in 1901 and began his career in musical scholarship in the 1920s).

15. Rangaramanuja Ayyangar, *History of South Indian (Carnatic) Music from Vedic Times to the Present* (Madras: By the author, 1972). In this work the author usually credits the source of recollections, and he includes dates frequently. His material is especially valuable because it includes, labeled as such, the author's personal recollections (he was born in 1901) and those of his famous preceptor Veena Dhanammal (b. 1868) and her contemporaries.

16. Copies of the *Hindu* back to its first issues (1878) are kept in the *Hindu* office in Madras, but the pre-1938 copies are so fragile that they cannot be handled. These early copies, according to the *Hindu* management, have been recently microfilmed and are available in Madras. As A.I.R. Madras started broadcasting in the early 1930s, data before that date can be collected only from concert announcements.

17. The tambura players are not included in the statistics on musicians as no musician specializes in playing tambura. The tambura player is usually a pupil of the principal performer.

18. For further description of the Carnatic concert, see the chapter on "katcheri dharma" in P. Sambamoorthy, *South Indian Music, Book 4,* 3d ed. (Madras: Indian Music Publishing House, 1963).

19. The sample of musicians identified as to caste is of course not technically representative of all musicians, as the sampling method used was nonrandom. Ideally, we would have personally interviewed those musicians who could not be identified by informants. We could not interview without a means of contacting the musicians, however, and the only document resembling a complete list of Madras musicians, the A.I.R. registry list, cannot be released by A.I.R.

The group of musicians using caste names did not differ significantly in caste distribution from the group identified by informants. The caste distribution for musicians identified by caste name was Brahmin (61%), Pillai (28%), other (11%), while that for the group identified by informants was Brahmin (70%), Pillai (21%), other (9%). The two distributions were compared using the chi-square test, which determines whether the difference between two distributions is large enough to be likely to be a true difference, or is better attributed to chance. In this case the difference was nonsignificant, i.e. better attributed to chance ($x^2 = 3.86$, $df = 2$, not significant).

A few observations may be made about the probable characteristics of the 45% who could not be identified as to caste. Since they could not be identified by any of the Madras informants, they were probably young and/or unimportant. They are largely vocalists. Of the 355 unidentified musicians, 242 (68%) are singers. Only 42% of the singers were identified, 42% of the veena players, 36% of the harikatha performers. In other specialties, over two-thirds of the musicians were identified. Women are overrepresented in this sample, as women use the caste name less frequently than do men. Since players of the nagaswaram, tavil, and clarinet almost always use the caste name, very few of the unidentified players would be in this group.

20. Caste names from Tamil Nadu are Chettiar, Mudiliar, Sarma (used by Saurashtrians who settled in Madurai some eight hundred years ago), and Asari (this man belongs to the caste of goldsmiths and is pointed out as a novelty). Caste names from Telugu-speaking areas are Naidu, Naicker, and Reddi. The name Rao is used by both Brahmin and non-Brahmin groups, so we did not include it in our list of caste names. Caste names from Kerala are Nair, Pandaram, and Panikkar.

21. P. Sambamoorthy, A Dictionary of South Indian Music and Musicians, vol. 1 (Madras: Indian Music Publishing House, 1952), p. 86.

22. Dubois (Hindu Manners, p. 587) describes the nagaswaram and ottu without naming them.

23. Ibid., p. 589; see also Thurston, Castes and Tribes, vol. 5, p. 59.

24. Sambamoorthy, Dictionary, vol. 1., pp. 86–87.

25. Ibid., vol. 2 (1959), p. 340.

26. Sambamoorthy, South Indian Music, Book 3, 6th ed. (1964), p. 200.

27. Sambamoorthy, Dictionary, vol. 2, pp. 248–49.

28. A clear discussion of the Devadasi system in various parts of South India, but especially Tamil Nadu, is quoted by Thurston (Castes and Tribes, vol. 2, pp. 125–30) from the 1901 Madras census. Dubois (Hindu Manners, pp. 584–87) also describes the system as he observed it in the southern part of the Tamil country and around Mysore.

29. Dubois, Hindu Manners, pp. 64–65.

30. Sambamoorthy, History, p. 132. The places listed are Bobbili, Ettayapuram, Karvetnagar, Madras, Mysore, Pithapuram, Puddukkottai, Ramnad, Sivaganga, Tanjore, Travancore, Udaiyarpalaiyam, Venkatagiri, and Vijayanagaram.

31. C. K. Srinivasan, Maratha Rule in the Carnatic (Annamalainagar: Annamalai University Press, 1944), p. 383.

32. P. Sambamoorthy, Great Composers, Book 1, 2d ed. (Madras: Indian Music Publishing House, 1962), p. 134.

33. Sambamoorthy's accounts of famous contests (History, pp. 95–105) make this point clear.

34. Ibid., p. 95.

35. Mysore was independent until the time of Indian independence, but the actual administration was taken over in 1831; when the rajah was reinstated in 1881, "very stringent regulations were made to prevent the country losing the benefits of British rule which it had enjoyed for half a century" (P. E. Roberts, History of British India, 3d ed. [London: Oxford University Press, 1952; reprinted, with corrections, 1958], p. 468). Travancore, Cochin, and Puddukottai, whose rulers early allied themselves with the Company, were the last states to lose their princely status, after Indian independence. They retained their positions as centers of music until nearly the end of the nineteenth century, as did Tanjore, where the rajah was relieved of his ad-

ministrative powers in 1779 and of his title in 1885 (ibid., pp. 247, 354). Most of the smaller states were taken over just before 1800, e.g. Palghat, (1790), Ramnad (1772), Dindigul (1792). See the *Imperial Gazeteer of India* (London: Government Printing Press, 1908) for information on other smaller states.

36. Raghavan, "Some Musicians and Their Patrons," p. 127.

37. Sambamoorthy, *History*, pp. 140–45.

38. E.g. see E. Krishna Iyer, "A Brief Historical Survey of Bharata Natyam," in *Classical and Folk Dances of India* (Bombay: Marg Publications, 1963), pp. 7–8. The dance personalities interviewed by Singer in Madras also subscribe to this view (*Great Tradition*, pp. 172–73, 181).

39. Singer, *Great Tradition*, p. 172.

40. Iyer, "Brief Historical Survey," pp. 8–9.

41. Sambamoorthy, *Dictionary*, vol. 2, p. 246.

42. Sambamoorthy, *History*, p. 102.

43. Ibid., p. 236.

44. Sambamoorthy, *South Indian Music, Book 4*, p. 273.

45. Sambamoorthy, *History*, p. 236.

46. Ibid., p. 149. The sabhas were Krishna Gana Sabha, Parthasarathi Swami Sabha, Bhagavath Katha Prasanga Sabha, and Bhakti Marga Prasanga Sabha.

47. Singer, *Great Tradition*, p. 171.

48. Ibid.

49. Rangaramanuja, *History*, pp. 316–17.

50. Ibid., p. 321.

51. A male Devadasi singer we interviewed in Madras says that he was the first of his caste allowed to sing Tyagaraja kirutis at the court of Travancore. This was in 1920.

52. Rangaramanuja, *History*, Appendix 1, p. xiii.

53. Dubois, *Hindu Manners*, p. 586.

54. Rangaramanuja, *History*, pp. 264–65.

55. Sambamoorthy, *History*, p. 145.

56. E.g. at Kalakshetra's music section between 1961 and 1964 there were four males and thirty females; in the University of Madras diploma course in music from 1962 to 1966 there were three males and thirty-seven females.

57. Matrimonial advertisements mention the prospective bride's skill in music nearly as often as they describe her educational level, her training in domestic duties, and her complexion. In many years of scanning matrimonial advertisements in the *Hindu* we have never seen a prospective groom's proficiency in music pointed out.

58. Adrian L'Armand earned his living as a cinemusician in Madras from 1963 to 1966. The information presented here comes from his personal acquaintance with nearly all the cinemusicians in Madras at that time.

59. *Report of the Ministry of Information and Broadcasting 1956–57*, quoted in E. Barnouw and S. Krishnaswami, *Indian Film* (New York: Columbia University Press, 1965), p. 202.

60. C. S. Mathur, *New Lamps for Aladdin: Mass Media in Developing Societies* (Calcutta: Orient Longmans, 1965), p. 127.

61. The approximate population in Madras in 1939 was 748,200; in 1949, 1,289,200; in 1968, 2,243,800. The increase in population from 1939 to 1949 was thus 72%, and that from 1949 to 1968 was 74%. These approximations

are crudely estimated from growth data from the census, which is taken every ten years.

62. Increase in concerts from 1949 to 1968 was 136%; increase in sabhas from 1949 to 1968 was 170%.

63. As pointed out in n. 19, the 1966–67 distribution by caste of musicians using the caste name did not differ significantly from the distribution by caste of those musicians who did not use the caste name but were identified by informants. The 1948–49 data similarly showed a nonsignificant difference in caste distribution between musicians identifying themselves and those identified by informants ($x^2 = .96$, $df = 2$, not significant).

64. E.g. Rangaramanuja (*History*, p. 317) lists twenty musicians active in 1900. All the rhythm players named used the caste name Pillai.

65. Sambamoorthy, *South Indian Music, Book 4*, p. 18.

Persian Classical Music in Tehran:
The Processes of Change

BRUNO NETTL

Ethnomusicology began almost a century ago. For much of its history this discipline, or subdiscipline, maintained a policy of studying the music of "primitive" and folk cultures, of isolated communities, because it sought to understand the traditions of these musics in forms untouched by Western and other outside influences. A generally accepted article of faith has been that the music of simple cultures—and, by extension, of the not-so-simple high cultures of Asia as well—has existed in two periods: an early one, stretching back far beyond historical horizons, which was static; and a recent one, beginning with the onset of Western influences, in which change has been very rapid. A certain amount of change —very slight and very slow—has been admitted for the earlier period, but it has been thought to be almost negligible, compared to the rapidity of recent developments. Curiously, the hypothetical period of no change has been considered the "life" of the tradition, and the subsequent era of rapid change has been considered its death—by both ethnomusicologists and the members of the cultures themselves.[1]

This equating of rapid change with the death of tradition may be the reason for change and its causes were rarely studied. Ethnomusicologists have continued to seek stable traditions; they have made enormous efforts to resurrect the older forms of a tradition from such sources as elderly informants who remember but do not

Bruno Nettl is Professor of Music and Anthropology, University of Illinois at Urbana-Champaign.

participate; and they have done their part to keep change at arm's length—to stave off death, as it were—and restore a measure of vitality through the antibiotic-injections of festivals and government-sponsored authenticity and through the intensive-care activities of collecting-projects and national archives. There are many other reasons for the ethnomusicologist's concern with stable, isolated, non-Westernized traditions. Even so, the scholarly neglect of musical change, and particularly the reasons for it, are significant to the history of ethnomusicology.

In the last twenty years, however, ethnomusicologists have generally followed the trends in the social sciences, particularly anthropology, toward involvement in the study of recent and contemporary change. Avoiding the conclusion that a tradition changed very much or very rapidly is a tradition deceased, they have begun taking an opposite point of view: that change is the rule rather than the exception and it is—somewhat paradoxically—the constant against which measurements are to be made.

Among the first to account for the reasons for change in musical traditions has been Alan P. Merriam, who divides the causes of change into those factors internal to the culture and those of external origin. On the internal factors, Merriam summarizes the theoretical thought up to his time of writing by citing three major points: (a) "The degree to which internal change is possible depends to a major extent upon the concepts about music held in the culture"; (b) within a music system, different kinds of music are more or less susceptible to change; and (c) variation within a culture contributes to change.[2]

As a matter of fact, practically all change studied by ethnomusicologists is the other, "external," variety. What is known about internal change comes from historical sources of only partial usefulness and from abstract theory. And we know of no changing culture in which some impact from the outside has not had at least a minor effect. Indeed, external forces have probably been the major factor in most cases. But, as Merriam states, little theory has been developed.[3] In almost all cases, statements about change in musical traditions indicate acculturation (a term used in rather broad definition by ethnomusicologists).[4] The most widely used theory of change resulting from culture contact is "syncretism,"[5] using measurement of degrees of compatibility between non-Western and contacting Western styles to explain the amount of change (i.e. degree of "death") of a tradition. Beyond this, only generalized statements about Westernization and modernization have been made.

Our task here is to try to refine a group of theoretical concepts in a culture that has changed substantially in the last one hundred years—the classical-music tradition of Iran, in its main area of provenience, the city of Tehran. Considerable literature in Persian and in European languages attests to the significance of this change and to the fascination it has held for observers and scholars.[6] This paper offers a model for analysis of these changes using concepts from anthropology and taking into account both the analytical views of outsiders and viewpoints from within the culture itself. In the past, Persian classical music, distinct from the rural folk musics of Iran, was primarily a court music of the emperor and the aristocracy.[7] Closely related to the musics of Arabic and Turkish cultures and more distantly to that of India, it also shares characteristics of Persian folk music. Persian classical music appears today in several styles, from serious and complex to light— from one that avoids all change to others that exhibit elements of modernization and Westernization. Despite its stylistic diversity, however, it does not, in the main, contend for the attention of most Iranians. More typically preferred, among the many musics of Iran, is the large body of popular music heard in nightclubs and on 45 rpm records, the classical styles remaining somewhat outside the mainstream of the typical listener's experience (see fig. 1).

Persian classical music is basically monophonic. Performed in solo and by small ensembles, it has several typical instruments: the lutes—setār and tār; the bowed kamāncheh and Western violin; the santour, a trapezoid hammered dulcimer; the nai, a Middle Eastern flute; and the zarb or dombak, a goblet-shaped drum. Other instruments are also used sporadically. Much of the music is improvised on the basis of a model called the radif, which serves as a repertory of melodic material, largely nonmetric, and which musicians memorize as students; but the term also refers to composed pieces based on this model. The music is organized in twelve modes, called dastgāhs (conceptually similar to the Indian raga), each of which is subdivided into sections, or gushehs. A dastgāh consists of a typical scale, motifs, and composed pieces. Much of

Fig. 1. Interrelationships of musical styles in Iran

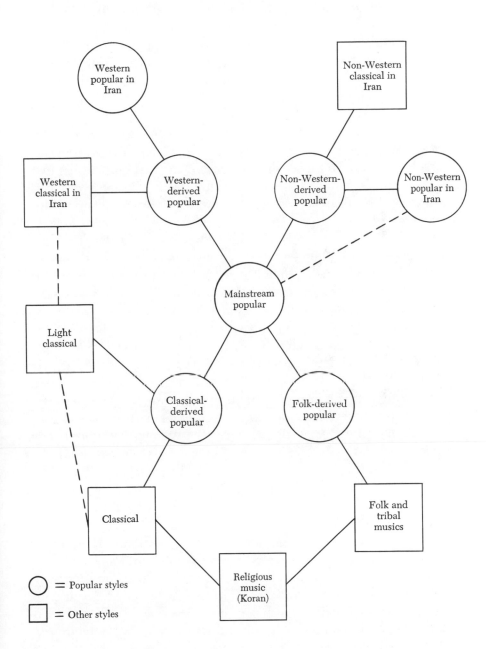

= Popular styles

= Other styles

the music is nonmetric; ornamentation, variation of motifs, and sequential treatment of phrases are important devices of composers and improvisors. The tone system is based on four intervals: the half and whole tones used in Western music, and approximate three-quarter and five-quarter tones.

What has happened to Persian classical music during the last century? Most important, it has been surrounded by other repertories emanating in part from Europe and North America; and it has centered itself almost completely in the city of Tehran. The impact that Persian classical music had on the population of Iran a hundred years or more ago is difficult to estimate. No doubt, it existed mainly in cities and at courts; but the musical competition, as it were, must have come mainly from folk music of largely rural origin. To what extent the music of other Asian cultures penetrated Iran is hard to say, but there is no doubt that Arabic and Turkish musics exerted some influence—just as Persian music and musical thought had a great impact on Arabs, Turks, and Indians. During the nineteenth century, Western music was introduced through the development of military bands and the teachings of French master-musicians in Tehran.[8] Today, Persian classical music occupies a small number of musicians—between one hundred and two hundred is an educated guess—residing largely in Tehran. The city also boasts a lively European-style concert life, including an opera house. There is a large popular-music establishment involving both Western and essentially Persian-style musics performed in a variety of nightclubs and music halls and issued on a number of 45 rpm records to which LP albums have been added the last few years. Persian classical music is thus now the music of a very small minority of performers and listeners; and while it has presumably always been so, its territory and influence have probably decreased in relation to other musics in the environment.

Specific changes in musical style and musical culture are many and interrelated. Some are readily documented, others known only from the impressionistic statements of contemporary musicians. In the following pages we wish to discuss a few of these at some length (although they have been more thoroughly described by Zonis and Massoudieh; see n. 6), and we have accordingly grouped them in three areas: (a) musical life, (b) music theory and composition, and (c) musical performance. In all areas it is the Western classical music system, with offshoots such as military music, that has produced change. Western popular and light classical music are also involved, but to a much smaller degree.

Changes in Musical Life

The typical performance of classical music in earlier times was at a private concert, attended perhaps by several dozen persons, at the court or in the garden of an aristocrat. This type of musical event persists, but other venues of performance have been added. A performance in earlier times evidently was relatively long; one to three hours might have been typical. Although small ensembles, consisting of two or three melodic instruments plus drum, were known, a performance was often carried out by a single performer: a tār player, for example, or a singer accompanied by tār and dombak. Especially at the court, larger groups of musicians were maintained, but to what extent they actually performed together is not known. Early in the twentieth century, public concerts were instituted in imitation of European practice. At first there were few, but by the early 1970s they occurred frequently.[9]

A concert arranged by Darvish Khān in 1906 under the aegis of a Sufi circle called Okhovvat is still frequently mentioned as a landmark. A number of well-known musicians were assembled, and a special genre of music, the *pishdarāmad*, a stately, metric piece designed to be played more or less in unison by an ensemble, was prominent in it. According to Tiersot, pishdarāmads were known before this concert, but oral tradition regularly ascribes its origin to this famous event.[10] This "first" large concert, held in a garden, did not suffer from the time-limitations of Western concerts, in which a performance of two hours exhausts an audience sitting in crowded chairs in a hall; it lasted, so it is said today, for twenty-four hours.

The desire to hear a number of musicians at one concert, and to hear ensembles, has continued and been intensified. Thus, two kinds of concerts are now frequently heard in various halls in Tehran, and particularly in Rudaki Hall, the opera house of the Ministry of Arts and Culture. One type consists of four or five pieces by different soloists or small combinations of musicians, each selection consisting of material from one dastgāh, and each lasting less than twenty minutes. Variety is emphasized. Contrastive dastgāhs appear, ensembles alternate with soloists, and drum solos are heard. Some performances consist of composed pieces such as the lyrical *tasnif*. This arrangement may perhaps be an imitation of the Western-style chamber-music concert, with its typical emphasis on variety of composers and periods and its alternation of pieces of differing lengths and moods. But the admixture of performers and ensembles gives it a flavor closer to Western "new music" concerts than, say, to the traditional string-quartet concert. An earlier traditional performance, by contrast, would typically have been composed of long renditions of one or two dastgāhs. Westernization is thus evident in program structure and in the brevity of the entire concert as well as of the individual numbers.

A second type of concert consists of orchestral performance in alternation with solos or small ensembles. The orchestra has approximately fifty players of Western strings and traditional Persian instruments, particularly violins, tārs, and santours. The music is in unison and octaves, and the pieces played by the orchestra are similar to the composed pieces of traditional solo and small ensemble performances (e.g. the pishdarāmad, along with occasional Western-derived pieces). Again, contrast and brevity dominate. Improvised sections are brief, and composed pieces are stressed and performed at great length, with repetitions. This type of concert is criticized by contemporary conservative musicians, and its music is sufficiently different in style from the traditional performance to have stimulated Ella Zonis to refer to it as "light classical music" and to question its quality.[11] Concert life, although contributing to the preservation of Persian music, is in itself a Western phenomenon, and its ramifications have in broad terms served to shape the style of the music.

Another era of musical life greatly affected by recent change is the place of the musician in society. Few details on the musician's role before 1900 are known. Contemporary musicians report that professional musicians of the nineteenth century usually had relatively low social status and were not highly educated beyond their musical training. There were also proficient amateurs who were often of the leisure class.[12] The Muslim proscription of instrumental music must not have been followed, for music was widespread; but the proscription does seem to have affected the status of musicians. Men and women who made their living as musicians were of low esteem; and frequently they were members of minority groups, such as Jews.[13] On the other hand, some men of high social status, including many Sufis, placed a high value on music. They felt that they could afford to ignore the proscription and were not penalized for this attitude.

Musicians today conform to this earlier social model only to a certain degree. Many people still hold musicians in low esteem, or respect only those who have attained stardom. And there are still a few well-to-do musicians who prize their "amateur status" because they can perform as, when, and for whom they choose, without following the directions of an employer or patron.[14]

Although such "amateurs" continue as a small, rarefied stratum of musical society, the majority of Persian classical musicians today occupy a role in society similar to that of the musician in Europe. They are held in higher esteem than in the past. Many are employed by state agencies committed to the preservation of the classical Persian heritage—the Ministry of Arts and Culture, the court, the University of Tehran, the Conservatory of National Music in Tehran, the national television corporation. For the majority, this employment is part-time. Many supplement their income through private teaching, occasional performances at private concerts in homes, instrument-making, and performing in other styles of music such as Persian popular or (more rarely) Western classical music.[15] The now-dwindling number of amateur musicians of high status is in a sense replaced in the sociomusical structure by the musician who holds a job in a respected nonmusical field, such as the civil service, banking, or law, and who practices his musical profession largely in the evenings, teaching and occasionally playing.

The proscription of music is still felt. On certain Muslim holidays, only the music department at the University of Tehran is closed, while other departments continue their work. On such days, musicians on the way to work or rehearsal dare not appear on certain streets with instrument cases.

Patronage of music has changed, but perhaps not as much as one might expect. The patrons of music of the past—imperial court, private aristocrats—are still active, but they have been augmented by various agencies of the national government, such as radio and television, the Ministry of Arts and Culture, and, most recently, record companies. There has not been a sudden radical change in patronage. That Iran, like many European nations, has made the government the primary patron of classical music is of course a significant factor. Parenthetically, a comparison of the Persian classical musician with the folk musician in Eastern Europe who performs for urban audiences reveals some significant similarities.

The attitude of the typical musician toward his art also seems to have changed, but musicians find difficulty in putting their finger on what has happened specifically. One transformation that appears to have taken place is in the way that music is ranked and regarded within the context of Iranian cultural activities. Once viewed as having a very close alliance with the literary arts and with philosophy, music now seems to be regarded as more of a craft, with technical vocabulary and paraphernalia. Music as a private and individual activity has been overshadowed in a musical life governed by ensembles and by corporate sponsoring agencies.

The musicians and the concert audience have, of course, been very much affected by the emergence of the mass media. Notations and their printed publication were the first of these to arrive, followed by large-scale recording, radio, and television. All of these, as has usually been the case in developing or recently developed nations, came suddenly and quickly compared with the Western European and American experience.

Radio has had its effects mainly in the shortening of performances, the imposition of the requirements of studio conditions upon performers, and the confluence of many different styles of music—Western, Persian classical, and Iranian folk traditions. But this medium—together with notation—has also brought about a substantial degree of standardization, partly because of a star system that has enabled certain performers, through radio exposure, to gain ascendancy over less competent musicians. This trend was reinforced by the introduction of other mass media—film, recording, and television—in both classical and popular music. Radio and to a larger extent television have assumed a didactic role, providing programs of instruction and "music appreciation" in Persian classical music. Another type of musical form, based on a sequence of composed and improvised materials, but with special emphasis on the composed, metric sections, seems to be the result of radio broadcasting more than of other media.

Electronic amplification, by way of the radio, which preceded live amplification, has certain important effects. In a live situation, for instance, it would be difficult for a speaker to intone soft phrases over a santour; and a nai alternating with orchestra is not effective without amplification. But the microphone makes all possible. Thus the radio has contributed to the development of new performance traditions within the framework of classical music.[16]

As in the West, the main vehicle for recordings of classical music is the twelve-inch LP record. At the time of this writing, there are perhaps no more than fifty LP discs of Persian classical music, fewer than half of them issued in Iran. The foreign records of Persian classical music are difficult to obtain in Iran, and except for three discs by the fabulous Delkash, a highly respected singer of both popular and classical music, no LP recordings were issued in Iran until 1969.

Western LP records of non-Western music—some of Persian music, but most representing other cultures—have only recently been issued for the listening pleasure of the general public. For years, their purpose was educational, intended mainly for the ethnomusicologist, the intellectual musician, and the student, whose interest, for better or worse, was to get a quick overview of the variety or homogeneity of a repertory. Thus, most recordings of non-Western music (78s as well as LPs) consist of short excerpts, which show one "how the music sounds" but rarely contain complete performances. And this holds true for Western recordings of Persian classical music. Iranians followed the Western practices when they began to issue LP records of their classical music. Few recorded performances last longer than ten minutes, and on each record there is a desire to present brief examples of several of the twelve dastgāhs, whether the performance be of a solo musician or an ensemble. The majority of LP records available to the Iranian thus present the music not as it would be heard in a live traditional performance, but as non-Western music is typically presented on recordings to the Westerner.

The mass media have sometimes reinforced characteristics of the older tradition—for example, the star system. The history of Middle Eastern music contains references to towering figures who were singled out by the shah and other potentates for special recognition or honor.[17] The sharply hierarchical structure of society, headed by the figure of the king, seems in some ways to have been reflected in musical life.[18] Middle Easterners, on the whole, do not respect musicians greatly, but they single out for special adulation a few of the best—the stars. In the Arabic world, such a star is Umm Kalthum; in Iran, the great vocalist, Delkash.

The Persian music-lover is exposed to a large number of performers through the media, and he is usually quick to make qualitative distinctions among them, to state, for instance, that there is only one good tār or santour or kamāncheh player, that this record or performance is good and that one bad. The making of qualitative judgments may have increased with the growth of the mass media and the ready access to a wide variety of performances.

Related to the emergence of the star system is the authority with which the media have imbued certain approaches to performance. Radio and television, having taken it upon themselves to disseminate classical music, have been able to select those styles and musicians they prefer; and these have to a large extent been accepted as authoritative by the audience. Thus, the media, like notation and modern institutions of learning, contribute to a growing standardization of performance; and even the adoption of new forms or subforms by Radio Iran could very quickly change a rather unorthodox experiment to a generally accepted standard type of performance.

Aside from standardization and authority, the mass media tend to reinforce the brevity of performances that itself was a result of other trends quickening the pace of life. The appearance of classical music on 45 rpm records is evidence of this trend. A "classical-derived" style of popular music represents perhaps the ultimate shortening of the once-leisurely classical performance.[19]

Changes in Music Theory and Composition

If the coming of the concert and mass-media culture and the new role of the musician in society represent obvious examples of change, a more subtle but musically perhaps more powerful force is exhibited in the body of technical and speculative thought known as music theory. A shift recently toward emphasis on musical theory in Persian classical music seems to have resulted from the introduction of European music and musical thought in the late nineteenth and early twentieth centuries.[20] The model Western musician, as he must have been presented to the Iranians in the nineteenth century by the succession of French composers and conductors who were brought in to Westernize military music, is a craftsman very much in control of things. His technical virtuosity obviously makes him a master of his instrument. Rhythmic control is exerted through systematic adherence to simple metric patterns (particularly, of course, in marches and nineteenth-century European dances such as the waltz). Notation permits him to standardize the essence of a musical work; and control in an overall sense prevails in his elaborate system of music theory that permits easy discussion and teaching of basic concepts. The traditional Persian musician was of course in control of his musical environment as well, but his authority was much less bolstered by a written tradition, and his control was not so tight. The way in which the Western musician was in control of his material must have seemed, to the typical Iranian musician, something musically desirable; and it may have reinforced the feeling that Western man was in firm control of *nonmusical* environment as well, more completely than was possible in a non-Western traditional culture.

Thus, the Westernization of musical thought, within a framework of Persian musical style and genres, must have seemed a highly desirable goal to some Persian musicians shortly before and after 1900. One of the most articulate was Ali Naqi Vaziri, a leading figure after 1920, whose publications amply exhibit the views of many Persian musicians.[21] There were and there still are opponents of Westernization who maintain that the intrusion of Western appurtenances such as notation is basically imcompatible with Persian musical thought. But the majority today have accepted the Westernization of Persian musical theory in several ways: Western notation has become widely used; a system of classification of musical phenomena has been established that is similar in style to Western ways of classifying modes, rhythms, and forms; virtuosity has become more prized; and metric pieces are more widely used.

Other factors have doubtless also been involved in establishing some of the changes mentioned. Thus, the increased importance of instrumental metric pieces results not only from the importance of meter in Western music, but also from the convenience of metric structure in the performance of music by ensembles. It should be noted that while most of the changes reflect Western influence, models for the innovations were already present in the tradition. Metric pieces, for instance, virtuosity, and music theory were by no means absent in the past; but their twentieth-century development was stimulated by contact with Western music.[22]

The greater stress on Western-style metric treatment has caused shifts in emphasis.[23] New genres have become prominent. They include the pishdarāmad; the *chahār mezrāb*, a virtuoso piece, usually with ostinato rhythm, composed or improvised, and used within a nonmetric improvisation or as a separate piece; the tasnif, a lyrical and often topical song (with words, but sometimes performed instrumentally) that may either be part of a larger performance or appear separately; and metric sections usually referred to as *zarbi* interpolated in the nonmetric improvisation, or *āvāz*. Thoroughly discussed in the literature, these pieces occupy a larger proportion of performance time, and they seem also to have a more prestigious role than in the past. Related to these are two other trends: the use of metric pieces such as chahār mezrāb as separate selections outside the context of a full-blown performance, and the increased popularity of solo drumming.[24]

The increase in metric performance represents a gradual change of emphasis in a Western direction. Even the development of the dastgāh system now in use may have resulted from a similar shift in musical thinking, coming from Western musical thought, but also affected by reform from within the Iranian musical community.[25] The organization of the gushehs of Persian music into the system of twelve dastgāhs is said to have come about in the late nineteenth century, under the leadership of Mirzā Abdollah.[26]

Whether such an organization of "small" modes into "supermodes" existed in earlier times is not clear. The literature on nineteenth-century practice refers rather indiscriminately to the forms now called gushehs or dastgāhs, implying that the two are more or less at the same level of organization; and even in the 1960s musicians outside Tehran were not always aware of the two-level organization. The grand hierarchical organization of the twelve dastgāhs is of course remindful of Western theory, with its prescriptions for forms and for successions of movements, its arrangement of modes, and its chord classifications. The coexistence formerly of a multitude of gushehs is much more suggestive of the relatively informal manner in which Arabic musicians west of Iraq today think of the *maqams* and their interrelationships.

If we maintain that the dastgāh system is recent and partially of European origin, this does not necessarily imply that the style of performance now associated with it is a recent phenomenon. (I refer to the playing or singing of successive gushehs in more-or-less stable and usually ascending order as the main and essentially nonmetric portion of a classical performance.) In all likelihood, the use of a stable group of gushehs that was preceded, followed, and occasionally interrupted by a principal gusheh, in a mainly nonmetric performance, precedes the period of Westernization. The arrangement is not very different, after all, from that of the Arabic *taqsim,* with its typical modulations to maqams related in various ways to its main maqam. And the use of extended improvisations in one mode that exhibits different focal points at various stages of performance is common to the entire West and South Asian group of cultivated musical traditions. A somewhat informally constituted system seems to have been first explained and finally, within the past century, made more rigid by a system of theory. Thus the growth of Persian theory in the course of the last hundred years has tended to make a more specific set of requirements for the performer, creating a certain orthodoxy; and it has also made musical thought a more complex phenomenon.[27]

The many-sidedness of the dastgāh system today relates it to Western musical thought; but so also does its rather standardized form. For, while Western music theory is admittedly complex, its complexity is mitigated by the fact that certain principles of musical structure are recognized almost universally throughout the occident. In a like fashion, as the dastgāh system has become more complex, it has also become more standardized.

Since the day of Mirzā Abdollah, seventy years ago, there has not come about a proliferation of radifs of the sort that seems to have existed in the oral tradition in earlier times. This fact is at least circumstantial evidence that Western music theory has had an impact on Persian musicians. But of course other factors—notation, the more conventional mass media, the need for quick learning—have also been involved.

Parenthetically, it may be of interest to cite the famous musician Nour-Ali Boroumand, who studied with many teachers around 1920 to 1950. He has declared (in a personal communication to the author) that he learned several quite similar radifs during the course of this training, but he also maintains that hardly anyone now knows the differences among these separate radifs. Furthermore, only older musicians today claim to teach individual, personal radifs; younger ones rely on the standardized versions available in publications, although they may use these publications more as reference tools than as primary notations from which to learn.

The explication of a rather complex system of scales and intervals in Arabic-Persian music has been uppermost in the minds of Middle Eastern music theorists for centuries.[28] It is difficult to ascertain to what extent the theoretical treatises reflect actual practices, or to what degree these treatises were actually affected by nonmusical disciplines such as mathematics. The discussion of interval sizes has continued into the present century. Ella Zonis has described the two main views: of Mehdi Barkechli, who calculated intervals on the basis of Pythagorean scales and used concepts of 24, 90, 114, and 204 cents; and of Ali Naqi Vaziri, who made use of tempered quarter tones.[29] In both cases, Western theory plays a part. Barkechli's attempts to state intervals with great precision, in cents, is of course directly related to the adoption of Ellis's cents system in Western ethnomusicology.[30] Quarter tones are also a Western concept based on the tempered chromatic scale. That a system of intervals is explained by two separate systems, neither precisely descriptive of musical practice, but both derived from recent Western music theory or scholarship, is significant and again indicates the importance of Western concepts in contemporary Persian musical culture.

Western musical traditions have decidedly influenced practice as well as theory. Younger musicians, more than older ones, tend to approach Western intonation; the accompanying change from the characteristic three-quarter tone to something closer to a halftone, at least in certain modes, is evidence of gradual change. In assessing the usefulness of this evidence, it should be borne in mind that precision of intonation in Persian music possibly did not become an issue at all until the introduction of Western musical thought, with its interest in the measurement and calculation of performed (in contrast to theoretical) intervals. In any event, the characterizing elements of a mode to the Persian musician are still not the intervals of the scales so much as the melodic motifs.[31]

Changes in the theory of melody and scale are accompanied by changes in the theory of rhythm. While metric pieces have long existed, the conceptualization of meter seems to have undergone great changes in recent times. In an earlier period, Persian music appears to have made use of the Arabic system of rhythmic modes subsumed under the term *iqa'* (or the Turkish term *usul*) and related to the theory of Arabic poetry and its meter. But most musicians today are hardly aware of this system. While metric material may have increased in prominence in the late nineteenth and the twentieth centuries, this development seems to have come not from a rediscovery of the old rhythmic modes, but from the desire to imitate Western ensemble music.

Metric pieces are now frequently classified in terms of Western meters; for example, a chahār mezrāb may be identified as in 6/8, 6/16, or 3/8 meter.[32] On the whole, in Western music, such differences in metric designation would imply only notational differences, or possibly tempo, but in Persian music, other differences in style seem also to be involved. A 6/8 piece is slower and more lyrical than one in 6/16, and other rhythmic distinctions may well be indicated. The naming of measured zarbi sections after Western models, such as the waltz, must also be mentioned. The modern metric classification is, of course, tied to the use of Western notation, without which Western theory could hardly have had an impact. While the rather complex theory of rhythmic modes of the Arabic-Persian tradition is replaced by modern Western

161

rhythmic theory (hardly complex or sophisticated), refinements are superimposed on this Western system that are perhaps derived from the older desire for close classification of rhythmic types.

Notation itself, apart from its role as a symbol of "modern" music-making, must also be discussed at least briefly in the context of music theory. Twentieth-century Persian musicians attach importance to notation as a means of controlling the musical environment. The diatonic principle inherent in the notational system of Western music is, of course, adaptable without too much difficulty to the seven-tone scales of the dastgāhs. But the variety of intervals existing in Persian music cannot easily be subsumed in a Western notational system. On a Persian stringed instrument, for instance, the tuning of frets is additive, not divisive—as would be the case with Western tuning—and in fact there are some intervals that can be equated only approximately to the halftone, three-quarter tone, whole tone, and five-quarter tone. Based on units that are divisible by halves, the Western system has the possibility of altering its basic pitches by a halftone—flat or sharp. Thus, the possibility of again halving these alterations resides within the system, and Persian musicians quickly discovered the convenience of using symbols that indicate a half-flat or half-sharp (*koron* and *sori*),[33] resulting in three-quarter and five-quarter tones. But the establishment of this notational device has caused a substantial difference between theory and practice. Some theory- and notation-minded musicians now think of the system as being based on units of a quarter tone as the common denominator; but in practice, use is made of intervals of various sizes clustering around half and whole tones.

Although notation is hardly new (it was introduced to Iran about 1840), its use in contemporary Persian classical music is still somewhat controversial.[34] A few musicians maintain that its introduction was harmful because it makes rapid learning possible. Most believe it is the best thing that could have happened, for precisely the same reason, and because they think notation is a symbol of the Westernization that is essential to the survival of the Persian tradition. Despite these vigorous opinions, the actual impact of notation on Persian classical music is not easy to assess.

One does not often see small ensembles typical of the older tradition using notation for performance, but orchestras playing Persian music—popular and semi- or "light" classical—do read music while playing. It is possible, however, that these orchestras use sheet music and music-stands more to exhibit their "modernization" than to aid the performance. The precise quarter-tone intonation is not reflected in practice, such as fretting the tār or setār, and indeed Vaziri foresaw and was willing to live with this discrepancy.

The impact of notation is felt most in teaching. The main task of the student of Persian music is to master his teacher's radif, the specific repertory of melodic material that is used as the basis of improvisation and composition. Compared to the repertory of violin music controlled by an advanced Western music student, or to the ragas known to an Indian musician, a radif is not a large corpus of music. Whereas each Persian musician in earlier times is said to have developed his own version of the radif, it is now rather standardized, largely because of the coming of notation, but also because in the period around 1900 it was restricted to a small group of musicians who carried on the tradition that had otherwise become largely neglected.[35] As it can be played in a matter of a few hours—perhaps eight to ten at most—notation makes possible the rather quick learning and the rapid visual control of this material. Thus notation would appear to be an aid to the retention of the tradition. Yet both standardization and speed of learning are regarded by conservative musicians as incompatible with the tradition.

The Iranian classical musician, who frequently lives in a Western-oriented segment of Tehran society, is likely to want to absorb a number of different musical styles. He participates in the various kinds of innovation in Persian classical music that are taking place, including the semiclassical performances current on radio and in concerts; he is likely to be involved in popular music; and he may even be performing Western music of various kinds— especially if he plays an instrument, such as the violin, that is used in both Western and Persian music. Efficiency and the need to save time are matters of high priority to him, particularly as he may have several different kinds of employment. As a student, he can probably devote only a small amount of his time to studying the radif. If he is studying Persian music full time, he is likely at least to have to take courses in the theory and history of Persian music in addition to performance. All of this results in a bustle of activity that is in striking contrast to the earlier form of music study, in which a student could devote himself single-mindedly to the radif. The modern musician, therefore, is bound to welcome the efficiency that notation provides for his learning of the radif, for he considers his musical work much more as a craftsman than did his predecessor.

An earlier stage in Persian music study is represented by a few older musicians. They are the ones who tend to denigrate notation, though by no means do they dismiss its benefits absolutely. In their view, quick learning of the radif is undesirable, because it makes impossible the contemplation that is essential for true understanding. The association of music with philosophy is important to them, and they regard music as the result of mystical experience. Performing music is in a sense identical with contemplation. Therefore, a student should learn only a small amount of material at a time, and he must learn it through hearing and thus decidedly "by heart." The defender of tradition would have the radif studied slowly and in great detail. The student should be required to internalize all aspects of it by memorizing them from the master's own performance. It is in this fashion that the student acquires a true depth of understanding, not through memorization from the printed page. Notation, it is held, thus militates against the kind of learning that is part and parcel of the older musical culture.

Finally, in the area of musical thought, let us mention the emergence, in Iran, of Western-style ethnomusicologists with a comparative approach. The peculiar role of this "specialist in non-Western (i.e. his own) music" in developing nations needs to be investigated; it too is a factor in the Westernization of Persian musical culture.

Musical Performance

Persian classical music continues to be performed on traditional instruments, although some Western instruments have been added

—particularly the violin, but also the piano, flute, clarinet, and occasionally others as well. Indeed, the violin has become the most widely used instrument in classical music. Some traditional instruments have had an interesting history during the last hundred years. Interest has been reawakened in the kamāncheh, at one time practically abandoned, having been replaced by the violin. The *gheichak*, once a folk and tribal instrument, has been drawn into the classical orbit. It has been standardized and has to a small extent replaced the violin during the last two decades. The Arabic *'oud* and the Arabic and Turkish *qanun* have been brought back after a period of neglect. This resurgence of older instruments may be attributed to modern nationalism; the accompanying antiquarianism has become a force in Persian music.

That Western instruments are now used in Persian classical music must be viewed against a background of the instruments' convenience and their prestige. Convenient they certainly are, if one takes into account that many musicians participate in both Persian and Western music. The violinist who begins with the study of Western music, for example, does not have too much trouble adapting his technique, later on, to the study of the radif. (It must be remembered, however, that Persian music does require the Western-style violinist to learn new intervals, tone quality, and ornament patterns.)

It is the prestige of the West, however, rather than considerations of convenience, that has probably had a greater impact. There are of course musicians who regard the *traditional* instruments as more prestigious, whether for nationalistic or other reasons, and their attitude has been reinforced by government institutions. Others, however, prefer the violin, or are proud of the occasionally anomalous or bizarre attempts that are made to play Persian classical music on other Western instruments. Additionally, one hears Western-oriented explanations of instruments. Thus a Persian may say: "We, in Iran, have a piano too; it is the santour"; or he may refer to "our Persian mandolin, the setār."

Three other aspects of the use of Western instruments should be touched upon: (*a*) the Western instruments themselves have caused changes in musical style and tuning; (*b*) Western sound-ideals and the emergence of the public concert as a milieu for classical music have evidently caused a shift in emphasis among

165

the traditional instruments; and (c) the tuning of fretted instruments—setār and tār—has been affected to at least a small degree by Western ideals.

The first of these changes involves the mood and general character of the music. Older musicians, and particularly performers on the traditional tār, setār, and kamāncheh, play music that can be described by the Western listener as contemplative, pensive, mystical, and "low-key" in character. Dynamics are fairly static, virtuoso technique is restricted, emotion is veiled. Performers on the violin, however, appear to have been influenced by Western violin technique and by the broader range of possibilities available on this instrument. Thus, Persian classical music played on the violin has elements of nineteenth-century European violin music—large dynamic range, wide melodic range, bravura technique, sudden changes in tempo, and, in general, a rather dramatic sound. Particularly to be noted (in entire performances and in sections) is the use of endings with an arpeggiated flourish, a figure surely not common in traditional performances. Players of the santour may have been influenced by Western piano music, for they too emphasize virtuosity, metric material, and dynamic contrasts. It is difficult to assess the degree to which different instruments gave rise to radically different performance styles in earlier music, but information available from older musicians and older recordings indicates that the differentiation among instrumental styles has increased in recent times; this again may be due to the Western model.

Aside from the violin, the most popular instrument for the performance of classical music is now the santour. But in earlier times, the tār and the setār are said to have shared this favored position. The ascendancy of the santour may be related to the increase in audience size after the institution of public concerts. The setār, indeed, is rarely heard in public, presumably because of its small voice. The ascendancy of the violin, again, while in part related to the prestige of Western instruments in general and its usability in both Persian and Western music, may also derive from its greater dynamic effect in the concert hall when compared to the tār, setār, and kamāncheh. Thus, as in other instances of change noted here, various factors have converged to move Persian instruments and their uses in a given direction.

Although difficult to ascertain, there is some evidence to suggest that the tuning of instruments and the intonation of scales has changed. The use of Western instruments with more or less fixed pitch using whole and halftones—piano, flute, clarinet—has encouraged Persian musicians to substitute halftones for three-quarter tones in many instances. This, along with the widespread availability of Western music and its scales, seems to have encouraged some performers on traditional instruments without fixed pitch (the kamāncheh and the 'oud) as well as the violin to decrease the size of the three-quarter tone to an interval approaching a tempered halftone.

Further, those instruments that have frets—tār and setār—have sometimes been modified in a Western direction. Thus, a few of these instruments have added frets so that instead of the sixteen intervals (of unequal size) per octave there are twenty-four intervals of equal size. More common, however, is the addition of only one fret at the low end of the scale, making possible the playing of a halftone above the open string instead of beginning the series of frets with a three-quarter tone, as is normally the case.

Finally, in the context of performance, we must mention improvisation. Whether its practice has changed can be ascertained only with difficulty, for discussion of it is lacking in the Persian literature, and the concept itself seems to have been verbalized only in recent times, by musicians acquainted with Western musical thought. The degree to which older musicians depart from the radif in their performances is generally greater than is the case among younger ones.[36] Thus it would appear that the amount of improvisation has decreased, but this trend may also be a function of the standardization of the radif. The increased prominence of composed pieces in the performances is further evidence. So also is the fact that concert and record performances, whose times are strictly limited, must be planned. Finally, the use of a rather small part of the radif in improvisations, which concentrate on the *darāmad* and two or three major gushehs, demonstrates that at least in the breadth of choice of materials from a dastgāh, improvisors now work in a rather restricted fashion. But these conclusions must be regarded as highly tentative.

Processes of Change

Thus far we have been concerned with summarizing data that are already available, for the most part, in various published sources. Our task now is to interpret these findings with respect to specific concepts.

The important changes that have taken place in Persian classical music in recent years have demonstrably been caused in one way or another by various Western influences. The broader processes by which the human condition has been shown to change in the contemporary world may, of course, also be related to musical style and behavior. Urbanization—the change from a rural, folk, or tribal lifestyle to that of a city—is only partly relevant to our problem, since Persian classical music has evidently been an urban phenomenon for centuries. It is a factor, however, in that Tehran itself has grown enormously and changed to a much more heterogeneous, national city during the last century; therefore, each music living in the city has had to interact with a variety of other musics. That these musics are in part Western is incidental.

Westernization, as has been noted, involves the conscious attempt of the indigenous musical system to become part of the musical culture of the West. Modernization, which overlaps greatly with Westernization, is nevertheless distinct in that it involves attempts to make an indigenous musical system compatible with a Western-derived economic and social mode of living and to make the indigenous system musically competitive while retaining its integrity.

Acculturation and diffusion account for change in a more general way. Diffusion, a conceptual tool of anthropologists of earlier times that deals with broad trends in cultural history, involves passing isolated culture traits from one society to another with which it is not necessarily in close contact. Acculturation, by contrast, is the result of substantial contact between two cultures. Considering the proximity of Iran and "the West," and the considerable contact made possible by modern communication, the changes in Persian classical music must be classed broadly as acculturation.

Urbanization

Most Iranians still live in villages and small towns, but Iran has had large cities for a long time. In the nineteenth century, according to a number of sources, Tehran was already a major center of musical activity, but what is known of it comes primarily from practices of the court.[37] The nineteenth century saw the transformation of Tehran from a small town to the national capital. In the middle of the twentieth century substantial change in the composition of Tehran's population occurred—the rapid growth from less than half a million to over three million in twenty years, and the development of Tehran into a central, national city that was greatly to outrank the other large cities of Tabriz, Isfahan, Shiraz, and Mashhad.[38] The additions to the population of Tehran came, as one would expect, from the countryside and the smaller cities; but in contrast to large cities elsewhere, the new residents evidently have not brought with them—or chosen to retain—much of their rural musical culture.[39] This situation may be related to the low status of music in the provinces. Instead, the new urban settlers joined in the rapidly developing popular-music culture. In a number of cases, the incoming population joined in the Persian classical-music tradition; some of the musicians in this sphere were born outside Tehran, and some were drawn to the capital by the opportunities for performance.

It is clear that Persian classical music survived best in Tehran because this city became Iran's focal center for cultural activity, owing to its size and the degree to which the patronage of government and wealth are located there. To what extent, however, are the changes that took place in this music the result of Tehran's growth as a city? Although a number of factors that inevitably accompanied urbanization—technological modernization, Westernization—have had great impact on music and musical life, the increase in the size of Tehran seems to have had only a few effects. But its role as a national city *is* involved.

A major need of many large cities with a great influx from the rural population is the absorption and homogenization of the new-comers. A city may absorb the incoming population and become relatively homogeneous, or it can maintain for a long period a number of minority enclaves. Music may play a part. In the United States, minority groups such as Germans, Jews, and Italians quickly came to dominate urban classical-music life, bringing with them the repertories of their homelands, which eventually became America's standard classical repertory. Black Americans coming from the rural and urban South became prominent musicians in the lives of all American city-dwellers, making the music derived from the black experience part of the mainstream of American musical culture. In Tehran, although information is fragmentary at best, there appears to have been no such flowering of immigrant-derived musical life. The classical-music culture, rather than becoming enlarged by the folk music of the country-side or the musical traditions of urban minorities (such as Armenians), tended instead to isolate itself, relegating to popular music the influence of these minorities. As Tehran became larger, the population involved with Persian classical music, as performer and audience, became larger, but the classical-music system itself was not similarly enlarged.

It radiated in other directions. For one thing, Persian classical music came to influence and participate in a popular music culture, which in turn was to feed into certain aspects of classical music, creating the genres of "light classical music" described by Zonis.[40] In other respects, the desire of individuals from minority groups, such as Armenians, to participate in a learned music has been more readily satisfied by the Western classical-music system —which in some respects tends to dominate Tehran's musical life.

The development of a middle class is a concomitant of urbanization and has had important effects on Tehran's musical culture —the coming of public concerts (also stimulated by Westernization) and a somewhat improved status of the musicians, many of whom moved from a lower class into the broad stream of professionals.

The present large size of Tehran, with its formidable traffic and communication problems, certainly has something to do with the need to produce brief musical performances, thoroughly planned, for large audiences. That Tehran has become a central national city is related to the rather considerable differences in both style and quality between the classical musician residing in Tehran and his counterpart in smaller cities. On the other hand, standardization has occurred because of the desire of classical musicians in other towns to study in Tehran. Thus, the urbanization of Tehran has clearly affected Persian classical music elsewhere.

We have discussed the response of music to the urbanization of Tehran; but one may also contemplate the urbanization of a musical style, that is, its fate in an increasingly urban environment. One way of characterizing the experience of urbanized musical styles and repertories in contrast to rural or tribal ones is to assess the amount of contact and interchange with other repertories in the city. In a sense (to paraphrase a widely held anthropological view of urbanization), when a musical style moves to a modern city it must learn how to interact with a large variety of musics. The music history of Tehran in the last hundred years certainly exhibits the absorption of new styles, from a variety of indigenous musics, Western classical and popular genres, and modern Arabic, Indian, and Russian musics. The classical practice has accepted some elements from other musics, while nonetheless keeping a posture of aloofness. It has been decidedly selective. It has accepted little or nothing from Indian, Arabic, and indigenous folk musics, but it has "borrowed" much from Western musics, more from the Western classical tradition than from the popular sector. While Persian classical music seems to have responded little to the growth of Tehran itself, it has perhaps changed in the process of urbanization because of the multiplicity of musics with which it has interacted.

Westernization and Modernization

In this discussion, the term *Westernization* refers to influences from Western culture that are accepted into a non-Western tradition and tend to make that tradition, in its own eyes, a part of the Western cultural system. *Modernization* also refers to a process in which Western elements are introduced into a non-Western society, but these elements are viewed in the culture as ways of continuing the tradition rather than changing it.[41] To the extent that becoming part of Western culture is itself a way of becoming modern, the two coincide, and a given phenomenon may be the result of either or both, and it may have different functions when viewed from either perspective. But it seems useful at least to distinguish between them, for there are certain ways in which Persian classical music has become truly Westernized; there are other ways in which it has, through modernization, maintained its integrity; and there are ways in which these forces have interacted and overlapped.

Is the Persian classical-music system now really a part of Western culture? That is, is it completely or essentially "Westernized"? To what extent have Western elements become part of the Iranian musical system *because* the musical community simply wished to take things from the West? And to what extent are these additions to Persian music, once incorporated, actually regarded as belonging to the Western sector of Iranian culture?

If we tried simply to enumerate all the characteristics of the classical Persian music system today (including what is usually called its "cultural context"), we would find that a great many of them, perhaps the majority, are directly derived from Western music culture; or, to put it more neutrally, they are identical with those of the West. These would include, for example, the hegemony of the violin, the use of large ensembles, Western-style concerts, dissemination through mass media, notation, Western-style teaching and music schools, and emphasis on metric pieces. From this point of view, and in comparison with, say, the classical musics of India or Indonesia, Persian music might well be considered part of the Western musical system. It would have to be regarded as a special local variety; but so would certain other musical systems, such as those perhaps of Scandinavia or, better, the Americas.

But in Scandinavia and the Americas, musicians and audience do regard themselves as part of Western civilization. What is the attitude in Tehran? No accurate data on attitudes are available, but both statements and behavior indicate ambiguity.[42] Musicians, characteristically, have a large variety of opinions. A very distinguished but conservative Iranian performer and scholar said to me that music is culture-bound and essentially untranslatable. In helping me in my studies, he maintained that while I might be able to grasp important elements of structure, there were certain essentials that only an Iranian could understand. He denied the same for Western music, which, he maintained, was already inter-cultural and international and could thus be understood by any-one. We have here an opinion that indicates differences not only in essence (each music is understood by its culture) but also in nature (Persian music for Iranians, Western music for all) between the two classical-music systems known in Iran. But the idea of mer-ger is also widely espoused, as, for example, by Zaven Hacobian, who recommends the hybridization of music.[43]

Various aspects of musical behavior in Tehran indicate a bi-furcation of musical systems. For example, record stores tend to separate Persian and Western music. Concerts of the two musics combined are rarely heard.[44] There are two conservatories main-tained by the Ministry of Culture, one for Persian and one for Western music. There are few attempts, if any, to subsume the two systems in courses on music theory. Contrary examples are also found, of course: musicians study both systems, and Western elements are borrowed and used by the Persian system. But total merging has been avoided, although it might not be difficult to effect. In other words, Iranians have specifically avoided the es-tablishment of a single, all-encompassing music system. They have kept the two systems intact by allowing them to relate to each other, composing Western music with Persian elements (folksongs, modes, motifs used in orchestral music) and borrowing Western elements for Persian music. But they feel that there is at some point a line between the two, although it is perhaps a curious line, inconsistent and vague.

The nature of this line of demarcation can be illustrated by the following. One distinguished santour-player has composed a con-certo for an orchestra of mainly indigenous Persian instruments (plus violins and cellos) with santour solo. Its style is difficult to clasisfy, but the most obvious source is the music of the eigh-teenth-century Viennese classicists. Nevertheless, the composer, when interviewed, maintained that it was Persian music, that he "was trying to do something new with Persian music." On the other hand, Alireza Mashayekhi, a young Iranian composer trained in Europe, has composed a piece of electronic music that he calls "Shur," since its most prominent feature is the main tetra-chord of this dastgāh. In certain respects it has much more in common with the radif than does the santour concerto. But the composer regards this as a piece of Western music for which he has borrowed Persian elements.

One might thus conclude that the *medium* of performance is a crucial factor in classification; but then it would have to be admitted that Iranians regard violins and cellos as "Persian" instruments. In any event, there continue to exist two discrete systems, labeled "Persian," and "international" or Western. But is the traditional-Western dichotomy appropriate for an objective appraisal? Or are both systems Western in essence, compared to an earlier system once widespread and now living an isolated existence in the memory of a few?

Accepting the principle that Iranians feel that they live with two classical-music systems, we must now inquire into the role that is played by the Western elements in Persian classical music and ask why these features were added. The elements introduced can perhaps be regarded as adaptive strategies to ensure the very survival of the Persian classical-music system. This point of view seems to be borne out by both events and behavior, and it is attested to by the "adaptors" themselves.

For example, we can again refer to the work of the distinguished Ali Naqi Vaziri. In the early part of this century, he studied Western music, theory, and counterpoint in France and Germany, then returned to Iran to introduce Persian music to the conservatory of Western music already there. He promulgated the use of Western-style notation and theory in Persian music and composed pieces of a mixed stylistic character. According to Zonis, Vaziri's intention "was not to teach Western music per se, but to use it for the revitalization of Iranian music."[45] Mehdi Barkechli indicates the need for using the techniques of Western music, such as notation, to assure preservation of the tradition.[46] Many statements made to me by musicians indicated the desire to use Western musical elements in Persian music in order to keep it intact. But in all of this, we have the impression that it is not the amalgamation, or Westernization, of Persian music that is desired, but the maintenance of a two-tradition culture. The indigenous tradition is changed—that is, modernized—in order to retain its acceptability, but the Western musical system is accepted, although it must keep its distance.

Let us try another approach. If we are to unscramble the rather complex distinction between Westernization and modernization in a musical system, we might do it with the use of the following model in terms of stylistic parameters. A musical style is not only modernized but also Westernized if the elements of Western music that are adopted into it are those that are most characteristic of Western music, in the view of Western musicians and audiences. A musical style is modernized but not Westernized if the elements that are adopted are not particularly characteristic of Western music, but rather are identical to or compatible with elements essential to the specific non-Western tradition. Using this model, we find outright Westernization very prominent. Western music, as seen by Westerners, seems to be most importantly characterized by the use of harmony, relatively simple metric rhythms, the use of large ensembles, and the precise composition and replication of pieces aided by notation. Now, these are actually the elements that were introduced into Persian music. There are other elements of Western music that are relatively compatible with Persian music, among them the existence of plucked instruments such as the guitar, the widespread use of chamber ensembles, experiments in microtonal arrangements of scales, jazz improvisation. But these were not to a large extent called upon by Persian musicians in order to form a syncretized style. Instead, the most characteristic Western elements, though they were also in some ways the least compatible, were used to change Persian music. There are also, of course, syncretistic tendencies, such as the adoption of the violin by kamāncheh players and the increased emphasis on standardization of non-Western intervals. But unlike the musics of certain Afro-American cultures, and like the musics of certain North American Indian cultures, Persian classical music seems to be a product more of outright Westernization than of syncretism.[47]

We must conclude the following: (a) Persian music was changed by the introduction of *characteristic* Western elements in order to make it part of the Western system. (b) Syncretistic elements were in the main avoided because a simple, combined style would be in essence traditional Persian. (c) The need for the maintenance of the national tradition was solved in a way typical of Eastern European music history, that is, by the establishment of two parallel, basically Western musical systems. (d) Modernization plays an important but sudsidiary role in its interaction with Westernization; it has a different role. There is then a case for the analysis of contemporary Persian classical music as a specifically Westernized phenomenon.

Though incorporating Western and Western-derived phenomena, modernization does not have ideological Westernization as its motivation. In the recent development of Persian classical music in Tehran, two forces seem most prominent: nationalism and the development of technology. Neither is necessarily tied to the Westernization of music or musical life, but each has inevitably been the cause of movement in the Western direction. But both have also been essential to the retention and promulgation of a traditional system as an alternative to the wholesale adoption of Western musical life, thought, and sound. Technologization and nationalism in music may thus be regarded as adaptive strategies whose purpose has been to allow the Iranian to say, "Yes, we do have a Persian music of our own," just as the forces of Westernization have enabled the Iranian to say, "Our traditional music is really part of the Western cultural system."

Western technology in music involves primarily the means of dissemination. Instruments with amplification (not widely used) permit a broadening of the audience, and the use of music-printing permits musicians to communicate their specific musical ideas more rapidly and efficiently. Radio and television, together with the record industry, have made Persian music more accessible and have provided a greater scope for the individual artist. And it is interesting to find that among all the elements of Western culture that have somehow come into Iranian musical life, it is those involving technology that have been most readily accepted by musicians, even the conservatives. For whereas Western-style music-teaching, standardization of the radif, and the adoption of large ensembles are criticized at least by some of the most conservative musicians as causing fundamental and unacceptable changes in Persian classical music, the use of the mass media is welcomed by almost all. The role of modernizaton is thus twofold: to facilitate Westernization, and to keep it under control.

Whether the ideology of nationalism is a Western import can be debated. No doubt Iran has long experienced this culture trait much more than have the surrounding areas of Asia.[48] Since the idea of the specifically modern nation-state, with its complex of international relationships, is an inherently Western phenomenon, it is thus tied to the very concept of Westernization. But nationalism of a different sort has been a feature of Persian culture since the times of the Achaemenids, a feature that was to varying degrees submerged in the intervening two thousand years, but one that seems to have come to the fore again in the era of the Pahlavi dynasty. Thus, while nationalism is related to Westernization, it is also a separable strand of traditional Persian culture.

It is likely that the system of Persian classical music was at one time more closely related to that of the Arabic countries and of Turkey than it is today. At one time, also, Western scholarship, in concentrating on what is known of Persian and Arabic music in the past, regarded the entire complex of Middle Eastern music as unified, referring to it as "Arabic," "Islamic," or even "Oriental." The intermixed use of Persian, Turkish, and Arabic terms in the musical traditions of all three culture groups is only one piece of evidence for close relationships; specific musical features are stronger evidence yet. But in Iran today, musicians, government agencies, and laymen alike emphasize the integrity of Persian music as a single and unique system. One rarely hears mention of "Middle Eastern music," and the separateness of Persian music from Arabic, Turkish, and, indeed, Indian musics is in various subtle ways emphasized over and over.[49]

Arabic and Indian musics are frequently said to be "monotonous" and to be "strange" to the Persian listener—in significant contrast to Western music, which every Persian claims to understand readily. Also stressed, for example, is the separateness of the Persian form, the pishdarāmad, from the somewhat similar Arabic and Turkish *peshrev*. That some of the gushehs of Persian music have pre-Islamic or specifically Persian names is brought out in conversation. The national provenience of certain instruments, such as the tār, setār, kamāncheh, and santour, is also emphasized, although analogous, if not indeed identical, instruments are found in neighboring countries.

One characteristic of modern nationalism in a large part of the world is the revival of traditional musical cultures, often with government encouragement and support. Evidence of this revivalism is found in Eastern European countries: national music and dance troupes have been formed to promulgate folk music and dance for urban audiences, and elaborate programs of collecting and research have been established by ministries of culture and education. In West Africa, national music and dance troupes attempt to bridge tribal differences and present native materials in the cities and abroad; and American Indians have revived traditional music in order to foster ethnic identity. Similar trends and programs, often with an antiquarian flavor, exist in Iran. The revival has been fostered largely by the Ministry of Arts and Culture, which employs musicians and has established collecting and archiving programs for folk music, as well as sponsoring concerts, publications, and schools.[50] It has also begun sponsorship of a program to revive and rehabilitate old instruments, such as the gheichak and kamāncheh, employing makers and teachers who adapt the traditional instruments to Westernized standards. Thus, the gheichak, once an instrument with up to eight strings, variously tuned, is now made with four strings and normally tuned in fifths, like a violin. Further, the instrument now appears in sizes so as to make possible a "gheichak family" analogous to the Western "violin family."

Conclusion

Mohammad Massoudieh, in his expert account of nineteenth- and early twentieth-century music history in Iran, as well as Ella Zonis, in her description of the contemporary system and its offshoots, indicate that while major differences set the twentieth century off from the more distant past, important distinctions are also found between the early part of the century and the most recent years.[51] Most prominent, of course, is an intensification of both the Westernizing and the modernizing trends, while at the same time the increasing urbanization of the nation has an impact. But in recent years there is also a tendency for the Persian and Western classical systems, once closer to merging, to become again more separate. In the days of Vaziri, when the motivation for change seems to have come from the need to assure the survival of the Persian system through Westernization, attempts were made to merge the systems through the establishment of harmony, notation, ensembles, and long composed forms. In recent decades, more attention has again been given to maintaining the integrity of the Persian system, through the establishment of separate educational institutions such as the Center for the Preservation of Iranian Music of the National Television Corporation. An example of separation is the issuance, by a prominent Iranian record company, of a series of LP records devoted to solo performances rather than to the ensembles that had become popular and standardized. This trend may again be regarded as a result of modernization, in contrast with Westernization, although the model may itself be the Western phenomena of nationalism and antiquarianism as exhibited in the Western institution of folk festivals and archives.

In Tehran we can see the forces of Westernization, modernization, and (to a smaller degree) urbanization all converging on the musical culture. What has happened is in some ways similar to events in other cultures of the Third World, in some ways unique. And what has happened can best be explained as interaction among the forces mentioned.

Perhaps what we have here is an identity crisis. The processes associated with change in recent times—Westernization, modernization, urbanization, syncretism—seem to have worked at cross-purposes. Perhaps this is due to the many forces operating in Iranian culture, and the symbolic roles played in the processes of change by various types of music: Persian classical, folk, popular, Western classical and popular, Arabic, Turkish, Soviet, and Indian. What may distinguish the role of the Persian classical system is its ambiguity in the Iranian-Western and the traditional-modern continuums.

Let me inject a final analytical note. We may view a musical system as consisting of a core (in Persian music, is it the radif and the system of improvisation?) and a surrounding superstructure (is this the venue of performance, the instruments, the role of musicians?). The role of the superstructure is somehow to maintain the core intact, at the expense of changing itself. Despite considerable change, the superstructure has been at least substantially successful, if not entirely so, using the ideas of Westernization and the techniques of modernization, but occasionally giving way to syncretistic tendencies in the core. The superstructure has been flexible and adaptable, while the core has remained relatively stable.

Had the core changed greatly, one could perhaps speak of the death of a tradition; but the changes that Persian classical music in Tehran has experienced demonstrate its continued vitality and the important symbolic role that it continues to play in the contemporary history of its country.[52]

NOTES

1. Regarding the question of life and death of traditions, especially in the high cultures of Asia, see Wolfgang Laade, *Die Situation von Musikleben und Musikforschung in den Ländern Afrikas und Asiens and die neuen Aufgaben der Musikethnologie* (Tutzing: H. Schneider, 1969), esp. pp. 18–20; William Kay Archer, "The Musical Bride," in *The Preservation of Traditional Forms of the Learned Music of the Orient and the Occident* (Urbana: University of Illinois, Institute of Communications Research, 1964), pp. 27–28 and passim. The general theoretical approaches to change in traditional musics held by ethnomusicologists before 1960 are discussed in Alan P. Merriam, *The Anthropology of Music* (Evanston, Ill.: Northwestern University Press, 1964), pp. 277–319. For a hypothesis regarding the "death" of Persian classical music, see Ella Zonis, "Classical Persian Music Today," in *Iran Faces the Seventies*, ed. Ehsan Yar-Shater (New York: Praeger, 1971) pp. 373–74.

2. Merriam, *Anthropology of Music*, pp. 307–9. See also Bruno Nettl, "Change in Folk and Primitive Music: A Survey of Methods and Studies," *Journal of the American Musicological Society* 8 (1955), 101–9, and "Historical Aspects of Ethnomusicology," *American Anthropologist* 60 (1958), 518–32.

3. Merriam, *Anthropology of Music*, pp. 314–16.

4. For perhaps the most inclusive summary of the conceptualization of acculturation in ethnomusicology, see Klaus Wachsmann, "Criteria for Acculturation," in *Report of the Eighth Congress of the International Musicological Society, New York, 1961* (Kassel: Bärenreiter, 1961), pp. 139–49.

5. For a summary of the use of the concept of syncretism, see Merriam (*Anthropology of Music*, pp. 313–15), who discusses mainly the contributions of Melville J. Herskovits and Richard A. Waterman.

6. Descriptions of recent change in the classical music of Iran are found particularly in Ella Zonis, *Classical Persian Music: An Introduction* (Cambridge: Harvard University Press, 1973), pp. 185–201; Zonis, "Classical Persian Music Today," pp. 365–79; Mohammad T. Massoudieh, "Tradition und Wandel in der persischen Musik des 19. Jahrhunderts," in *Musikkulturen Asiens, Afrikas und Ozeaniens im 19. Jahrhundert* (Regensburg: G. Bosse, 1973), pp. 81–91; Khatschi Khatschi, *Der Dastgah* (Regensburg: G, Bosse, 1962); Bruno Nettl, "Attitudes toward Persian Music in Tehran, 1969," *Musical Quarterly* 56 (1970), 183–97; Bruno Nettl and Bela Foltin, Jr., *Daramad of Chahargah* (Detroit: Information Coordinators, 1972), pp. 32–38.

7. Several important surveys describe the essentials of the Persian classical-music system: Zonis, *Classical Persian Music;* Hormoz Farhat, "The Dastgah Concept in Persian Music" (Ph.D. diss., UCLA, 1965); Nelly Caron

and Dariouche Safvate, *Iran* (Paris: Buchet/Chastel, 1966); Nettl and Foltin, *Daramad of Chahargah*. A particularly relevant article is William O. Beeman, "You Can Take the Music out of the Country, but . . . : The Dynamics of Change in Iranian Musical Tradition," *Asian Music* 7:2 (1976), 6–19.

8. Massoudieh, "Tradition und Wandel," pp. 73–80, 85; Zonis, *Classical Persian Music*, p. 186.

9. Some information regarding early concerts of Persian music is found in Ruhollah Khaleqi, *Sargozasht-e musiqi-ye Iran* (Tehran, 1954). On recent concerts, see the Iranian music magazine *Majale-ye musiqi* and, in English, the daily newspaper *Kayhan International* (Tehran). See also Massoudieh, "Tradition und Wandel," p. 91.

10. Ella Zonis, "Contemporary Art Music in Persia," *Musical Quarterly* 51 (1965), 646, gives information on the circumstances under which the pish-darāmad is said to have been invented; her information is based on Khaleqi, *Sargozasht-e musiqi-ye Iran*, vol. 1, chap. 8. See also Khatschi, *Der Dastgah*, p. 154, n. 48. Zonis dates the first performance of pishdarāmad in 1906, Khat-schi in 1909. However, see also E. P. L. Tiersot, *Notes d'ethnographie musicale*, vol. 1 (Paris: Fischbacher, 1905), p. 109, which indicates that the name had been in use before 1900. It seems likely, also, that the Okhovvat, cited by Massoudieh ("Tradition und Wandel," p. 78), had in earlier times had the practice of giving twenty-four-hour-long concerts, but these appear to have been private.

11. Zonis, "Classical Persian Music Today," p. 376.

12. Massoudieh, "Tradition und Wandel," p. 80; Zonis, *Classical Persian Music*, pp. 7–8.

13. Laurence D. Loeb, "The Jewish Musician and the Music of Fars," *Asian Music* 4:1 (1972), 4–6. There is no special census of Jewish musicians in Tehran. According to various musicians interviewed, a good many Jews are musicians. The classical-music sector appears to have a smaller proportion of Jews, however, than does the popular-music sector.

14. Nour-Ali Boroumand, personal communication.

15. Bruno Nettl, "Persian Popular Music in 1969," *Ethnomusicology* 16 (1962), 221. It is interesting to survey the musicians found in *Iran Who's Who* (Tehran: Echo of Iran, 1972). Over a hundred individuals are listed as musicians; this is about 3 percent of the total listing. The vast majority are involved in Western, popular, or film music. Only a half-dozen are active in Persian classical music. These figures—considering that this source may not be representative of widespread opinion—indicate that musicians are not held in low esteem now, but also that Persian classical music is not high in the scale of values held by the Westernized sector of society that uses such a publication.

16. *Iran Almanac and Book of Facts*, 7th ed. (Tehran: Echo of Iran, 1969) gives information on radio transmitters and sets, amount of government sup-port, etc. See also Daniel Lerner, *The Passing of Traditional Society* (New York: Free Press, 1958), pp. 394–96, for a summary of government use of a policy toward the mass media. Robert Stephen Blum, in "Musics in Con-tact: The Cultivation of Oral Repertoire in Meshed, Iran" (Ph.D. diss., Uni-versity of Illinois, 1972), pp. 219–24, postulates a relationship between the government's efforts to "tame the people" and the standardization of musical styles characteristic of the programming of government radio. Although Blum addresses himself mainly to "folk" music, the hypothesis appears applicable

to classical music as well, and may help explain the emphasis upon a mixture of classical, folk, and Western elements in the type of performance typical of radio and television.

17. See e.g. Henry George Farmer, "An Outline History of Music and Musical Theory," in *A Survey of Persian Arts,* ed. Arthur Upman Pope, vol. 3 (London: Oxford University Press, 1939), pp. 2783–804.

18. The role of music as a reflection of basic social and economic structures has been widely though impressionistically discussed in ethnomusicological literature. The most recent attempt to come to grips with this problem is by Alan Lomax and his staff in the cantometrics project, which is described in detail in his *Folk Song Style and Culture* (Washington, D.C.: American Association for the Advancement of Science, 1969); see particularly pp. 117–69 and 227.

19. Described in Nettl, "Persian Popular Music in 1969," pp. 226–27.

20. Massoudieh, "Tradition und Wandel," pp. 81–82. Massoudieh does not assert the growth of theory in itself; rather, he indicates that a large body of theory was created in order to reflect changes that had come about in practice, but had gone unrecognized. The volume of theory in the period before and after 1900, and the evident desire to consolidate it, is also exhibited throughout Khatschi, *Der Dastgah.*

21. Among Vaziri's publications, we mention only *Dastur-e tār* (Berlin, 1913); *Dastur-e violon* (Tehran, 1933); *Musiqi-ye nazari* (Tehran, 1934); and *Nouvelle méthode de tar* (Tehran, 1936).

22. For a summary of traditional Middle Eastern rhythmic modes, see Zonis, *Classical Persian Music,* pp. 205–8. As indicated in Gen'ichi Tsuge, "Rhythmic Aspects of *Āvâz* in Persian Music," *Ethnomusicology* 14 (1970), 205–27, rhythmic theory based on the medieval model system and on the theory of Arabic poetry is still important in Persian vocal music.

23. Zonis, "Classical Persian Music Today," pp. 364–65; Massoudieh, "Tradition und Wandel," p. 81.

24. See Caron and Safvate, *Iran,* pp. 133–40, for occasional bits of information on the rhythms of drumming. A school of zarb players who specialize in extended drum solos that have little to do with Persian musical traditions but exhibit the large varieties of technique available to the drummer has been developed by Hossein Tehrani and his students.

25. Many of the sources giving information about the reforms are given and used in detail by Khatschi in *Der Dastgah.* See also Massoudieh, "Tradition und Wandel," pp. 81–84.

26. Khatschi, *Der Dastgah,* gives information on the life and role of Mirzā Abdollah; see pp. 1–3 and pp. 147–48, fnn. 2 and 3.

27. The role of Persians in the development of Middle Eastern theory—usually called "Arabic" theory—is very great, as indicated in numerous studies, such as those of Henry George Farmer. It seems that the nineteenth century did not produce very much in the way of theoretical writing by Persians, however. The twentieth century saw an increase, beginning e.g. with Vaziri, *Dastur-e tār,* M. Hedayat, *Majmā'el Adwwar* (Tehran, 1928), and Forsat-od-Dowle-ye-Shirazi, *Bohur el Alhan* (Bombay, 1913), and continuing with works by Ruhollah Khaleqi, Mehdi Barkechli, and others. Musicologist-theoreticians such as Hormoz Farhat, Mohammad T. Massoudieh, Dariouche Safvate, and others who have studied in the Western orbit of academic life must also be included in this list, since they did not study

Persian music only as outsiders, but strove to establish a theoretical basis for Persian musicians in addition to providing an explanation of the system for the outside world. No doubt the resurgence of Persian music occasioned by the work of Mirzā Abdollah and his school was in part responsible for this flowering of theoretical writing. It is my contention, however, that the contact with the large and well-organized body of Western music theory has also provided an important stimulus. Khatschi (*Der Dastgah*, chap. 4) indicates the way in which the Mirzā Abdollah school of musicians gradually came to standardize the radif.

28. At least this appears to be the case in the considerable number of treatises preserved, as described by Henry George Farmer, "The Music of Islam," in *The New Oxford History of Music*, vol. 1 (London: Oxford University Press, 1957), pp. 456–64. For early and more recent interval theory applied more specifically to Persian music, see Mehdi Barkechli, "La musique iranienne," in *Histoire de la musique*, ed. Roland-Manuel (Paris: Encyclopedie de la Pleiade, 1960), vol. 1, pp. 460–504. See also, for an exposition by a practicing Iranian musician (Safvate), Caron and Safvate, *Iran*, pp. 25–37.

29. Zonis, "Contemporary Art Music in Persia," p. 640.

30. For an exposition of the "cent" system, see Jaap Kunst, *Ethnomusicology*, 3rd ed. (The Hague: Nijhoff, 1959), pp. 4–11; and Fred Lieberman, "Working with Cents, a Survey," *Ethnomusicology* 15 (1971), 236–41.

31. Zonis, "Contemporary Art Music in Persia," p. 638. Many of my own field experiences corroborated present this statement.

32. Ma'aroufi's radif, which appears in Mehdi Barkechli, *La musique traditionelle de l'Iran* (Tehran: Secretariat d'Etat des Beaux Arts, 1963), includes chahār mezrābs in 6/16 and 3/8 meter. Sabā's radif, parts of which appear in numerous sheet-music publications printed in Tehran, includes chahār mezrābs in 6/8, 3/8, 6/16, and 12/16. Metrically, all of these materials are similar, and all could have been notated in 6/8 or 6/16. The rhythmic character of the pieces distinguished by different meter signatures, however, differs in subtle ways.

33. According to Zonis ("Contemporary Art Music in Persia," p. 640), Ali Naqi Vaziri is credited with the invention of the designations *koron* and *sori*. Vaziri's article, "Notation: Means for the Preservation or Destruction of Music Traditionally not Notated," in *Preservation of Traditional Forms*, ed. Archer, pp. 251–57, discusses this system and proposes its use for Asian music in general.

34. Massoudieh, "Tradition und Wandel," p. 89. Zonis (*Classical Persian Music*, p. 40) maintains that "Vaziri set out to modernize Persian music. For this purpose, he adapted Western staff notation to Persian music. . . ."

35. The voluminous information given by Khatschi (*Der Dastgah*, chaps. 2–3) states unequivocally the importance of the Mirzā Abdollah school for the preservation of the Persian system around 1900. His discussion of the relationship between this tradition and others present in Iran at the time allows us to extrapolate the weakness of other traditions. Caron and Safvate (*Iran*, p. 15), are much more specific, indicating that in the period of Nasred-din Shah (1831–96), knowledge of the classical tradition was confined to two families of court musicians, one of which was that of Mirzā Abdollah's father, Aliakbar Farahani.

36. Nettl and Foltin, *Daramad of Chahargah*, pp. 36–38.

37. Massoudieh, "Tradition und Wandel," pp. 73–74.

38. Information on the population growth of Iran and Tehran, and the relationship of urban to rural populations, is available in *Iran Almanac and Book of Facts*, 7th ed., pp. 98, 493–96, and 10th ed. (Tehran: Echo of Iran, 1971), pp. 101, 265, 509, 516. Since World War II, the population of Tehran has increased from about five hundred thousand to about three million.

39. For bibliography on the music of minority groups in American cities, see Bruno Nettl, "Aspects of Folk Music in North American Cities," in *Music in the Americas*, ed. George List and Juan Orrego-Salas (Bloomington: Indiana University Research Center in Anthropology, Folklore, and Linguistics, 1967), pp. 139–46. Few publications have dealt specifically with the role of urbanization in the history of a traditional music. A landmark is *African Urban Notes* 5:4 (Winter, 1970), which contains several relevant papers. Regarding the urbanization of Iran, see W. D. Fisher, ed., *The Land of Iran*, *The Cambridge History of Iran*, vol. 1, (Cambridge: Cambridge University Press, 1968), pp. 468–85, and Paul W. English, "Culture Change and the Structure of a Persian City," in *The Conflict of Traditionalism and Modernism in the Muslim Middle East*, ed. Carl Leider (Austin: University of Texas Press, 1966), pp. 32–48, esp. p. 45, fn. 2.

40. Zonis, "Classical Persian Music Today," p. 371.

41. Daniel Lerner, in *International Encyclopedia of the Social Sciences*, (New York: Macmillan, 1968), vol. 10, pp. 386–87, defines modernization as "the process whereby less developed societies acquire characteristics common to more developed societies," and subsumes Westernization within it. The distinction between the two is difficult to make, but occasionally insisted upon, as in Lloyd I. and Susanne H. Rudolph, *The Modernity of Tradition* (Chicago: University of Chicago Press, 1967). For definition, commentary, and bibliography see *International Encyclopedia of the Social Sciences*, vol. 1, pp. 20–27, and vol. 3, pp. 554–58.

42. Nettl, "Attitudes toward Persian Music in Tehran, 1969," is a small introductory attempt at sampling opinion.

43. Zaven Hacobian, "La tendance à l'hybridation," in *Preservation of Traditional Forms*, ed. Archer, pp. 148–62.

44. Evidently, however, they were heard in earlier times. See Zonis, *Classical Persian Music*, pp. 186–88. According to Massoudieh ("Tradition und Wandel," p. 85), concerts of European music mixed with arrangements of Persian music were known in the nineteenth century. William S. Haas, *Iran* (New York: Columbia University Press, 1946), p. 187, states that "the Academy of Music intends to introduce and to cultivate Western music and to transpose Iranian music into polyphony with the idea of evolving something that will do more than merely imitate the West." However, the "mixed" performances appear to have made use of Westernized Persian music along with the Western, and they have omitted Persian classical music in its more traditional forms. Attempts to mix the styles were stimulated more by Vaziri than anyone else, and after his influence waned, they also receded.

45. Zonis, *Classical Persian Music*, pp. 186–88.

46. Mehdi Barkechli, "Introduction to the International Congress," in *Preservation of Traditional Forms*, ed. Archer, pp. 55–56.

47. For an example of American Indian Westernization, see Alan P. Merriam, *Ethnomusicology of the Flathead Indians* (Chicago: Aldine Press, 1967), pp. 123–47. For Afro-American music, see Richard A. Waterman,

"African Influence on the Music of the Americas," in *Acculturation in the Americas,* ed. Sol Tax, *Proceedings of the 29th International Congress of Americanists,* vol. 2 (Chicago, 1952), pp. 207–18.

48. The degree to which religious minorities participate in the Iranian nationalist movement is discussed in Richard W. Cottam, *Nationalism in Iran* (Pittsburgh: University of Pittsburgh Press, 1964), pp. 75–101.

49. Historical studies like the large number of works by Henry George Farmer constantly stress, both explicitly and by implication, the unity of Middle Eastern music. Even as recent a work as Hans Hickmann, "Die Musik des arabisch-islamischen Bereichs," in *Orientalische Musik, Handbuch der Orientalistik,* ed. B. Spuler, part 1, supp. vol. 4 (1970), pp. 1–134, still maintains this unity. To what extent this insistence is justified depends on the measuring devices for stylistic similarity that are used, but there is certainly a vivid contrast between it and the constantly heard assertion in Tehran that Persian music is independent and, indeed, very, very different from Arabic and Turkish music.

50. The basic structure of the ministry is outlined in *Iran Almanac and Book of Facts,* 7th ed., p. 152. Zonis ("Classical Persian Music Today," pp. 369–71) describes the history of some of the government's efforts in behalf of Persian music.

51. Massoudieh indicates a change of mood when he says ("Tradition und Wandel," p. 91), "Im zweiten Drittel des 20. Jahrhunderts sind Veränderungen, die die persische Musik des späten 19. und frühen 20. Jhdts. geprägt haben, voll zum Tragen gekommen." Zonis (*Classical Persian Music,* pp. 192–94) also implies a difference in the musical life between these periods. The enormous changes in social and economic life have obviously played a part.

52. This paper was written while the author was an associate of the University of Illinois Center for Advanced Study. Field research on which it is based in part was carried out in 1968–69 and again briefly in 1971 and 1972, under a Fulbright grant and with support from the University of Illinois Center for International Comparative Studies and Research Board. After the bulk of work toward this paper was completed, two publications that in many ways cover the same ground—Massoudieh's excellent article "Tradition und Wandel in der persischen Musik des 19. Jahrhunderts" and Ella Zonis's fine survey, *Classical Persian Music*—appeared in print. It nevertheless seemed appropriate to summarize the basic data, with frequent reference to these publications, since the ultimate purpose of this paper is different, namely, to analyze the processes involved in the changes that have been described by many authors, but particularly by Massoudieh and Zonis. For a later stage in my thinking, see my article "Some Aspects of the History of World Music in the Twentieth Century: Questions, Problems, and Concepts," *Ethnomusicology* 22 (1978), 123–36.

Gharanas: The Rise of Musical "Houses" in Delhi and Neighboring Cities

DANIEL M. NEUMAN

It has long been recognized that cities comprise a particular kind of environment, one that is seemingly constant in some respects for all urban areas and presents, consequently, comparable conditions to which city inhabitants have had to adapt.[1] Much of urban anthropological research has focused on the specific ways in which people adjust to the demands of city and town life. In thus examining the process of adjustment, anthropologists have concentrated on recent migrants while largely ignoring the already-adjusted. Fox, in his critique of urban anthropological studies, makes the point that such interest in people peripheral to the city as a whole continues a tradition in anthropology of pursuing the exotic; although it is "the basis of anthropology's strength in the past, the form it takes in contemporary urban anthropology often means that little can be said about city and society or urban organization and national culture."[2] He argues instead for an urban anthropology treating the city holistically and concentrating on two major problems: studying "the ideological ties which bind the city to the countryside and vice versa . . . [and viewing] the city as a socio-economic and political factor in the organization of the society; it is both product and producer of particular political alignments, economic sectors and social structures."[3]

This paper is an attempt at an urban ethnomusicology that takes into account this latter perspective. The case in point is the

Daniel M. Neuman is Assistant Professor of Anthropology, Dartmouth College, Hanover, New Hampshire.

186

effect of cities on the social organization of North Indian art musicians and, in consequence, on the musical system itself. Specifically, this is a study of an urban sociomusical phenomenon, the *gharanas* (musical houses) of North Indian music. In this part of India the primary means by which an individual conveys his identity as a classical musician is to name his *gharana* (literally "of the house"), by which he usually means the stylistic school of which he is a member and his performances a representation. When discussing these gharanas with artists, one gains the distinct impression that gharanas have great *depth:* through space, including as they do musicians throughout North India; through time, extending back along ancestries that sometimes reach the eighth century A.D.; and last, in significance, giving musicians the authority of a tradition as well as a tradition of authenticity.

It turns out, however, that gharanas as we know them now did not appear before the middle of the last century, and the term itself probably did not gain currency until after the beginning of the present century. Gharanas are almost always named after cities, and, contrary to the impression of depth in space, they virtually all have their origins in urban centers within a two-hundred-mile radius of Delhi.[4]

The present study is about the rise of these gharanas and the role of cities in their formation; for cities, as I intend to argue, have been crucial in the way they have affected the social organization of *Hindusthani* (North Indian) music. The first part of this study examines the different concepts attached to the term *gharana* and the different kinds of musicians that comprise the gharanas. Important here is the hierarchical distinction between soloists and accompanists and the caste-like social units from which they have been recruited. Most hereditary musicians in North India belong to either of two major social groups. One of these is called *Kalawant,* a category usually reserved for those musicians who claim a long and pure ancestry of soloists. The other, *Mirasi,* is comprised of accompanists, some of whom have gone on to become soloists, but virtually all of whom are descended from rural "folk" musicians. The second part is an analysis of the urbanization of musical specialists during the last century based on Indian census data from 1881 through 1931. This analysis is followed by a description of the migration of rural Mirasis to the cities and their transformation from folk to classical musicians. This movement is significant due to the importance of Mirasis as music innovators. The third part is a discussion of social changes in Indian society beginning in the middle of the last century and the implications that these changes have had for the emergence of gharanas. This is concluded with an interpretation of the condition of hereditary musicians today.

Gharanas

The formation of gharanas is appropriate to the interest of the ethnomusicologist, since, like ethnomusicology itself, the definition of gharana incorporates the features of both the musical and the social world.

To the sophisticated Indian listener, the significance of gharanas lies in the characteristic performance styles of each. Thus, the Gwalior Gharana is known for its "open-throated singing and straight movements." The Agra Gharana is also characterized by open-throated singing and an emphasis on rhythmic syncopation. In addition to differences in the emphasis of musical features, styles are distinguished by the structure of performance practices as well. For example, unlike the Gwalior Gharana, those of Agra sing the *alapa* before the *khayal*.[5]

Gharanas also denote the families of musicians who are its exponents. As a social unit, the gharana is based on a core lineage (*khandan*) founded by a known ancestor (or ancestors), from whom membership in a gharana is established by a claim of descent—in principle, through the male line, but in fact, commonly through cognatic descent relationships. An outsider can become a member of a gharana by being a disciple of its representatives, but he or she will still be distinguished from those who have inherited their gharana status through birth and are known as *gharanedars*.[6]

It is difficult, if not impossible, to give an exact number or list of gharanas, since, as with Indian castes, they exist at a number of different conceptual levels. Consequently, one discovers that many more gharanas are claimed than any single individual will recognize. This disparity is due primarily to ambiguities in the meaning of the term and a variety of strategies in the use of it. For example, while an individual may claim membership in a particular gharana, another may refuse to recognize the validity of the former's claim ("he does not really belong") or the validity of the gharana itself ("it is not a real gharana").

The definition of authenticity depends, of course, on who is making the judgment, a question we will consider below. There are certain gharanas, however, that are universally accepted as genuine and can be termed "classic" or established gharanas.

The oldest of these gharanas is the Gwalior Gharana, founded by two brothers and (perhaps) a cousin.[7] The two brothers, Haddu and Hassu Khan, were well known in their own day and are celebrated by a mid-nineteenth-century contemporary of theirs, Mohammad Imam.[8] Through marriage and discipleship, the Gwalior Gharana is related to virtually every other major gharana (see fig. 1).

Delhi, as the center of political power for most of the period of Islamic rule, had a number of families of musicians. For this reason one noted authority discusses the khandans of Delhi rather than the Delhi Gharana.[9] Nevertheless, others will often refer to the "Delhi Gharana," using the term in at least one of three major senses. An elucidation of these will clarify the semantic space that the term *gharana* occupies, while providing the reader an understanding of the manner in which gharanas evolved.

The Delhi gharanas

The most famous Delhi contemporary of the founders of the Gwalior Gharana was the great Tanras Khan. He was court musician to Bahadur Shah Zafar, the last Mughal king (1837–58). When the latter was exiled from Delhi after the Mutiny of 1857, Tanras Khan migrated to the Hyderabad court, where he died in 1890. When some speak of the Delhi Gharana, they are referring to Tanras Khan and his descendants. Some of his descendants, including his great-grandson, are living in Delhi today, but as artists they have been obscure for the last two generations. Those descendants who have remained musicians are specialists of the *qawalli* (Muslim devotional song) genre and are therefore outside the mainstream of the classical music tradition.[10]

There is, however, another group of musicians who claim to be the representatives of the Delhi Gharana. When outsiders refer to this gharana, they call it the Delhi Gharana of Mamman Khan to

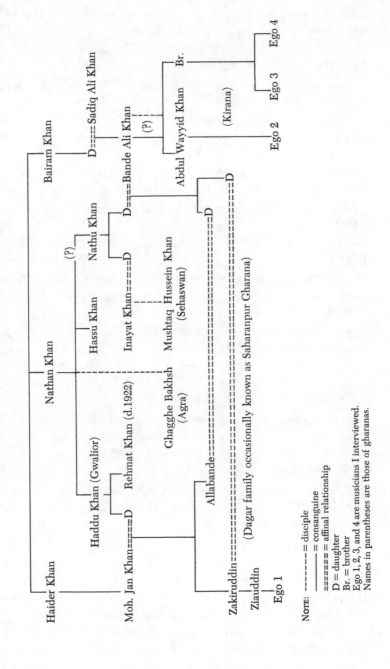

Fig. 1. The Gwalior Gharana and its relationships to other gharanas

NOTE: ------ = disciple
　　　 ———— = consanguine
　　　 ====== = affinal relationship
　　　 D = daughter
　　　 Br. = brother
　　　 Ego 1, 2, 3, and 4 are musicians I interviewed.
　　　 Names in parentheses are those of gharanas.

distinguish it from the Delhi Gharana of Tanras Khan. This is the second meaning that *Delhi Gharana* conveys.

The Delhi Gharana of Mamman Khan is particularly interesting because it is still in the process of formation, that is, establishing itself as an authentic gharana. Members of established gharanas and their allies among musical connoisseurs, however, raise three main objections to recognizing this group as a legitimate gharana; and these reservations prevent its complete acceptance as an established gharana by musical society. A review of these objections will provide us with an orthodox conception of the prerequisites of a gharana.

The first objection is that the Delhi Gharana of Mamman Khan does not have the requisite genealogical depth. Minimally, three generations of distinguished artists maintaining the integrity of a coherent and recognized style are said to be necessary to establish a legitimate gharana. Mamman Khan, considered the founder of this gharana by its members, died only in 1940. His son, Ustad Chand Khan (b. ca. 1895), is the doyen of this gharana, but he constitutes only the second generation (see fig. 2). There are several artists among Chand Khan's agnatic descendants, one of whom is well known as a distinguished vocalist. Nevertheless, purists maintain that only in the succeeding generation, "when one can look back at three generations," will this gharana's credentials (perhaps!) become valid.

The second objection relates to the first. Some insist that this gharana does not represent or embody a truly original style. One descendant of Tanras Khan claims that Ustad Chand Khan is a disciple of the Tanras Khan Gharana, and therefore the ustad can only claim to be a member of the Tanras Khan Delhi Gharana. Ustad Chand Khan says somewhat the same thing, but from a different perspective. He recognizes that Umrao Khan (Tanras Khan's son) was the previous chief exponent of the Delhi Gharana, but now claims that status for himself. In other words, he does not acknowledge being a *disciple* of the Tanras Khan Gharana; rather, he considers himself its *extension*. Only outsiders, as I mentioned above, add the qualifier "of Mamman Khan" to the label "Delhi Gharana." Members themselves just say that they are the Delhi Gharana. Their justification is further reinforced by the claim of

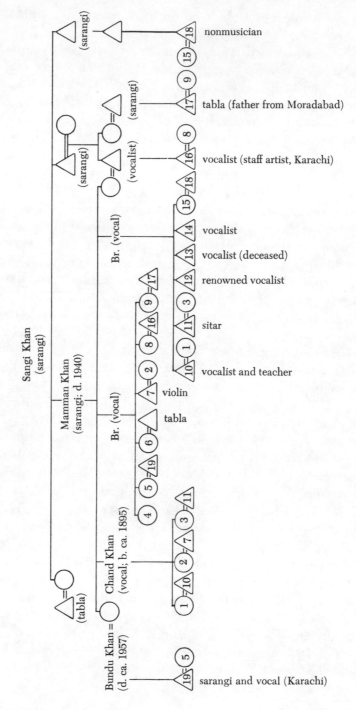

Fig. 2. The Delhi Gharana of Mamman Khan

NOTE: The numbers are the "names" of individuals; where repeated, they are both descendants and affines.
Br. = brother

192

Chand Khan and others in the family that they are descendants of Mian Aachpal, who was a teacher of Tanras Khan.

The previous objections—like the definition of gharana itself—revolve around a juxtaposition of musical and social criteria. Musical style, its distinctiveness, age, and origin, are combined with the prestige, genealogical depth, and originality of its practitioners as determinants of a gharana's legitimacy. The third objection is of a different type. The ancestors of today's Delhi Gharana were sarangi and tabla players, being therefore accompanists, not soloists.[11] Gharanas as stylistic schools are represented only by soloists, claim the critics; and although contemporary exponents of this Delhi Gharana are soloists, their musical traditions are those of accompanists, and they therefore cannot claim to be members of an authentic gharana.

Although all the lineal male descendants of Mamman Khan are soloists (see fig. 2), this family is part of a much larger kinship group called a *biradari* (brotherhood), the male members of which are almost all accompanists. Many in this brotherhood are tabla players, and they have evolved a distinct style of tabla playing that is known as the Delhi *baj* (style). Since these tabla players are related to the soloists of the Delhi Gharana of Mamman Khan, they also claim to be its members. They have their own distinctive style—the Delhi baj—and the kinship connections to the Mamman Khan lineage, which make their claim seemingly valid. Thus, the third sense in which the term *Delhi Gharana* can be understood is as a tabla gharana. The use of the term *gharana* for tabla styles is quite recent, however—having been in use for perhaps no more than two decades, if that long.[12]

The objection that the Delhi Gharana of Mamman Khan cannot be considered a legitimate gharana because of its accompanist heritage raises a number of important questions. Not the least of them is this: What is it about being descended from accompanists that (in the eyes of many) automatically disqualifies descendant soloists from forming a legitimate gharana? By implication, how is it that some soloists have no accompanists as ancestors? And more generally, how are these music-specialist categories—accompanist and soloist—related to the formation of stylistic schools? Or, put a different way, what relevance do these categories have for an understanding of the rise of gharanas in urban centers during the last century? A summary answer to these questions is that soloist and accompanist musicians are different kinds of musicians —one could even say different castes, having different social origins and occupying different ranks in the social hierarchy. And, as I will attempt to demonstrate, musicians of accompanist backgrounds are descended from rural musicians who migrated to urban centers during the cast century. In the city they entered the ranks of classical musicians, and one of the means by which they achieved this status was in the formation of musical houses. In order to understand this development, however, we have to go back to Ustad Chand Khan, the doyen of the present Delhi Gharana, and listen to his story.

Accompanists and soloists

It is important to note that Chand Khan never denies the definition of a legitimate gharana as put forward by the members of established gharanas. As we have seen, he does not claim descent or discipleship from the older, established Tanras Khan Gharana, but validates his own position by surrounding the period of Tanras Khan's ascendancy with time: time in the past, to which he connects via descent to Tanras Khan's teacher; and time in the present, in which he embodies the extension of Tanras Khan's (or rather his son's) reputation. Chand Khan uses a similar strategy to overcome the "three generation rule," by tracing his descent back to the eighth century, when his ancestors entered India at the time of the first Islamic incursions (A.D. 712). His ancestors were given the position of "divider of inheritance." Inheritance is *miras* in Arabic, so his descendants have come to be known as *Mirasi*.

The authenticity of this claim is unimportant. What is important is that it provides great genealogical depth for his family, together with a legitimate origin for Mirasis. The significance of Mirasis, as we shall soon see, lies in the fact that the majority of sarangi and tabla players throughout Northern India, and all of the rural migrants that we will be discussing, are called Mirasis. Thus the accompanist-musicians' "caste" is called Mirasi and is separate from the "caste" of soloists, who have no accompanists as ancestors.

The question now arises of how Chand Khan can claim a legiti-

mate gharana if his ancestry includes sarangi and tabla players—
accompanists—a fact too recent and too well known for him to
deny. He again uses the strategy of time to encompass the historical reality of recent time. The sarangi, for example, enters his family almost by accident. In Chand Khan's own words:

> According to a legend when, after the 1857 uprising in Delhi,
> some of the leading sarangi and bin players of Delhi including
> Mamman Khan's *maternal* grandfather, Ghulam Hussein Khan,
> migrated to Ballabh Ghar, Mamman Khan's paternal grandfather
> treated these relatives rather shabbily because he disapproved of
> their association with a lowly instrument like the sarangi. This
> hurt the feelings of Mamman Khan's father, Abdul Ghani Khan.
> As a protest against his father's and uncle's behavior, Abdul Ghani
> Khan decided to take up the sarangi. This annoyed the elders who
> turned Abdul Ghani out of Ballabh Ghar. He then came back to
> live in Delhi with his father-in-law [Mamman Khan's maternal
> grandfather]. He turned his back on ancestral property and de-
> voted his entire talent to the improvement of the sarangi. His de-
> votion to the sarangi earned him the name, Sarangi Khan, which
> became Sangi Khan, by which name he is still known. Bundu
> Khan, one of his grandsons, took to the sarangi after his grand-
> father, but the other grandson [the present narrator, Chand
> Khan], in deference to the wishes of his great-grandfather (who
> was finally reconciled to his son's passion for the sarangi)—and
> with the approval of his grandfather, *resumed* the vocal tradition
> of his ancestors under the guidance of his grandfather and grand-
> uncles. [Emphasis added.][13]

According to Chand Khan, therefore, his musical tradition is
actually a vocal, soloistic tradition through the male line. The sarangi appears recently and through the *female* side of the family
only. His paternal ancestors, although originally prejudiced against
sarangi playing (as are many musicians today), were finally rec-
onciled to and accepted the sarangi.[14]

Chand Khan further emphasizes his claim for the integrity of
his gharana by distinguishing between those who were teachers
of his ancestors and those who were not: "Mamman Khan [the
founder of this gharana] received his musical training from his
paternal grandfather and grand-uncle and later from his father
and maternal grandfather, Ghulam Hussain Khan. It is wrong to
say that he got any training from Mian Kallu Khan of Patiala or

Imdad Khan Sitariya or Chajju Khan Amar Shah. He had great respect for these masters, but he owes no debt of learning from them."

Not only does Chand Khan disclaim disciple obligations to those outside his lineage, but he also makes the point that Mamman Khan, who was a sarangi player, first learned from his *paternal* ancestors, who were *soloists,* and only later from his maternal side and his own father, who as sarangi players were accompanists. In effect, then, Chand Khan is able to skirt the issue of his gharana's accompanist ancestry by stressing that his patrilineal ancestry is comprised of soloists and precedes in time his accompanist ancestry.

I have said that accompanists constitute a separate "caste" called Mirasis. Soloists, like those of the Agra Gharana or Saharanpur Gharana, also constitute a separate, caste-like, social unit. They intermarry among themselves, as do Mirasis, and make it a point that there be no marriage with accompanists. Thus they can point to pedigrees that include no connection to accompanists. Such soloist lineages can be referred to as *Kalawants.*[15] The gharanas of Kalawants are the "classical" gharanas, and almost all are vocalist lineages. Theirs were the earliest gharanas, and by being the oldest, members claim to be carriers of the most authentic musical traditions. Although these Kalawant soloists are all Muslim (like Mirasi accompanists), they recognize their origins (unlike Mirasis) as Hindu, usually Brahmans and sometimes Rajputs.[16]

What we discover, then, are two kinds of social organizations, what I have called "castes,"[17] corresponding to the two primary musical performance roles in Hindusthani music: soloist and accompanist. These roles are indeed quite distinct and mutually exclusive. An accompanist cannot also be a soloist, and vice versa. Such separateness is well exemplified by an older musician, who recalls an occasion when this rule was broken:

> There is one thing about musical sittings which I still remember. Sarangi players were not allowed to take the tampoura and sing. . . . in one such *Mehefil* [musical gathering] a sarangi player who sang very well started singing in the mehefil. The sponsor of the mehefil asked him to stop singing and told him to stop playing the sarangi, and then only would he be allowed to sing in all the mehefils. So he completely stopped playing sarangi and started

singing. After that he was praised by good vocalists and became famous. By mentioning this I mean to say that in those days [early twentieth century] music was the purest and highest form of education, and it was very necessary to respect it.[18]

It is important to note that an individual can change roles if he abandons his original role. (In practice, the switch is unidirectional, since for a soloist to become an accompanist would result in a marked decrease in status.)

Chand Khan claims that in the past, hereditary families of musicians included all kinds of specialists, and there was no distinction between them. More recently, he adds, schisms in a family because one of its members has become a sarangi player (as happened in his case) have not been unusual.[19] His assertion that specialties were undifferentiated in the more distant past is indirectly corroborated by the mid-nineteenth-century observer of musical life referred to above.[20] Although lineages of Kalawants (among them Tanras Khan's) are described and accorded generally more prestige than other groups of musicians, the fundamental distinction between soloists and accompanists is not evident. Furthermore, there is no mention of Mirasis.[21]

Thus it appears that *social* differentiation between soloist and accompanist families is fairly recent. The formation of gharanas as social units has been the result, I would suggest, of closely intermarrying lineages. A closed marriage circle is thus formed. Such a strategy for upward social mobility has been used by other Muslim castes as well.[22] This practice also explains why hereditary gharana musicians are always Muslims.[23] Cousin marriage of any type among Hindus in North India is strictly prohibited, whereas among Muslims it is allowed: indeed, among Muslim musicians it is the preferred form of marriage, and it is stated by them to be an explicit strategy by which musical knowledge is kept within the family.[24] It would appear, from an outsider's vantage point, that such intermarriage has been an important way in which gharanas have maintained the integrity of their musical styles.

Figure 2 demonstrates how a lineage can close in upon itself, keeping accompanist kin relations outside, while allowing only male soloists. In the most recent generation, all marriages of this patrilineage are with close relations, most in fact being first cousins.

There are other gharanas, now "established," which originally were formed by lineages of accompanists. One of the most famous of these is the Patiala Gharana, founded by two cousins known collectively as Alliyu-Fattu. These two were disciples of Tanras Khan of Delhi. Upon returning to Patiala, they developed their own style, which has become very popular in North India. This style is original enough, the genealogical depth long enough, and some of its exponents famous enough, that there is no longer any question of the gharana's legitimacy. The Patiala Gharana is recognized and respected everywhere. Most important, its accompanist heritage has been obscured through time; and only the specialist would know that today's hereditary representatives are descended from accompanists.

One manner by which origins are "forgotten" is perhaps accomplished by altering or obscuring pedigrees. For example, the Kirana Gharana was supposedly founded by Bande Ali Khan, a descendant of a soloist Kalawant lineage. This gharana became famous in the 1930s through two vocalists, Abdul Karim Khan and Abdul Wayyid Khan. Although both were very famous (and also brothers-in-law), they belonged to a community of accompanists. Abdul Wayyid Khan's son and nephews are sarangi players at All India Radio in Delhi today. However, all members of this community of accompanists claim Bande Ali Khan—a Kalawant—as an ancestor. Yet other musicians who are Kalawant soloists say that Bande Ali Khan was only their *ustad* (teacher), not a relation. The fact that Bande Ali Khan was both a bīn player and a sarangi player (thus a specialist of both a soloistic and accompanimental instrument) does not add any light to the confusion. But again, the Kirana Gharana is an established gharana, and the fact that there are accompanists in the family is irrelevant, or unknown to the public. Its authenticity as a gharana, however, is nothing if not further corroborated by the claim that Bande Ali Khan was its founder.[25]

The point I wish to underline here is that, although gharanas are, in principle, stylistic schools of hereditary solo specialists, the claim that their authenticity rests on a pedigree unblemished by accompanists is in fact unfounded. In actuality, most of the viable gharanas today were indeed founded by Mirasi accompanists, a fact that becomes especially significant when one learns that Mirasis were (and are) a caste of rural musicians who began to enter the cities and the classical tradition only during the last century. In order to substantiate this assertion, we must examine the urbanization of musicians generally and Mirasis in particular from about the 1870s on.

Cities as Musical Centers

The urbanization of musical specialists

India has always been known for its relatively slow rate of urbanization and its high proportion of a rural population.[26] On the

TABLE 1. POPULATION CHANGES BETWEEN 1881 AND 1931

	1881		1931		
	Population	Percent urban	Population	Percent urban	Percent growth
Lucknow City	253,729	36	274,659	35	8
Lucknow District	696,824		787,472		13
Delhi City[a]	173,393		365,527		111
Delhi Province[b]					
Kanpur City	155,369	13	243,755	20	56
Kanpur District	1,181,396		1,212,253		3
Agra City	160,203	16	229,764	22	43
Agra District	974,656		1,048,316		8
Bareilly City	115,138	11	144,031	13	25
Bareilly District	1,030,936		1,072,379		4
Meerut City	99,911	7.6	136,709	8.5	37
Meerut District	1,299,333		1,601,918		23
Moradabad City	63,309	5	110,562	9	75
Moradabad District	1,155,513		1,284,108		11
Saharanpur City	59,194	6	78,655	7	33
Saharanpur District	979,882		1,043,920		7

[a]The figures for Delhi City include only Old Delhi, and not New Delhi, which would increase the rate even more, to 153%. The New Delhi population for 1931 was 73,663.

[b]Delhi became a separate province in 1912, but was not separately enumerated until 1931. The growth rates since 1881 were listed as percent gains between decades as follows:

	1881–91	1891–1901	1901–11	1911–21	1921–31
Delhi Province	6	9	2	18	30
Delhi urban	11	8	12	31	47
Delhi rural	2	9	−8	2	3

If in 1931 Shadara had been listed as a village, as it was in the 1921 census, the 1921–31 growth for Delhi rural would be 6%.

TABLE 2. MALE MUSICIANS IN MUNICIPALITIES AND CORRESPONDING DISTRICTS

| | 1881 Number[a] | | | 1901 Number | | | 1911 Number | | | 1921 Number | | | 1931 Number | | |
	City	District	Percent urban	City	District	Percent urban	City	District	Percent urban	City	District	Percent urban	City	District	Percent urban
Lucknow	417 (16)[b]	692	60	356 (14)	649	55	548 (22)	870	63	108 (4)	341	32	677 (25)	759	89
Delhi[b]	567 (28)	761	74	502 (22)	618	81	764 (33)	987	77	414 (15)	531	78	652 (18)	772	84
Kanpur	295 (19)	1041	28	51 (2)	436	12	250 (14)	561	45	180 (8)	391	46	132 (5)	190	69
Agra	258 (16)	1280	20	278 (15)	699	40	185 (10)	371	50	219 (11)	567	39	150 (6)	432	35
Bareilly	192 (17)	930	21	197 (15)	755	26	207 (16)	838	25	145 (11)	465	31	143 (10)	470	30
Meerut	526 (53)	2726	19	433 (36)	1517	28	349 (30)	499	70	187 (15)	734	25	208 (15)	876	24
Moradabad	442 (70)	1569	28	120 (16)	1010	12	160 (20)	1177	14	111 (13)	959	12	180 (16)	987	18
Saharanpur	97 (16)	1233	8	307 (46)	773	40	252 (40)	1104	23	82 (13)	459	18	110 (14)	826	13

[a]The numbers for 1881 include the category of actor, automatically included in subsequent censuses.
[b]Parentheses indicate the number of musicians in cities per 10,000 population.
[c]For 1881, the Delhi figures are listed under "towns" and "villages," not Delhi City and Delhi District.

other hand, musical specialists (in North India) were probably already relatively urbanized from the beginnings of Islamic rule and certainly after the middle of the last century.

In table 1, I have listed eight cities (all important as centers of musical activity and the homes of known musician-communities) and their respective districts, showing their population growth between 1881 and 1931.[27] All (excepting Lucknow) have increased in the proportion of their urban population to the surrounding district, although, considering the fifty-year interval, the growth is far from dramatic.

In table 2[28] one can compare the figures for musicians (male only) and their rate of "urbanization."[29] Even though musicians are already more urban in 1881 than the population as a whole, in all but one instance (Moradabad) their proportion of urban growth has accelerated even more quickly than the rest of the population.

One cannot fail, however, to note the striking decrease in the absolute number of musicians, a phenomenon not limited to those cities and districts, but existing throughout India.[30] The figures for Lucknow and Delhi are significant exceptions, suggesting that larger urban centers were attracting an increasing proportion of music specialists. These two cities also have the highest number of musicians compared to the total population, Lucknow and Delhi having 25 and 18 per 10,000, respectively. Further corroborating the importance of absolute size of urban centers is the correlation between the rank size of the cities listed and their respective proportions of urban musicians.

Although the overall decrease in the absolute number of musicians is difficult to account for, the fact that a higher percentage of musicians was urban in 1931 implies either that urban musicians were more likely to remain musical specialists than were their rural counterparts[31] or that there was a migration of rural musicians to the cities. In either case, it seems clear that there were greater opportunities of "making it" as a musician in the city than in the countryside.

A similar conclusion is supported with reference to the absolute size of a city. Not only is there the aforementioned correlation between rank size and the proportion of urban/rural musicians for cities and districts in 1931, but the highest percentage of urban musicians over the five decades in a given city corresponds to the size of cities as well. Thus, the smallest urban centers listed (Moradabad and Saharanpur) had the highest proportion of urban musicians in 1881 and 1901. The next three larger cities (Meerut, Bareilly, and Agra) have their highest proportions in 1911 and 1921. The three largest cities (Lucknow, Delhi, and Kanpur) reach their highest point in 1931. This suggests the *possibility* that musicians were migrating to successively larger urban centers through this fifty-year period. Thus Moradabad, which experienced the only overall decline in the urban proportion of musicians during this period (and the most marked decrease in the proportion of musicians to the population as a whole—from 70 to 16 per 10,000), may have done so only because many of its musicians migrated to Delhi and other large urban centers. This shift is indicated today where one finds many Moradabad musicians living in Delhi and Jaipur and at least some others in Lucknow and in Bombay.

Although the census data that I have presented here must be interpreted with some caution,[32] the broad outline strongly supports the contention that music specialists of North India were becoming even more urbanized in this period than they had been previously. This contention is also corroborated by data that I was able to gather through interviews with over seventy musicians, in addition to my own genealogical and census data.[33] Thus, of the musicians I interviewed who were living in Delhi, the overwhelming majority claimed an origin outside of Delhi. Typically, they name the village (*gaon*) and/or the district they came from. Also, many tend to name smaller urban centers like Moradabad, Saharanpur, or Bulandshahar, which they consider their ancestral homes. At the same time, they recognize that before coming to these smaller urban centers, their ancestors lived in the countryside, although the particular locations are often forgotten.

Migrating Mirasis

An example of Mirasi migration is the case of a sarangi player who now lives in Delhi, having been brought there as a child by his father back in the 1930s. He comes originally from Moradabad, where many of his relatives continue to live and where he still owns an ancestral home. He was vaguely aware that his family had come to Moradabad in the distant past, but he had no idea from where. It was only when I was interviewing an elderly uncle on his mother's side that I (and he) discovered that the family was originally from Sialkot district in Punjab, some two or three generations back. This pattern of migration, from the rural hinterlands to urban centers, has been characteristic of most of the Mirasi families that I came to learn about.[34]

We know about the rural origins of Mirasis from other sources as well. On the basis of the descriptions in ethnographies, earlier census reports, and other sources,[35] it appears that the traditional role of the Mirasi was that of genealogist to the lower castes (recalling Chand Khan's ancestors becoming the "dividers of inheritance") and musical entertainer at festivals, weddings, and other important social functions. Mirasis were originally from the Punjab, where they were part of the village *jajmani* (patron-client) system, each Mirasi group serving a number of villages in a given territory.[36]

The term *Mirasi* had, then as now, a pejorative connotation. As Tandon recalls in *Punjabi Century,*

> another Muslim caste in the Jajmani system was that of the Mirasis. The Mirasis beat drums and played the shehnai [oboe] . . . at weddings and other auspicious occasions, but their specialty was wit and repartee, which they could exercise with traditional immunity on the highest and lowest in the society. . . . Men and women sang praises of the family and recited its genealogy at weddings. They were also the vehicle of old ballads and songs. *The word Mirasi in the Punjabi language has come to mean witty and funny in an overdone, vulgar manner.* [Emphasis added.][37]

Once in the towns and cities, Mirasis tended to come together in the same neighborhoods. These neighborhoods or wards (*mohallas*) continue to exist today, so that in old Delhi, for example, the Mirasis and also some other musicians live mainly in three or four wards.

The groups that shared a common locality were and are organized into the biradaris that I mentioned before.[38] These brotherhoods are composed of a number of lineages that share an identity based on common territorial origin. Thus an individual who was born in Rampur (or whose father was born there) is a member of the Rampur brotherhood, even if he now lives in Delhi.

A particular Mirasi brotherhood is not, strictly speaking, an endogamous unit, although there is a commonly expressed sentiment that marriage within the lineage or, lacking that, within the brotherhood are favored arrangements. There is a sense, albeit subtle, of solidarity between members of a given biradari. For example, all are especially invited to participate in or attend weddings, funerals, and other ritual occasions within the biradari.

The brotherhood as described here is essentially an urban phenomenon. This distinction becomes clear through a comparison with contemporary rural Mirasis. Although little is known about the latter, it is clear that their social organization is quite different, most notably in the area of marriage. Among urban Mirasis, cousin marriage (both cross and parallel) is a preferred form and occurs quite regularly. Rural Mirasis, on the other hand, like their Hindu neighbors, prohibit any kind of cousin marriage and practice village exogamy as well. They do have brotherhoods, but these are differently organized; they extend over a relatively wide area of villages, and their internal organization is much more complex.[39]

In the cities, Mirasis have been known traditionally as the accompanists of the singing and dancing girls of the courtesan tradition. Even today one can find them as accompanists to courtesans, this role being the major reason for the stigma attached to the sarangi and tabla as instruments and to the specialists who perform on them. The Mirasis were (and still are) considered by courtesans as their ustads, since they learn their music from them.

The earliest reference to Mirasis as art musicians that has come to my attention dates from 1872.[40] In Imam's extended description of musical life and musician communities in Lucknow before the Mutiny of 1857, there is, as I have said, no mention of Mirasis. It would appear, therefore, that Mirasis entered the cities and the "great tradition" of art music during the latter half of the nineteenth century, having been preadapted as specialists of the "little tradition" of rural music.[41]

How Mirasis entered the art-music world can now only be adumbrated because the details are not fully known. That this metamorphosis was achieved via the salon tradition of the courtesans, however, seems quite certain. The line between the classical music of the courts and the music of the courtesans has never been very distinct. Imam describes the female vocalists (they were never instrumentalists) of his day in premutiny Lucknow as highly respected artists. Nonetheless, it appears that they were considered courtesans.[42] Even today, many of the famous female vocalists are descended from and recognized as courtesans; and the music of this tradition (primarily the *thumri*, and to a lesser extent the *ghazal*) are today categorized as "light classical"[43] musical forms. The ordinary courtesan singers of today perform the thumri and ghazal, but more commonly they sing the distinctly popular film songs. In the past, it is likely that the "popular" music of that day was the music of the countryside, what would now be called *lok geet* (folk music, or, more literally, songs of the people).

Given this range of musical forms available in the courtesan tradition, it seems reasonable to suppose that Mirasi accompanists migrating to the cities were able to offer their own talents and repertoires to the courtesan music tradition.

We do know that Mirasi musicians attempted to learn classical music from established Kalawant solo specialists. One learns this from the stories that Mirasi musicians give with an eye to persuading the listener of their own distinguished learning traditions and from the claims of Kalawant soloists that Mirasis are all ultimately their disciples. Furthermore, from both perspectives one hears of the great difficulty that Mirasis had in becoming disciples of the Kalawants, for the latter were not enthusiastic about providing more competition for their own families. How Mirasis succeeded could probably be explained only in individual histories. However, in one case, which may be typical, a Mirasi musician was the brother of a Kalawant's mistress, and through her influence was able to become the Kalawant's disciple. Other means that were employed included payment of money, although this by itself was no guarantee that an individual could become a disciple.

Whatever the methods, it is quite certain that some Mirasis learned the classical tradition from established art musicians, and then were able to go on to become soloists and form their own gharanas as well. Other Mirasis could become knowledgeable about performance practices merely through the experience of accompanying. One renowned sarangi player, Bade Ghulam Sabir (who died in the 1950s), was famous for the accuracy and speed with which he was able to follow heterophonically the vocalists' complex melodic lines. He was also known for the fact that he knew nothing about the theory of Hindusthani classical music, not even knowing the names of the ragas that he performed! Yet he was considered a great musician who understood the music so thoroughly that he was able to anticipate what a vocalist would do and therefore follow with unerring skill.

What emerges from this somewhat reconstructed history of Mirasi musicians is part of the story of the way cities have affected the musical culture of North India. Urban centers, already home to many musicians, clearly afforded opportunities that had declined in the countryside. As the birthplace of gharanas, cities were where Kalawant soloist musicians could consolidate their musical traditions by limiting the marriage network of their lineages. And in some cases Mirasi accompanists were able to become soloists, by separating their lineages through specialization and perhaps by selective marriage as well. But to say simply that cities were the locale of these developments does not in itself adequately portray the role of these urban centers in the changing nature of Hindusthani musical culture during the last century. We know that cities attracted migrants and that the gharanas therein allowed for a measure of social mobility for some. What is left is to describe how cities, as centers of social change, provided the conditions that led to the rise of gharanas, and their continuing evolution as adaptive social structures for musical specialists.

Social Changes

We are now ready to answer the following, as yet implicit, questions. Why did gharanas arise at all? Why were they born in the cities, and why after the middle of the nineteenth century? My argument in brief is that gharanas were the *result* of a number of adaptive strategies that musicians employed as a response to rapidly changing social conditions that originated almost exactly in the middle of the last century.

Endogamy and identity

In 1853 the first rail line in India, 21 miles long, commenced operations. By the Mutiny, four years later, there were 200 miles of track, and by 1871 the British (spurred on by the events of the Mutiny) had 5,074 miles completed. Four years later, Delhi was connected with Calcutta and Bombay.[44] The growth of the telegraph was perhaps even more remarkable. The first experimental telegraph line, 82 miles long, was built in 1851. In only four years Calcutta, Agra, Peshwar, Bombay, and Madras were connected through 3,050 miles of line and forty-one other offices.[45]

For musicians the implications of these developments were profound. No longer need a musician be dependent on a single patron. Nor, for that matter, need a patron be limited to his resident musicians. Other musicians could be called for and brought with ease. Voyages of months were cut to days, and messages to hours. Whereas musicians' careers were formerly limited to a very few patrons, performers could now spend a few months in one court, then move to another, performing for dozens of patrons in a lifetime. (However, an artist could—and usually did—have a primary patron from whom he would take leaves of absence when called to perform in other places.) Cities were also the home for the newly rich classes who had gained their wealth through government service under British rule[46] and were now sponsors of musical evenings, always important in India as a symbol of affluence and refinement.[47] Where else, then, to have one's center of operations but in the city? The urban environment offered the maximum opportunity for patronage and performance, as well as serving as the hub of transportation and communication networks.

These, then, are some of the motivating forces that made the urbanization of musical specialists even more adaptively significant than it had in the past. But then, what was the special significance of gharanas, which were now coming into being? It would appear that their significance lay in two sequential functions that they fulfilled.

The first of these was a means to control competition between the largely undifferentiated classes of musicians that existed before. A possible inference that can be drawn from the drastic reduction in the absolute number of accounted-for musicians between 1881 and 1931 is that there was a corresponding decrease in sponsorship and an increase in the competition for the remaining patronage. But even if this inference should prove invalid, the diversity and spread of performers now available to listeners must have expanded the competition for *any* given musical niche. Ten musicians, having available to them the modern communication and transportation links, could now cover the same territory of patrons that previously required several score musicians. In order to succeed under these new conditions, musical knowledge—always the source of some secrecy in the Hindusthani musical tradition—was kept within the bounds of certain musician lineages, resulting in a monopoly of repertoire and style and perhaps at the same time maintaining the music's "information" value as a function of scarcity.[48] The success of these lineages can be attributed only in part to the monopoly that their members exercised over particular musical styles. Even more significant was the control over recruitment of musical specialists in exercising the principle of hereditary rights to musical knowledge. By limiting the range of marriage relations through the practice of cousin marriage, a generation of music specialists was able to limit the number and extent of their obligations to teach descendants and secure positions for them. Viewed structurally, a man's son-in-law, who was also his brother's son, collapsed two kinds of kinship obligations in the person of one individual. The efficiency of this strategy over several generations becomes even more apparent. Consider, for example, the case in which a man's (Ego's) son-in-law is also his sister's son. If Ego's sister, furthermore, is married to her (and Ego's) father's brother's son, her son is thus a member of his father-in-law's (Ego's) patrilineage. Here we find three kinds of kinship roles—namely, son-in-law, nephew, and agnatic descendant—with their concomitant obligations assumed in one person. Not only did this kind of efficiency result in the limitation in number and extent of musical specialists, thus reducing competition, but it also allowed the concentration of teaching time and energies on fewer individuals—a very important element of the master-disciple tradition—making them that much more highly adapted to the niche they were born to.

The other function of gharanas relates to the newly mobile artists and their requirement for a sociomusical identity that was meaningful to new listeners. Since there were now many more artists whom a listener would have occasion to hear, and there were many more audiences before whom an artist would perform, the personal reputation of a name in most instances would no longer suffice.[49] As a consequence, artists were identified, and identified themselves, with reference to their ancestral homes, in much the same manner that others in India identify themselves in new places. Thus, so-and-so is of the Agra house and by extension the Agra family of musicians, and by implication performs in the style of that family. In other words, gharanas became labels, which, as I have said, came to be used in this sense only after the beginning of the present century, a period that also marks the start of truly public performances of classical music in India.[50]

The role of gharanas today

As sociomusical identities and as a source of stylistic diversity, gharanas continue to be important today. As lineages of hereditary musicians, by contrast, gharanas are not so active as they had once been. Many hereditary musicians emigrated to Pakistan (a few later returning to India) during and after partition. In India a new consciousness has made music a central symbol of the nation's cultural heritage, and music as a profession has become eminently respectable.[51]

Yet, to be sure, there are still many hereditary musicians performing today, and among professional musicians they probably constitute the majority. Although they no longer completely dominate the profession in the way they once did, perhaps up into the 1950s, they remain the most important in numbers and prestige among top-ranking artists. However, while some gharanas are flourishing, others have become inactive or have died out. In order to understand why this is so, we must look at the developments in Hindusthani musical culture during the present century.

From the musician's perspective, what has changed profoundly during this period is the strategy for "making it" as a professional. Especially since independence, the older, personal patronage system has virtually collapsed, and new types of institutions have taken over its supportive functions.

The most important of the new patronage systems is All India Radio, which employs thousands of musicians throughout India.[52] In 1969 All India Radio in Delhi alone had 715 musicians on its roll, 556 of these being North Indian musical specialists, the others being South Indian. Although All India Radio is an important source of income for many musicians, only 97 of the North Indian musicians were full-time employees at the Delhi station.

Music schools and private tuitions are other important remunerative sources, with many musicians earning a portion of their income from teaching. Music festivals, public concerts, and the private gatherings of music societies provide additional income for many. A surprising number of musicians have also traveled abroad, some spending months and even years in the West—establishing schools, teaching in colleges, and giving concerts, sometimes thereby establishing the basis of a new wealth.

The even greater significance of cities should be apparent: along with disciples, there are now schools, radio stations, train stations, airports, and concert platforms, all concentrated in the urban environment.[53]

The gharanas that have adapted least successfully to these changes are those that were the first to make cities their homes: the Kalawant soloist gharanas. As purveyors of musical styles, some are flourishing, through nonhereditary disciples, but as musical lineages, they are largely defunct. The reason is that being exclusively soloists, and especially by being in most cases vocalists, they have become too highly specialized and consequently unable to take advantage of new opportunities. Thus, of the ninety-seven full-time musicians at All India Radio, Delhi (in 1969), only fourteen are (or call themselves) vocalists. But not a single one actually performs vocal music on a full-time basis. Rather, they have entered auxiliary specialties, seven, in fact, being *tampoura* (drone instrument) players, and the remaining being administrative officers of the station. Even more significantly, not one of these vocalists is descended from a Kalawant lineage.[54]

Because of loyalty to the purity of their musical traditions, Kalawants are often reluctant to exploit the novel possibilities made available as a result of the new, large, and typically unsophisticated listening publics. Thus, one vocalist of this tradition made it clear that he would not perform lighter varieties of music, such as the ghazal, even though audiences often demanded them. Another artist, relying on the reputation of his father, waited for disciples who never came. He was unknown to the new classes of students who find their teachers through public performances.

He was rarely on the podium because, as he himself admitted, he refused to cultivate the "new music brokers,"[55] that is, those who have the power to book concerts.

Ironically, the hereditary musicians who seem to have done the best are the accompanists. Because of the stigma attached to their specialties, they have not had the competition from nonhereditary musicians that soloists have had.[56] In addition, accompanists are less specialized musically than soloists, this being the result of the music structure itself. The soloist defines the performance, while the accompanist need only follow. Thus, the role of the accompanist is in principle interchangeable where that of the soloist is not. What this means is that All India Radio can maintain a pool of accompanists as full-time employees, who are always available for the "guest artist" soloists who make up the bulk of the "casual" (not full-time) musicians who perform on radio.[57]

Less successful accompanists can also find alternative positions, such as accompanying singing girls and performing in restaurants and for private parties—employment that "respectable" soloists would be reluctant to accept.

The gharanas of former Mirasi accompanist lineages have also done relatively well. As we have seen, the descendants of Tanras Khan have become obscure qawalli singers, finding thus a low-prestige but respectable alternative for Kalawant soloists.[58] The descendants of Mamman Khan, the sarangi player, on the other hand, are now all soloists. One of them is a successful concert artist, and others have found employment in radio and in a music department.

Most of the important solo instrumentalist lineages are also descended from Mirasi or some other similarly modest social background. The question naturally arises as to why soloists of this background have flourished while the traditional elite of the musical world have not. I would suggest two major reasons.

The Mirasi lineages are, as stated earlier, part of a larger network of kin known as a biradari. These brotherhoods were initially formed in urban centers as well, and membership is determined by the principle of common territorial origin. Thus, like gharanas, the biradaris are named after the cities in which they were originally formed. Although not all the members of a particular brotherhood are considered actual relatives, they do constitute a social group with its system of rights and obligations. It is my hypothesis that this larger network of relatives has provided both support and social contacts, encouraging individuals to *attempt* success as soloists. Although we know of only the successful attempts, there have undoubtedly been many that have not succeeded. In the highly probable event of failure, an individual can always return to his accompanist role. And during the study and reputation-building period of an attempt, an individual can be financially dependent on his relations and have access to a large number of contacts through the brotherhood as a whole. Indeed, such a strategy is quite common in the present day. Many of the accompanists at All India Radio, for example, have secured their positions through their brotherhood relations.[59]

Such a modus operandi is not of course limited to Mirasi brotherhoods. Kalawant soloists, for example, follow a similar pattern. But in their case a much smaller pool of musicians is available. All the Kalawant lineages together constitute only one brotherhood,[60] whereas among Mirasis, there are a score or more brotherhoods scattered throughout the towns and cities of North India. Thus, as specialists of the accompanist traditions, the brotherhoods of Mirasis were able to become very large and widely dispersed. Given the new opportunities that were becoming available in modern India, Mirasis had a wider (if not as prestigious) range of connections, which they were more willing to cultivate, and they have consequently offered many more candidates for any given position.

There is another important factor that accounts for the Mirasis' success under these new conditions: they have been less committed to the orthodoxy of the classical music tradition and, perhaps because of their diverse heritages, musically more innovative. For example, one of the most important stylistic developments during the last century was the evolution of the *Imdad-khani baj*. It is named after Imdad Khan, who made the style famous, having learned it from his father, Sahabdad Khan. The latter was a sarangi player turned sitar player, and he is considered the originator of this style. The style was innovative because it was based on the romantic khayal vocal style (which a sarangi player, as an accompanist, would be familiar with), in contrast to the more classic and formal Dhrupad style (which typically did not use sarangi accompaniment) of the older sitar tradition. Imdad Khan's grandson, the justly renowned Vilayat Khan, has continued this innovative tradition through his elaboration of the *gayaki* (vocal) style on the sitar.[61]

There are numerous other examples of the innovative spirit of accompanists who have transformed themselves into soloists. Space does not permit elaboration of this point, but one suspects that the entrance of rural musicians into the Great Tradition of Indian art music is not in itself a new thing in the country's history. What *is* new is the entrance of, for want of a better word, *modernity* into the musical culture of North India. And it is the interaction of this process—some would call it a juggernaut—with a cultural system that celebrates its antiquity that inevitably arouses our curiosity.

Summary and Conclusion

I stated at the beginning of this paper that the *idea* of gharanas implied great depth in space and time and, by extension, in significance as the focal point of Hindusthani musical tradition. Yet we have also learned that as social systems, gharanas have evolved fairly recently, and they continue to undergo transformations even now. (Recall the quite recent practice of describing tabla styles as gharanas.) These findings support the views of an increasing number of social scientists that social change and cultural change are interrelated but different processes. As Gould has pointed out in his rethinking of the tradition-modernity model, we must "distinguish between traditional social structures which *qua* structures are patently incapable of assimilation to modern social structures and the mobilisation of traditional values, skills or artifacts in behalf of modernisation. . . . Social systems cannot be mutually reinforcing when they rest on different, mutually exclusive levels of social evolution, *but idea systems can.*" [Emphasis in the original.][62]

The appearance of gharanas in the mid-nineteenth century signaled the birth of a new kind of social structure. To view gharanas as identical to preexisting social structures, however, is to confuse "phylogeny with evolution," as Fox has said in the context of Indian castes.[63] Yet at the same time, such a "confusion" is important, perhaps even necessary, because only then are gharanas able

213

to incorporate their depth through the phylogenetic relationships musicians make for them. The musical tradition exists as a continuity, *as an idea system*, while being fitted to new social structures, as the increased numbers of nonhereditary musicans are even now transforming gharanas. Thus, the social organization of music, and the music itself, can undergo fairly extensive change as long as it does not appear to change. We find neither the proverbial old wine in new bottles nor its opposite; rather we find that both wine and bottles are new. They simply *appear* to be old.

Like Delhi itself, gharanas are divided into "old" and "new," each providing the other with part of its meaning. They are enduring ideational systems and modifiable social systems, and thus lies their significance in inheriting the old and being born in the cities they were named after.

It is in the cities that soloists searched for new sources of patronage, and it was here that they settled with their families. And it was to the cities that the formerly rural Mirasi accompanists came with *their* families, eventually arranging close marriages to other Mirasis and forming brotherhoods defined ultimately by common residence in the city. For both soloists and accompanists, this pattern was quite opposite from that of the typical Indian migrant.[64]

Put another way, the occupational speciality of art music became urbanized and in that sense—among others—"modernized." Once in the cities, the soloist lineages put down roots and established a sociomusical identity that would come to be known as a gharana. For their part, rural musicians also settled in the cities, forming brotherhoods; and some eventually formed soloist lineages and then also gharanas.

We still do not know in detail how the patronage system in the cities was organized, but musicians must have been among the first to recognize the potentials of the new technology that would yield the media through which they could communicate their art. The radio, gramophone, film, and music conference, all enabled by the new technology and nurtured in the cities, attracted specialists and transformed the basis upon which they had been previously organized.

This rearrangement and recombination of musical material provided the foundation for musical innovation and change. It is per-

haps not too extreme to claim that the musical houses of the Kalawant soloists provided the traditional musical framework upon
which the less traditionally committed accompanists worked their
new ideas.

Musical styles continue to be passed on, from father to son, uncle to nephew, and master to disciple, and it remains for the student of this process to examine in detail the stylistic features of
particular houses and the manner in which these are transmitted.
For ethnomusicologists, straddling as we do the fields of anthropology and musicology, questions concerning the movement of
music—"inherited" through blood, transmitted as dowry, and com-
municated to disciples—would appear fundamental if we are to
understand the dynamics of this musical system. Lacking records
of musical style, can we learn about the changing patterns and
tastes of the listening public and the cultural values inherent in it
by a study of the variegated careers of musical lineages and the
musical traditions inherent in them? Perhaps the answer is to be
found in the words of an old master of the past: "Music? You are
asking what changes have occurred in our music? Nothing changes
in our music, it is always the same; it is we who change."

NOTES

1. The data for this paper were gathered in India in 1969–71 and 1973.
Many of the subjects introduced here are discussed in more detail in my
dissertation, "The Cultural Structure and Social Organization of Musicians
in India: The Perspective from Delhi" (University of Illinois, 1974). The research was supported by grants from the National Institutes of Health, the
Department of Anthropology at the University of Illinois, and Dartmouth
College. I would like to express my appreciation to Hoyt Alverson, Howard
Erdman, James Fernandez, Nelson Kasfir, and members of the Asian Studies
Seminar at Dartmouth for reading and commenting on earlier drafts of this
paper. I also wish to thank my student Lawrence Rosenshein for his help
in the compilation of the census data.

2. Richard G. Fox, "Rationale and Romance in Urban Anthropology,"
Urban Anthropology 1 (1972), 206.

3. Ibid.

4. There is one major exception to the gharanas named as cities: the Senia
Gharana is named after Tansen, the great court musician of the Moghul
emperor Akbar in the latter part of the sixteenth century. This constitutes
a strange exception, for a number of reasons, which are discussed in my
dissertation. Virtually all solo instrumentalists claim some connection to this
gharana, although there are no longer any musicians among blood descendants. The use of the term *gharana*, when referring to Tansen's lineage, is

215

also recent and reflects one of the ways in which the concept of gharana has been expanded. As for the two-hundred-mile radius of Delhi, one need only mention the names of the most prominent gharanas; a look at the map will bear this out: Agra, Atrauli, Jaipur, Gwalior, Patiala, Kirana, Seheswan, Saharanpur, Hapur, Khurja, and Rampur. Exceptions are musicians who have claimed a new gharana, such as Indore and one gharana in Bengal called Vishnupur Gharana. They have all been founded by musicians who came from within this two-hundred-mile radius of Delhi. Other exceptions are "gharanas" that do not suit the term as discussed in this paper but are now being called such. I mean here, in particular, the tabla styles, such as the Benares *baj* (style) which is now sometimes called Benares Gharana.

5. B. Chaitanya Deva, *An Introduction to Indian Music* (New Delhi: Publications Division, Ministry of Information and Broadcasting, 1973), p. 38. The alapa is an improvisatory section of a performance, and khayal is the major form of vocal music in Hindusthani music.

6. Gharanedars carry greater authority in matters musical than do disciples. Often they and their performances will be referred to as *khas khandani:* genuinely of or special to that lineage.

7. Deva, *Introduction,* p. 38. Deva puts in writing what is generally recognized—namely, that the Gwalior Gharana is the oldest. It is not clear whether the "cousin" was not perhaps another brother.

8. Hakim Mohammad Karam Imam, "Melody through the Centuries," *Bulletin, Sangeet Natak Akademi,* nos. 11–12 (1959), pp. 13–26; "Effect of Ragas and Mannerism in Singing," ibid., nos. 13–14 (1959), pp. 6–14.

9. Vilayat Hussein Khan, *Sangitagyon ke Samsmaran* (A remembrance of musicians) (New Delhi: Sangeet Natak Akademi, 1959).

10. Thus, technically, the Delhi gharana of Tanras Khan as a musical style is extinct.

11. Accompanists and soloists make up the most fundamental music-specialist categories in the North Indian tradition. They are fundamental for a number of reasons; one reason not discussed here is that for any *bona fide performance* (not demonstration) of Hindusthani music, minimally two performers are required: a soloist and an accompanist. The soloist is either a vocalist or an instrumentalist, while the accompanist must be a rhythmic specialist, usually a tabla player. A vocal soloist will often have a melodic accompanist as well—either a *sarangi* (Indian fiddle) or a harmonium player, sometimes both—who provides a heterophonic line in the performance.

12. In my experience, older tabla players do not use the term *gharana,* but younger performers and listeners do so increasingly.

13. This is a paraphrased translation from the original Urdu by Harbans Mathur. It comes from a pamphlet that Chand Khan had published concerning his family's musical tradition.

14. Bundu Khan, the other grandson mentioned in the story, was in fact one of India's most respected and famous musicians, such a position of esteem being a rare accomplishment for a sarangi player.

15. The label *Kalawant* is in fact rarely used, since the distinctions I am making are rarely publicly discussed. The term is also applied to the descendants of four important court musicians of Akbar, according to Imam, "Melody through the Centuries," p. 14. See n. 20.

16. Kalawants even know in some cases the subcaste of Brahman or Rajput to which their ancestors belonged. Mirasis almost always claim descent

from Muslims outside of India, as is the case with Chand Khan, but there are exceptions here as well.

17. My reticence in labeling these social groups as castes is due, in part, to the considerable theoretical difficulties with the term *caste*, not to mention the question of whether Muslims may be said to have castes at all. Used here, the term refers to endogamous groups having members who are hereditary occupational specialists. There is only one group of Kalawants, while there are many groups (what I have called brotherhoods) of Mirasis. Put more formally, Mirasi and Kalawant are *social categories,* the brotherhoods and lineages, respectively, being the largest social units one could identify as *social groups.*

18. Kahn, *Sangitagyon,* p. 5. The translation is by myself and Arundhati Neuman.

19. His case, however, is the only one I have personally heard about.

20. Imam, "Melody through the Centuries," pp. 14, 18, 20–25. Both accompanists and soloists are mentioned in the text (as one would expect), but the distinctiveness of their roles does not appear very clear-cut. Thus there are musicians who both play sarangi and sing, or whose names indicate they come from soloist lineages but play the sarangi (e.g. Himmat Khan Kalawant). There is also a sitar player (Nabi Baksh) who comes from a nonsoloist community and vocalists who come from accompanist backgrounds. Significantly, there is no mention of musical houses in the text. What is mentioned are famous families of musicians of the emperor Akbar (1556–1605). Also described are major communities of musicians: *Kalawant, Dhari, Qawwal.* According to Imam, authentic Kalawants were descendants of one of these four major court musicians of Akbar, and there were only a very few left in his day. However, as Imam states, there were many musicians who "call themselves Kalawants, but their claims are baseless. It is interesting to note that in practice they do what is taboo in a Kalawant family, i.e. they openly accompany dancing girls, thus putting even the devil to shame." Dharis are said by Imam to be the oldest community of musicians, originally Rajputs who converted to Islam. They were vocalists, but "now for all practical purposes the serious type of music has left this community. Most of the Dharis earn their living by accompanying dancing girls." From these fragments it is clear that there were hereditary musicians and a few distinguished lineages whose members did not do accompanying. For the most part, however, there seems to be much overlap between specialists; and the only evidence of stylistic schools are the four *banis,* originating with the four Kalawants at Akbar's court. For most musicians there does not seem to be much that stylistically distinguishes them except for their personal reputations.

21. Imam's discussion of Dharis makes them appear very much like Mirasis. The term is occasionally used interchangeably today by outsiders, but I have never met a musician who was called or who called himself a Dhari. One musician suggested that *Dhari* was a term from the eastern United Provinces (now eastern Uttar Pradesh) for musicians who are "like" Mirasis, which would explain their importance in Lucknow in Imam's time. Quite frankly, how they are related to Mirasis, if at all, is still a puzzle. For a more extended discussion of this problem, see Neuman, "Musicians in India," pp. 153–60.

22. For discussions of such marriage circles, see Imtiaz Ahmed, "En-

dogamy and Status Mobility among the Siddique Sheikhs of Allahabad, Uttar Pradesh," in *Caste and Social Stratification among the Muslims*, ed. Imtiaz Ahmed (Delhi: Manohar Book Service, 1973), p. 190; E. A. H. Blunt, *The Caste System of Northern India: With Special Reference to the United Provinces of Agra and Oudh* (Oxford: Oxford University Press, 1931), pp. 196–97; Ghaus Ansari, *Muslim Caste in Uttar Pradesh* (Lucknow: Ethnographic and Folk Culture Society, 1960). Cora Vreede De Steuers calls these marriage circles *biadhari*, a term none of my informants was familiar with (*Parda: A Study of Muslim Women's Life in Northern India* [Assen: Van Gorcum, 1968]).

23. There are other "castes" of musicians that are Hindu in origin, such as the *Kathak* of Benares. Such groups, however, have not formed solo gharanas as have the Mirasis.

24. Thus musicians will often say that, in the old days especially, marrying close relatives was a way to keep musical secrets in the family. The descendants of Tansen are said to have passed on Tansen's "book" on compositions as a dowry, so it was important that daughters not marry outsiders. I have not, however, come across any evidence that such a "book" actually exists.

25. When asked about this discrepancy, one Kalawant musician told me that Bande Khan was a close friend of an accompanist whose name was similar to his. As a result, descendants have confused the two.

26. Thus between 1891 and 1931 the average percentage gain per decade of the proportion of urban to rural population in places of 20,000 or more and 100,000 or more was 4.2 and 7.3, respectively. In the U.S., by contrast, the figures between 1870 and 1930 were respectively 17.3 and 18.5. See Kingsley Davis, "Urbanization in India: Past and Future," in *India's Urban Future*, ed. Roy Turner (Berkeley and Los Angeles: University of California Press, 1962), pp. 4–10.

27. The other reason these cities were chosen was that comparable data between 1881 and 1931 were available for them and not for other musically important centers. The source for all cities and districts with the exception of Delhi is the *Census of India, 1931, United Provinces of Agra and Oudh*, vol. 18, pt. 2, table 2, pp. 6–8, and table 4, pp. 16–23. For Delhi, see *Census of India, 1931, Delhi*, vol. 16, pt. 2, table 4, p. vii. For Delhi's growth rate, see ibid., pt. 1, pp. 12–13.

28. For the following sources on populations of musicians, I am including the microfiche card numbers in brackets. Data from the 1891 census were not included, since for that census actual workers and dependents were lumped together, so that the figures are not comparable.

For district figures:

Census of India, 1881, Northwest Provinces and Oudh, Supplement, table 12, pp. 120–259. [579–82]
Census of India, 1901, Northwest Provinces and Oudh, vol. 16A, pt. 2, p. 483. [1758]
Census of India, 1911, United Provinces of Agra and Oudh, vol. 15, p. 528. [2387]
Census of India, 1921, United Provinces of Agra and Oudh, vol. 16, pt. 2, table 17, p. 322. [2786]
Census of India, 1931, United Provinces of Agra and Oudh, vol. 18, pt. 2, table 10, p. 369. [3271]

For city figures (from the *Census of India* for the years indicated):
    1881: *Supplement,* table 13, pp. 172–259.   [580–82]
    1901: Vol. 16A, pt. 2, table 15, pp. 340–49.   [1754]
    1911: Vol. 15, pt. 2, table 15, pp. 408–23.   [2383–84]
    1921: Vol. 16, pt. 2, table 17, p. 375.   [2788]
    1931: Vol. 18, pt. 2, table 10, p. 430.   [3273]
For Delhi City and District figures (from the *Census of India* for the years and places indicated):
    1881: *Punjab,* vol. 2, table 12A, p. 70.   [615]
    1901: *Punjab,* vol. 17, pt. 2, table 15, pp. 188, 49. [1791, 1787]
    1911: *Punjab,* vol. 14, pt. 2, table 15, p. 372.   [2352]
    1921: *Punjab,* vol. 15, pt. 2, table 17, p. 347.   [2765]
    1931: *Delhi,* vol. 16, pt. 2, table 10, p. 39. (These are province figures.) [3221]

29. Only male musicians were considered, for three reasons: (*a*) The musical lineages that are the focus of this paper include only males as musical specialists; (*b*) data on female musicians are even less reliable than those for males, since the line between prostitute and singer was drawn differently for every census (see n. 30 for an example); and (*c*) there were no data on female musicians in 1881.

30. E.g. between 1911 and 1921 in the United Provinces of Agra and Oudh, the decrease is so marked (−41.8%) that the census commissioner makes a special note of it—the occupation rarely elicits any comment in the census reports—without, however, offering any reasons. In the 1901 census, Risely, the census commissioner, suggests that many musicians could have been entered as prostitutes, since in the all-India figures there was a 14% decrease in the number of musicians and a 14% increase in the number of "disreputables," namely prostitutes and procurers. Cf. *Census of India, 1921, United Provinces of Agra and Oudh,* vol. 16, pt. 1, p. 166, and ibid., *1901, General Report,* vol. 1, pt. 1, p. 216. On the other hand, in the Punjab census of 1911 (vol. 14, pt. 1, p. 519 [2341]), there is a marked increase in the number of musicians, from 46,582 in 1901 to 128,071 in 1911. This increase is due to the inclusion of *Bhats* (genealogist-bards) and Mirasis; the latter figure includes both actual workers and dependents, of both sexes.

31. Nelson Kasfir brought this alternative to my attention.

32. Aside from the ordinary uncertainties about the accuracy of enumeration and the different types of specialists included within the occupational category "musicians" (see nn. 29 and 30), it should also be noted that a great diversity of musical specialists was always included and that the classical musicians discussed probably made up only a minor proportion of the total. Thus there is no way of knowing to what extent classical musicians reflect

	Musicians	Dancers	Singers	Teachers	Actors	Total
Lucknow	163	251	0	1	2	417
Kanpur	255	18	17	0	5	295
Agra	180	60	0	0	18	258
Bareilly	69	103	11	0	9	192
Meerut	193	301	16	0	16	526
Moradabad	425	11	6	0	0	442
Saharanpur	36	25	3	0	33	97

the total figures given here. Only in the 1881 United Provinces census are subcategories of musicians provided and enumerated. For purposes of comparison, I have combined these, as they were automatically in later census reports. The table on p. 219 gives the 1881 figures for the four categories of musical specialists for seven of the eight cities listed. Delhi is not included because these categorical distinctions were not made for the Punjab census, which covers Delhi.

Another note of caution about the definition of *urban:* in table 2 I have included only the proportion of the main municipality and the district in which it is located to determine the urban proportion, e.g. Lucknow City and Lucknow District. There are other urban centers besides the ones listed here, but data are unfortunately not available after 1881, and so I was limited to the larger urban centers. But if towns are included, as they are in the 1881 census, then for the United Provinces of Agra and Oudh there were 9,554 "musicians" in towns and 18,224 in villages. Thus about a third of the musicians in the United Provinces would be in this sense urban. This includes only the category "musicians" and not singers, dancers, ballad singers, teachers, or actors. See *Census of India, 1881, United Provinces*, pp. 1–37 [569–70].

33. In all, I have data on well over five hundred musicians.

34. The exceptions are certain lineages in Delhi who claimed to have been there since the period of the Delhi Sultanate (thirteenth century).

35. For caste descriptions, see W. Crooke, *Tribes and Castes of the North-Western Provinces and Oudh*, vol. 4 (Calcutta, 1896), p. 367; Sir Denzil C. J. Ibbetson, *Panjab Castes* (Lahore, 1916), p. 234; George W. Briggs, *The Doms and Their Near Relations* (Mysore: Wesley Press and Publishing House, 1953), p. 93; and Rev. M. D. Sherring, *Hindu Tribes and Castes as Represented in Benares* (London: Trubner, 1872), p. 275. For the contemporary village context, see McKim Marriott, "Caste Ranking and Food Transactions: A Matrix Analysis," in *Structure and Change in Indian Society*, ed. Milton Singer and Bernard S. Cohn, Viking Fund Publications in Anthropology, no. 47 (New York, Aldine, 1968); Adrian C. Mayer, *Caste and Kinship in Central India: A Village and Its Region* (Berkeley and Los Angeles: University of California Press, 1960); Zarina Bhatty, "Status and Power in a Muslim Dominated Village of Uttar Pradesh," in *Caste and Social Stratification among the Muslims*, ed. Imtiaz Ahmed (Delhi: Manohar Book Service, 1973), pp. 93, 94, 104.

36. Prakash Tandon, *Punjabi Century* (New York: Harcourt, Brace & World, 1961), pp. 79–80. See also Bhatty, "Status and Power," p. 104.

37. Tandon, *Punjabi Century*, pp. 79–80.

38. Biradaris have been discussed extensively in the literature on India. See e.g. Bernard C. Cohn, *India: The Social Anthropology of a Civilization* (Englewood Cliffs, N.J.: Prentice-Hall, 1971), pp. 125–26, for a very illuminating discussion of the structural relationship between biradaris and the caste system; for a discussion of biradaris in the village context, see Mayer, *Caste and Kinship.*

39. These observations are based on an intensive interview with one rural Mirasi and discussions with other, urban Mirasis. Though fairly extensive, these data require more corroboration. In the Punjab census of 1901 (vol. 17, pt. 1, p. 329 [1773]), Mirasis who serve Hindu families are said to observe

the "four-*got*" rule: they cannot marry in the same clan as any of their grand-parents.

40. Brian Silver, personal communication.

41. Cf. Milton Singer, *When a Great Tradition Modernizes: An Anthropological Approach to Civilization* (New York: Praeger, 1972).

42. Imam, "Melody through the Centuries," pp. 21–22. The names of these female vocalists all end with *-bai*, which implies that the women belong to a courtesan community.

43. The category "light classical" is common in India and is a formal category used by All India Radio.

44. *Imperial Gazeteer of India*, vol. 3, *The Indian Empire* (Oxford: Clarendon Press, 1908), p. 411.

45. Ibid., p. 437.

46. Bernard S. Cohn, "Structural Change in Indian Rural Society," in *Land Control and Social Structure in Indian History*, ed. Robert E. Frykenberg (Madison: University of Wisconsin Press, 1969), pp. 76–80. Cohn points out that most of the large landowners in the Benares region in 1885 were "new men" and that new purchasers of land in another district in 1851–52 were "overwhelmingly nonresident. Typically they were urban." It should be noted that this region, the eastern United Provinces, lies somewhat outside the area I have been discussing. The latter area is the western part of the United Provinces, known before as the Northwestern Provinces, which came under British rule a half-century earlier than the eastern United Provinces. For a brief discussion of land policy in the Northwestern Provinces, see Thomas R. Metcalf, "Social Effects of British Land Policy in Oudh," in *Land Control and Social Structure in Indian History*, ed. Frykenberg, pp. 157–58.

47. This is beautifully illustrated in Satyajit Ray's film *Jalsaghar* (The music room).

48. E.g. musicians even now "revive" a long-forgotten raga or composition that they will claim as part of their gharana's heritage. The scarcity or the extent of esoterica presumed known by a representative of a gharana enhances his prestige. Such musical knowledge will often be referred to as khas khandani (see n. 6).

49. Iman lists scores of names—many, if not most, presumably known to interested readers of his day.

50. The first major music conferences were held in the 1920s. Perhaps the earliest was the All-India Music Conference in Lucknow in 1925.

51. In neither North nor South India did "respectable" families allow their children to perform music except as an avocation. The stigma on accepting money for music performances is evident in the Iman's mid-nineteenth-century story of a nobleman who demanded fees and was laughed at as a result ("Melody through the Centuries," p. 23).

52. J. C. Mathur, *New Lamps for Aladdin: Mass Media in Developing Societies* (Calcutta: Orient Longmans, 1965), p. 127.

53. The film industry concentrated in Bombay (for North India) is also an important source of "patronage" for a number of musicians.

54. The only recent case of a Kalawant vocalist working at All India Radio was an individual who was a "composer" (i.e. conductor-arranger) of "light classical" music. He quit because it was inappropriate and unfulfilling for him.

55. Neuman, "Musicians in India," pp. 253–55.

56. This lack of competition is less true for tabla players, since in the last generation a number of nonhereditary tabla players have gained prominence, most of them from Bengal.

57. "Casual artist" is the category that All India Radio gives for musicians who broadcast intermittently, usually between three and twelve times a year. "Staff artist" is the category given for full-time employees of the station.

58. Since qawalli is a devotional song type in principle (although not always in fact), its performance is a respectable alternative, certainly in comparison to accompanying singing girls. It is low in prestige for two reasons. First, many qawalli singers come from disreputable backgrounds (there is also a caste specializing in qawalli singing); and second, it is the most obvious symbol of failure for a formerly classical musician.

59. The "older brother" at the station will prepeare his "younger brother" for the rigors of auditions, introduce him to others at the station, and in general teach him how to succeed in the new system.

60. As with the term *Kalawant* (see n. 15), the term for brotherhood (*biradari*) is not ordinarily used because one rarely has occasion to refer to all the intermarrying lineages of Kalawants. But when the subject does come up, *biradari* is the term employed.

61. Sharmistha Sen, "String Instruments (Plucked Variety) of North India" (Ph.D. diss., Visva Bharati University, Santini-ketan, 1972), pp. 177–78.

62. Harold A. Gould, "Is the Modernity-Tradition Model All Bad?," *Economic and Political Weekly* 5, nos. 29–31 (1970), 3.

63. Richard G. Fox, "Resiliency and Change in the Indian Caste System: The Umar of U.P.," *Journal of Asian Studies* 26 (1967), 579 (quoted by Gould, "Modernity-Tradition Model," p. 2).

64. Typically the Indian migrant to the cities is a male who leaves his family behind in his ancestral village. He visits the village from time to time on extended leaves and eventually retires there.

Music Clubs and Ensembles
in San Francisco's Chinese Community

RONALD RIDDLE

Studies of social and cultural aspects of overseas-Chinese communities have rarely touched upon the phenomenon of organized music-making by amateur groups. From the observation of the vigorous activities of music associations in San Francisco's Chinese community, one might readily infer that inattention to such groups thus creates a substantial gap in the literature that seeks to provide an understanding of the cultural life of overseas Chinese. The present study is essentially exploratory and descriptive, attempting to paint a general picture of the role of music clubs and other musical groups among San Francisco's Chinese.[1] The information gained on such groups has been mainly through the oral accounts of musicians and others in the Chinese community who have either been directly involved in music-making or who have watched and listened intently. It would be useful to supplement and compare these findings with other studies and observations, but such sources are virtually nonexistent at the present writing. Music societies in overseas-Chinese communities have been noted in passing by sociologists,[2] but their activities have gone mostly unchronicled in either scholarly literature or the popular press. Musical goings-on at parades and other public functions in San Francisco's Chinatown are duly noted by newspapers and magazines, but scant notice is taken of Chinatown's everyday musical life, though it is remarkable in many respects and probably

Ronald Riddle is Assistant Professor of Musicology, New College of the University of South Florida, Sarasota.

eclipses that of any other urban neighborhood in North America for the sheer quantity of non-Western music played on non-Western instruments. In turn, the musical associations of Chinatown are essentially private organizations that seldom seek publicity. It is known that Chinese music societies function in a similarly active and unpublicized fashion in other North American cities (such as New York, Honolulu, Los Angeles, and Vancouver, B.C.), but as yet there is little in print that would permit comparisons with them. It is hoped that the burgeoning interest in the music of urban ethnic minorities might eventually lead to ethnographic surveys and comparative studies that could help shed light on the musical culture of overseas-Chinese communities in general. The present localized study would thus take its place as raw material in a more comprehensive investigation of the musical life of the overseas Chinese.

The Community

The government census of 1970 recorded a total of 58,696 Chinese living in San Francisco. A true figure, however, would probably be closer to 70,000 or even 80,000, owing to the reluctance on the part of many Chinese to give census information[3] and also allowing for population growth by mid-decade. In any case, the Chinese make up at least 8 and probably from 10 to 12 percent of San Francisco's population, one of the largest such percentages in any city outside of Asia.[4] The heart and headquarters of San Francisco's Chinese community is Chinatown, an area of central San Francisco inhabited by approximately half of the city's Chinese residents. Since the arrival of California's first Chinese, in the late 1840s, there has been a flourishing residential, commercial, and cultural enclave of Chinese in San Francisco. Chinatown has indeed become one of the city's most publicized tourist attractions.

For the most part, San Francisco's Chinese hail from southern China, either directly or ancestrally. Like the majority of the world's immigrant Chinese, they derive their language and culture from Kwangtung province.[5] A little over half of San Francisco's Chinese were born abroad (in Chinatown itself, a large majority are foreign-born), and a continuing influx of immigrants serves to provide direct contact with Chinese cultural patterns.

This continuing immigration also perpetuates the need for such a protective environment as Chinatown, in which it is possible to conduct most of one's affairs in the Cantonese tongue and to have little contact with non-Chinese.

As a family prospers, however, it rarely elects to remain permanently in Chinatown. Eventually, when finances permit, the family will relocate in one of the middle-class residential districts of San Francisco.[6] Some will choose to move even farther way, to such areas as Oakland and Berkeley to the east or to suburban communities between San Francisco and San Jose to the south. The ties to Chinatown are by no means severed by such moves, however. Visits to Chinatown are frequent, as the relocated Chinese stay in touch with friends and relatives, shop for Chinese groceries, and maintain their connections with the multitude of Chinese clubs and organizations based in Chinatown. More than an ethnic neighborhood, Chinatown is the headquarters for virtually every Chinese association—family (clan), political, commercial, social, and cultural. The area's complicated infrastructure of such organizations is to some degree a vestige of earlier years when Chinatown existed as a virtually self-contained principality, governing itself in many respects and remaining effectively sealed off from the larger community by barriers of language and custom, as well as by discriminatory laws that discouraged any attempt of Chinese to move from the protective ghetto.[7] While such restrictions have crumbled and Chinese have made a gradual exodus from Chinatown, the elaborate network of social and quasi-governmental organizations remains, though many of its institutions have diminished in their usefulness as Chinese have become assimilated into the larger society. Among the associations headquartered in Chinatown that continue to serve much-needed functions for their members are the community's numerous music clubs, whose private activities provide a lively world of socializing and amateur music-making.

Music in the Community

In the Chinatown of an earlier day, the Chinese theater was the conspicuous center of musical activity, as it offered Cantonese opera every day of the week, an attraction well attended by the Chinese and also de rigueur for tourists. Chinese opera troupes began coming to San Francisco in 1852, and the area supported full-time professional Chinese music-drama continuously for nearly a century. At times there were as many as four theaters devoted to Cantonese opera.[8] After World War II—with the return to China of many Cantonese actors and musicians who had been stranded here during the war—interest in the theater dwindled. The institution was undercut by the lure of the movies and television and by the increasing expense and red tape involved in importing Chinese theatrical groups. In the present day there are still visits of Cantonese-opera companies—now exclusively from Hong Kong—but such visits occur only once or twice a year, with performances offered only for a week or ten days.

That such visits continue at all, of course, attests to a degree of continuing interest in Cantonese opera among segments of the community, as does the sale of phonograph records of this type and also the popularity of radio broadcasts of Cantonese opera and an occasional opera-film at one of Chinatown's movie theaters. Moreover, the opera becomes an even more direct element of many individuals' lives through their participation in music clubs whose main fare is Cantonese opera.

Most Chinatown music clubs are formally organized but informally conducted. The formalities include a charter, by-laws, an elected slate of officers, dues and initiation fees, and a specified procedure by which new members may be admitted. Such clubs commonly maintain a rented headquarters, which serves for general social get-togethers as well as music-making. Foreign-born Chinese form a large majority in almost all of the music clubs. There are presently about fifteen music clubs in active existence. The clubs are of three general types, as will be discussed below: Cantonese opera, Peking opera, and instrumental music.

Less distinctively Chinese but not to be overlooked in any study of Chinatown's musical mannerisms and tastes are those organizations that are cast in a Western mold and exist as part of larger institutional programs: for instance, the choirs of Chinatown's eight Christian churches; the drum-and-bugle corps that are sponsored by Chinese-language schools and civic groups; and the marching bands and other musical organizations of the local public schools.

Among sources of musical learning, in addition to the public schools, are programs of instruction sponsored by the Chinatown YWCA, the San Francisco Community Music Center, the Chinese Recreation Center, and other recreation and social-service institutions in the Chinese community. Instruction in music, Chinese and Western, is also readily available with private teachers in the community. Additional to both the organized clubs and the instructional groups are informal aggregations of young musicians who simply get together in random numbers to make music in one convenient meeting-hall or another. In such groups, one often finds no real coordination, but rather simultaneous practice of unrelated pieces. The resulting cacophony is perhaps a manifestation of gregariousness, perhaps of the crowded quarters in Chinatown that make impractical the practicing of an instrument at home.

Community Organization in Chinatown

Music clubs in Chinatown are distinguishable by type, with respect to the sorts of music cultivated. In order to understand their functions in the Chinatown society, however, one must also distinguish such groups in general from other types of associations and view them in an overall social perspective. In some cases, the functions of clubs ostensibly organized for musical purposes will be seen to overlap with other types of clubs. In other cases, one may note definite interaction between music clubs and other types of organizations.

The most all-encompassing and powerful of Chinatown's associations is the Chinese Consolidated Benevolent Association, usually referred to as the Six Companies. The Six Companies was formally organized in 1882 as an amalgam of district associations (or hui-kuan) representing the principal areas of Kwangtung province that are the ancestral homelands for Chinatown's residents. In earlier years the Six Companies had an all-important administrative and adjudicating role in the Chinese community, serving as advocate and go-between with the larger community. However, its power and importance have receded in the years since World War II, as Chinatown has become less socially insular and families have moved elsewhere. The district-association constituents of

the Six Companies are in turn made up of groups whose membership is based on a common surname (thus "family association,"
whether or not actual kinship) or common origin from within a
given area of the district in question. By virtue of surname and
region of ancestral origin, every Chinese is thus an ipso facto
member of several organizations. In practice, many Chinese, especially the American-born, do not choose to participate actively
in these homeland-oriented groups. Some ignore them completely;
others pay only nominal acknowledgment (as with attending only
the annual banquet of the family association).

Separate from immediate regional and surname considerations
are the fraternal societies often known as tongs (or "Chinese ma-
sonic lodges"). These groups, descendants of Chinese secret societies, emphasize ceremonial and social functions. They were once
a powerful force in Chinatown life, largely through control of
gambling, prostitution, and other illegal activities that flourished
in the community's earlier years. Like the Six Companies, the
tongs have seen a decline of power and purpose over the past
decades (the last of the notorious West Coast "tong wars" ended
in the 1920s) and now consist mainly of middle-aged and elderly
members. The tongs own a great deal of Chinatown's property,
as do the family associations, and continue to exert a degree of
influence through such ownership.[9]

Among other organizations are political associations (such as
the Kuomintang), religious groups, merchant associations (such as
the Chinese Chamber of Commerce), and a wide variety of clubs
organized for social services, hobbies, athletics, and other common
interests. It is in this category of social or "voluntary" organizations that we find music clubs.

It is typical of members of music clubs to emphasize the au-
tonomy of their groups. Heavily stressed is independence of political ties and general avoidance of political issues. The validity
of the claims notwithstanding, there are many interactions and
interconnections between music clubs and other organized groups
in the Chinese community. For instance, one orchestral group is
given a rent-free place of rehearsal by a family association. Another ensemble is provided quarters by the local Salvation Army;
still another meets in the headquarters of a political party (though

the ensemble itself has no official ties to the party). Music-club groups are hired by the Chinese Chamber of Commerce for functions involving parades or ceremonial events. A family-association banquet will typically feature a hired performance by music-club members. Athletic activities provide a notable overlap of functions between music clubs and other groups. Some music clubs put much emphasis on interclub sports (volleyball and bowling are common) and hold competitions with other clubs, some of them musical groups, some not.

A music-club member not uncommonly belongs to at least one other voluntary organization in the Chinese community. However (with rare exceptions), no one is formally a member of more than one music club at a given time. Observed by custom in any case, this exclusivity is written into the by-laws of at least one of the music clubs (Nam Chung). However, such restriction does not apply to the participation of members in other clubs as guests. Sitting in as a musician with another club is indeed quite common. Generally, music clubs do not make it a practice to unite for common purposes as organizations. There are exceptions, however, such as interclub cooperation during war-bond drives and other patriotic functions during World War II and, in more recent years, the working together of several Peking-opera clubs in order to stage a production.

Music Clubs in the Present Day

One approaches the categorizing of Chinatown's music clubs with some caution, as the types mentioned are not always mutually exclusive. Instrumental solos and ensemble pieces are sometimes played at Cantonese-opera clubs, for instance; and instrumental-music associations will typically feature a vocal selection or two—sometimes from Cantonese opera—on a program. Further, one could make a case for lumping Cantonese and Peking opera clubs into one general "music-drama" classification; yet the differences extend well beyond musical styles, techniques, and instrumentation, as will be discussed. In taking a variety of factors into account, then, one does find a fairly clear division of types into (*a*) Cantonese opera, (*b*) Peking opera, and (*c*) instrumental music.

In the last-named category, we include several groups whose repertoire is mainly or entirely Western music but whose membership is Chinese.

Cantonese-Opera Clubs

The Cantonese-opera clubs are the oldest and most populous of local Chinese-music associations, the Cantonese traditions of course reflecting the South China origins of almost all of San Francisco's Chinese. These groups are the most culturally insular of the music clubs. The spoken language is Cantonese. The music is generally for the membership only. Privacy is valued and publicity shunned. While a club's policy is ostensibly to promote the appreciation and performance of Cantonese opera, in practice the association typically serves a more heavily social function. Each of these groups has a rented headquarters to which every member has a key. Thus the meeting-place serves as a locus for social gatherings, with or without music. It is a club room that any member can repair to, as a place to relax and chat, drink tea, play mahjong, or listen to records. Though members may bring family and guests at will, the clubs are not otherwise open to nonmembers.

There are presently six Cantonese-opera clubs in San Francisco's Chinatown.[10] Membership figures, as given by members of the respective clubs, vary from ten to slightly over two hundred, but such figures are necessarily approximate, as "membership" may be held by individuals seldom or never seen: such a member will always pay dues initially but become eventually inactive, with respect to both finances and participation. In some cases, members have moved to distant states or to other countries, yet are not dropped from the membership rolls. In practical terms, no more than twenty or thirty active members of the clubs could function comfortably in the rather uniformly small quarters: typically one general-activities room (with couches, chairs, and a small stage for singers and musicians) and one or two other smaller rooms in which mahjong and general socializing can go on. Kitchen facilities are ubiquitous. Hot coffee and tea are always available at social get-togethers, and various snacks are sometimes brought or prepared in the kitchen. The largest club, Nam Chung, serves a full meal to its members at midnight on Saturday nights.

Actual performing ability in Cantonese opera is never a requirement for membership, and many members are devotees only, with
no special training in music or acting. The experience of those who
do perform is often limited to amateur participation in the club
itself. Every club can boast of at least one member who has a professional background in the field, however, and some have a number of such members. The former professionals serve as a guiding
force musically and provide instruction and coaching to other
members on an informal level. Not infrequently, they are among
the elected officers of these clubs.

During the days when professional opera was flourishing in
Chinatown, there was initially little direct interaction between
the professionals and the local amateurs. It was in the nature of
the professional performers to associate only with their own colleagues and to guard jealously the various secrets of their trade.
In time, however, a degree of association did develop between
amateurs and professionals. When the Nam Chung club was first
formed, in 1925, its members would frequent the Chinese theater
in hopes of learning techniques by watching and listening. Members would secure seats as close as possible to the performers.
Particularly important to the aspiring amateurs was learning the
actions of the orchestra's percussionist, whose role is central and
directive to the other performers, as in other Chinese-opera traditions. Such learning-by-observation was the only recourse for the
early Nam Chung members, as the aloof professionals refused to
give direct instruction in their esoteric and oral-tradition art. After
a night of intense observation, the Nam Chung members would
return immediately to their club and spend hours in imitation of
the techniques they had been observing. Alternately, members
would listen to recordings of Cantonese opera and play along with
them. They were otherwise limited to the rudimentary techniques
that a few of the members had learned in their Kwangtung villages and in Canton.

After some months of this imitative self-teaching, the Nam
Chung neophytes were able to persuade members of an opera
company to come to the club headquarters to hear the amateurs
perform. The professionals were surprised to find at least occasional competence on the part of the fledgling players. This initial
encounter led to friendly relations between professional perform-

ers and Nam Chung members. In time, it was not uncommon for theater musicians and singers to visit Nam Chung in off-hours and join in with the amateurs.[11] Such a relationship continues to this day, as members of the—now infrequent—visiting troupes are guests at this club, which has acquired an international reputation among Cantonese performers and in time has welcomed a number of professionals and former professionals to actual membership in the club. This association has been of considerable benefit to the competence of Nam Chung performers, who eventually developed the ability and confidence to stage occasional full-scale opera productions, renting a local theater for the night for the purpose. (In thus giving actual public performances, Nam Chung has been unique among the Cantonese-opera clubs. Such large-scale undertakings have ceased in recent years, however, owing to their logistical complexities and increasing expense.)

The musical activities of the Cantonese clubs center in large part on scenes from operas that members recall from performances in San Francisco and elsewhere. During informal sessions on Saturday nights, the accompanying orchestra will consist simply of anyone who shows up. (In Nam Chung, the largest club, the orchestra rarely numbers fewer than seven and sometimes includes as many as fifteen musicians.) The Cantonese tradition does not have stringent specifications for melodic instruments, and the typically versatile players will sometimes switch from instrument to instrument, even as singing is in progress. The favored instruments are the Chinese spike fiddles of various sizes (especially the erh-hu), transverse and straight flutes, the yang-ch'in, and the san-hsien. Notated music is rarely in evidence, but singers will sometimes read texts from a sheet or keep one handy for reference. Singers always use a microphone, and each club has an amplification system. It is characteristic of the Cantonese clubs to have a stock of musical instruments for performers to play, though musicians may occasionally bring their own.

It is rare that one hears a non-Chinese instrument in such clubs. This situation is in interesting contrast to an earlier period, which reached a peak in the 1940s, when the use of Western instruments in Cantonese opera was a vogue. In Nam Chung, which has used the same quarters almost since its founding in 1925, there is a decorative, glass-fronted display case for instruments that is prominently placed near the stage. This case has been there for nearly the whole history of the club. In a commemorative volume published by Nam Chung for its members in 1945,[12] a photograph shows the display case to contain, in addition to Chinese instruments, a tenor saxophone, a trumpet, and a clarinet. (For a while during this period, a xylophone was also put to use by the club, and Nam Chung even possessed a grand piano for a number of years.) Today only the clarinet (unused for years) remains. In spite of the continuing use of Western instruments in some Hong Kong operatic troupes, San Francisco clubs gradually abandoned the use of such instruments. "We learned from the Communists," states one opera-club member. It seems that much of the Cantonese-opera music from Mainland China (prior to the Cultural Revolution of the middle sixties) was held in high regard by San Francisco opera fanciers, whose interest in the genre transcended political considerations. Recordings from the Mainland, generally obtained through Canadian sources, featured only Chinese instruments; and the local clubs followed suit in gradually abandoning the Westernization of their orchestras. An exception is the Western violin, which has found a more-or-less permanent place amidst the Chinese instruments in present-day accompanying groups. Occasionally one also finds the Western four-string banjo used interchangeably with Chinese plucked instruments.

Instruction in Cantonese-opera techniques is given both formally and informally in the opera clubs. The apprenticeship system, which still holds sway in professional Cantonese opera, is obviously impossible for part-time enthusiasts. Each of the Cantonese clubs has at least one person who will teach on a fairly regular basis. One of the smaller clubs (Hoy Fung), which has had the financial problems and dwindling membership that characterize these groups, now remains in existence in large part to provide a place for the club's president to teach. Another club (Chung Sing) has formed in recent years as, in effect, an alumni club of students who studied with the teacher Wun Gee-chung, who taught in San Francisco in the late 1960s.

Though each club has its own special features, one can generalize a Saturday-night get-together that would not be unlikely at any of the clubs. One will witness a number of activities in progress at once. While a group of musicians accompanies a singer,

233

children will be playing games and running to and fro. In the midst of this—in the main room—several members may read newspapers or magazines, others will chat, a few will sit (perhaps with eyes closed) and listen to the music. In an adjoining room, the punctuating click of mahjong tiles will be heard. In the kitchen, other members may be putting together a snack or late supper. Hot coffee and tea, the only beverages in use, are being consumed in large quantities. The mélange of children's cries, mahjong, and kitchen activities is of no apparent consequence to musicians and singers as they proceed uninterruptedly through twenty- or thirty-minute musical sections of a Cantonese-opera scene. As members tend to bring their whole families to such meetings, there is a mixture of sexes and generations. (It may be noted, however, that singers and musicians are unlikely to be under forty.)

Such a picture is in striking contrast to what meetings must have been like in the earlier days of Cantonese-opera clubs. The most noticeable difference is the presence of women and children. The Cantonese-opera clubs of earlier decades were founded in a predominantly male society. Even the married men were de facto bachelors, as their wives were constrained to stay in China, owing to immigration restrictions that generally excluded women. (Only with the lessening of such restrictions since World War II has the ratio of men to women tended to approach that of the rest of the United States population.) Women were in any case not considered for membership in Cantonese-opera clubs, though they might be brought as guests. (The male-only tradition was breeched in 1943, when Nam Chung began admitting women as members.)[13] The clubs served as centers for social and recreational activities for their men without families. During the war years, many clubs were often active around the clock, as jobs were plentiful in Bay Area defense industries, and many workers were employed in shifts that necessitated seeking recreation at varying times of the day and night.[14] Today's club members remember the early forties as a sort of golden age of opera-club activities, with music going on every night of the week, in contrast to today's entertainment only on Saturday nights.

The gradual decline of activities in the Cantonese-opera clubs following the war years may be attributed in part to the relaxation of immigration laws in 1945 and 1946, one result of which was to admit thousands of Chinese women as war brides.[15] As members of the opera clubs became married and increasingly involved in family life, the need for such gathering places diminished; and the presence of wives and children gave a changed character to those clubs whose members did continue to attend.

Music per se is not always the predominant concern of some of the present-day associations. General socializing and mahjong occupies the time of many of the members. Not a few regard the club mostly as a place to congregate with friends, a place for any member to stop in, whatever the hour, when he has an hour free. For those who no longer live in Chinatown, the club is useful as a stopping-off place, before or after shopping or appointments, and as a generally convenient place to relax. In several of the clubs, athletic pursuits are emphasized. Trophy cases, celebrating triumphs in bowling or volleyball, are conspicuously displayed in such clubs. Picnics and excursions also occupy members' time. Thus music as a specific activity varies in importance from club to club. In all cases, however, a stage, instruments, and sound-amplifying equipment are available for whoever wishes to perform; and there is a core of the membership that continues to perpetuate the musical traditions within the club.

What singing and playing does go on is rarely heard outside the circle of club members. Indeed, their performances might quite literally be termed "underground music," as clubs tend to be located in inexpensive basement quarters. (Such subterranean meeting places, reached from an outside entrance, are common in Chinatown, an area where the efficient utilization of space has always been notable. Lacking access to light and air, such dwellings are not legally allowed for residential use and rent for low rates to many types of clubs.) Even the most reclusive of clubs, however, will generally surface around the time of the Chinese New Year. It is during this period that the family associations of Chinatown give their spring banquets, and it is traditional for a Cantonese-opera club to provide performers for these affairs. The family association in turn makes a donation to the club's coffers. The income that a group derives from such a performance is an important part of the club's annual budget, usefully supplementing the dues and donations that pay the rent and other expenses.

It is thus as the Chinese New Year approaches that many get-togethers may assume the character of rehearsals. Otherwise, musical activity, when it exists, is a decidedly private affair. It is no easy matter for a nonmember to gain admittance, as doors are locked to outsiders. (One club has a special signal for doorbell-ringing and a latched peephole in the door through which the visitor may be viewed.) Notwithstanding this emphasis on privacy, many club members are welcomed as performers in other clubs. At the Saturday-night meetings of the well-attended Nam Chung club, the opera orchestra is often made up in large part of guests from other clubs. In some cases, members of the smaller groups utilize their own clubs for convenience and conviviality but go to Nam Chung to make music.

In general, the membership of San Francisco Cantonese-opera clubs is middle-aged or older. Though children and other younger relatives are often brought to club functions, interest in Cantonese opera among younger people is in rare evidence.

Most of the clubs require regular, standardized dues of their members. Annual dues typically range between $10 and $25, but additional donations are sometimes solicited. One club has no set requirements for dues but expects each of its members to make a pledge twice a year, at which times the contributions range from $5 to $500. Money problems are said to be endemic among the opera clubs. Over the years, many clubs have quietly expired, having been crushed between rising expenses and dwindling income from members who have lost interest in the club's activities.

As previously mentioned, ability to play or sing Cantonese-opera music is never a requirement for membership in a club. In all cases, a prospective member must first be recommended for membership by at least one member of the club; his application is then voted upon by the club at large. Typically, such votes must be unanimous. In mentioning desirable qualities for new members, present members put high priority on good character and the ability to get along with others. Also stressed is the apolitical nature of the club (at least one association forbids membership to any member of a tong or purely political group). While "love of music" is mentioned as desirable in a new member, no other musical criteria apply.

The Cantonese-opera clubs are of course prime sources for audiences when an opera troupe visits San Francisco from Hong Kong. As a rule, such a troupe will come to San Francisco for a ten-day run, often beginning its American tour here, then moving off to Los Angeles, New York, and sometimes Houston, Seattle, Boston, and other cities. The act of distributing tickets has evolved into a special kind of ritual in San Francisco. While tickets are available to the general public at the theater box-office, opera-club members will often receive tickets directly from the opera performers themselves—ostensibly as a gift—the tickets having previously been purchased from the opera company by the performer. Well in advance of the opening night of the performance, individual singer-actors from the company will be brought as guests to opera clubs and to other associations in Chinatown. During such a visit to an opera club, the performer will sometimes sing with the group's orchestra and will distribute tickets as gifts to individuals in the club. In earlier years, club members would respond with flower corsages as tokens of gratitude to the ticket-giver, who would wear these adornments during the subsequent opera performances. In about 1950, however, opera-club members devised the practice of making flowers, fans, and other decorative objects out of dollar bills, so that a player might thus be reimbursed as well as ornamented. These are given to the performer by the ticket-recipients and worn as part of the singer's costume during opera performances. The custom of creating fanciful costume-adornments out of dollar bills is said to have been inspired by the practice of Honolulu opera clubs of making flower-leis of money to be worn by opera performers.

Peking-Opera Clubs

Chinese of North China origin, whose dialect is Mandarin, have never formed a sizable part of the Chinese population of the San Francisco Bay Area. Those who now reside locally are for the most part immigrants from the 1950s and 1960s, many of whom were admitted to the United States originally as parolees who had previously immigrated to Hong Kong from the Mainland. These immigrants, typically middle-class merchants and professionals, have generally settled not in Chinatown but in other sections of the city or in other communities in the Bay Area. That such individuals have been relatively rare in this area is reflected by the fact that no locally organized performance of Peking opera had been held until the 1960s. Late in 1960, a lecture-demonstration of Peking-opera techniques was given in Berkeley by David Huang, a Berkeley radiologist who had immigrated to the United States two years previously. The interest aroused by Dr. Huang's demonstration led to the formation of the Chinese Center Opera Group in the same year. The group held monthly meetings at the Berkeley Chinese Center, an organization founded in 1959 as a volunteer-staffed agency for assistance to newly arrived Chinese immigrants. The Opera Group's meetings were informal, as participants simply met to make music together rather than rehearse for public performance. (The members of this group continue to meet to this day for informal sessions of singing and playing, though the Chinese Center itself is no longer in existence.)

In 1963, coinciding with a Peking-opera performance in Berkeley by the Fu Hsing Opera Company of Taiwan, a group of the Center Opera Group members decided to form an independent club that would devote itself to perfecting Peking-opera techniques and to rehearsing for eventual public performances in the Bay Area. The new group found quarters in San Francisco's Chinatown and began holding frequent training sessions and rehearsals. Members pooled their resources to buy costumes and instruments necessary for the mounting of full-scale productions. In 1967 the San Francisco group was incorporated and registered with the State of California as the San Francisco Chinese Opera Association. (It remains the only Chinese music club that is formally incorporated.)

In the same year, one faction of the new association resigned to form a separate group, giving itself the title of the Mandarin Opera Society of San Francisco. Thus by the end of 1967, three Peking-opera groups—two of which were actively performance-oriented—had been formed in the Bay Area. Since that time, both the San Francisco groups have grown in size and resources, and each has professional instructors with long experience in the genre. In the course of the past eight years, both audiences and numbers of performances have increased for both clubs. In addition to full-scale opera presentations, from which each group receives a substantial part of its income, both associations give less formal demonstrations of Peking-opera techniques for civic organizations and educational institutions in the Bay Area.

Markedly different in attitude and approach from the Cantonese societies is the Peking-opera groups' penchant for public performance and goal-directed training and rehearsing (for which, unlike the Cantonese clubs, they collectively own their own theatrical costumes). The Peking-opera clubs are anxious to bring this aspect of Chinese cultural tradition to the attention of non-Chinese as well as to Chinese in the Bay Area. Also, in contrast to the more mutually insulated existence of Cantonese groups, the Peking-opera clubs sometimes join forces to assist each other and have also presented works jointly with Peking-opera clubs in Los Angeles and Seattle. The meetings of the San Francisco Peking-opera clubs are more likely to be intensively musical affairs, less purely social than those of the Cantonese societies. Such contrasts do not extend to the age groups of memberships, however. Like the Cantonese clubs, the Peking-opera groups comprise mostly middle-aged or older individuals. They have not significantly elicited an interest of younger-generation Chinese in carrying on the traditions of Peking opera.

In general, the sociological aspects that characterize members of Peking-opera clubs are those of the Mandarin-speaking community as a whole: largely first-generation immigrants, middle-class, often college-educated, and living in outlying residential areas of San Francisco or in suburban communities—rarely in Chinatown itself. Contact between the two types of opera club is almost negligible. There have been a few instances of Cantonese-speaking Chinese who have attended meetings of Peking-opera groups out of curiosity and a desire to extend their understanding of different aspects of Chinese culture. There is no evidence that members of Peking-opera clubs have shown similar interest in the Cantonese opera. In general, there is no significant mixing of the two operatic traditions, just as there is little social interaction of any sort between local Chinese of northern and southern backgrounds.

Instrumental-Music Clubs

In 1961 Ho Ming-chung, a versatile musician and teacher from Taiwan, visited the United States for six months. In the course of his visit he gave Chinese-instrument lessons in San Francisco and formed a Chinese-music ensemble, which met at the Chinese Recreation Center in Chinatown. After Ho's return to Taiwan, the group continued to meet and was organized in 1963 as the Chinese Classical Music Club, which rented a basement hall and commenced to meet for weekly rehearsals. Using sheet music from Hong Kong and also arrangements by Lawrence Lui, one of the club's founders, the group assembled a repertoire of works of both northern and southern Chinese origin. The club would perform frequently during the Chinese New Year period and was invited for performances for the Chinese Chamber of Commerce, for family-association events, for public schools, and for such institutions as Stanford University and the state universities at San Francisco and San Jose. The members also made radio and television appearances. From an original membership of seven, the group grew in size to about twenty-five members.

At the time of its optimum membership, in 1971, the club experienced a breakup of personnel, and several splinter groups were formed by former members of the original club. The group that has retained the title Chinese Classical Music Club continues to rehearse in its rented quarters, meeting informally on weekend nights. While maintaining a repertoire of older traditional music, this group has been devoting increasing attention to current popular songs that emanate from Hong Kong and Taiwan. Several female vocalists regularly sing with the group, using the microphone and sound system that is set up in the club. In performing current, commercially popular selections, the group sometimes makes use of such Western instruments as the amplified guitar, the Hawaiian steel guitar, and Western-style trap drums. In the summer of 1973 a group of the club members, featuring a female vocalist and announcer, played weekend professional engagements in a local nightclub that offered occasional Chinese, Japanese, and Korean musical acts.[16] In their professional work at the nightclub, the players used a program comprising classical Chinese instrumental music and popular and traditional songs sung by the female vocal-ist-announcer.

Adhering to a more conservative repertoire is the recently formed Chinese Music Association, which was started in 1973 by former members of the Classical Music Club. The newer group meets for frequent rehearsals at the headquarters of a family association to which several of its players belong. Neither Western instruments nor Westernized Chinese popular music are encountered with this group, whose practice sessions are characterized by a sense of concentration and intensity of purpose rarely evidenced in other Chinatown clubs. Most of the group's sheet music has been arranged by Lawrence Lui, a member of the new ensemble, often as transcriptions of instrumental-music recordings from the People's Republic. Both the original Classical Music Club and this newer offshoot make much use of the p'i-p'a and the cheng, instruments rarely heard in the opera clubs. The newer group sometimes finds a use for the shrill sonorities of the hu-ch'in, the principal melodic instrument of Peking opera, in arrangements from that genre. Also notable in the new group is the use of the ancient Chinese mouth-organ, the sheng, an instrument of northern preference that is seldom encountered in Chinatown ensembles. Both the original Classical Music Club and the recently formed association were founded by middle-aged musicians, but both groups include a number of younger members, some in their teens.

Still another faction that had split off from the original club turned its collective attention to the training and rehearsals of musicians to accompany the Chinese Folk Dance Association, a group of young dancers who in their previous activities had to rely on tapes and phonograph records for musical accompaniment. The musicians in the accompanying ensemble—the Chinese Folk Orchestra—meet once a week with the dancers and also hold separate rehearsals twice-weekly, one of the latter meetings being devoted to the accompaniment of a choral group. The twenty-odd instrumentalists meeting in this ensemble are carefully coached and are painstaking with regard to intonation and ensemble coordination. It is notable, in the context of Chinatown musical groups, that this ensemble is made up almost entirely of youths in their teens and twenties. To a greater degree than is the case with most other groups in Chinatown, this orchestra's repertoire reflects the contemporary trends in Mainland China music. Most of the repertoire has been transcribed directly from Mainland recordings.

Also deriving its music from the People's Republic is the musical ensemble of the Chinese Progressive Association. This group is formed mainly of young people, most in their teens, totaling about fifteen musicians, many of whom are beginners. It would be more accurately described as a semi-instructional group rather than a performing ensemble. Their meetings are characterized by practicing that is only occasionally coordinated by a leader, as the emphasis here is presently on individual instrumental development.

An instrumental group that concentrates almost entirely on popular music from Hong Kong is the Chung Sai band, consisting of high-school and college-age youths. The group is an offspring of one of the Cantonese-opera clubs (Chung Sing) and is coached by several members of the older group. The band's repertoire consists mainly of recent song hits made popular by Chinese recording stars. The Western string bass, trap drums, and amplified guitar are used to augment the Chinese instrumentation of yang-ch'in, erh-hu, and ti. The group, which holds twice-weekly rehearsals, advertises itself as the Contemporary Chinese-American Band, offering (on its business card) "live music at your party."

The Flowing Stream Ensemble

Perhaps the most well-publicized of the instrumental groups over the past few years has been the Flowing Stream Ensemble, whose repertoire is Chinese, as are the majority of its members (American-born), but which has included black, Caucasian, and Japanese players. All of its musicians are also experienced in Western art music, and several also perform professionally in jazz.[17] The group's inception stems from an eight-week instructional session in Chinese instruments held in the summer of 1971 by David M. Y. Liang, then a member of the faculty of the San Francisco Conservatory of Music. Subsequently, several members of Liang's group gathered together the musicians who would become known as the Flowing Stream Ensemble. This three-year-old group has performed extensively throughout the San Francisco Bay Area in concerts and in conjunction with dance presentations. Its repertoire is eclectic, reflecting both North and South Chinese styles, and its instrumentation is entirely Chinese, including flutes, spike fiddles, the yang-ch'in, the cheng, and the sheng. Some of the group's members have been actively involved in teaching classes in Chinese instruments for children and young adults, through the sponsorship of the San Francisco Community Music Center (a United Fund agency that offers many varieties of music instruction throughout the city). Five musicians form the core of this group. These are joined by guest players and singers at concerts.

One aspect of the Flowing Stream Ensemble's work that appears to characterize this group alone among local Chinese ensembles is the compositional activities of its members. Several in the group compose works for Chinese instruments, and some of these pieces have become incorporated into the Ensemble's repertoire. Experiments in collective improvisation have also engaged their attention. At rehearsals, the ensemble's concentration on the work at hand is not unlike that of a Western chamber-music group. The players' precision and discipline, which contrasts with the somewhat more casual approach of the older Chinese groups, particularly the Cantonese-opera societies, derives in part (according to one member) from the players' rigorous backgrounds in Western art music.

The Flowing Stream Ensemble's performances are usually for the public at large rather than for exclusively Chinese audiences. One of its players has noted that the interracial nature of this group has caused difficulties in its gaining acceptance by the older Chinese in the community. The musicians feel, however, that the ensemble's participation in the Chinese New Year festivities of 1973 marked its acceptance by the Chinese community in general. Several musicians from older instrumental clubs in Chinatown assist the group, providing both coaching and musical arrangements. Despite its new departures, the ensemble thus maintains links and continuity with more settled traditions in the musical community.

The Cathay Club

Now existing in semiretirement is the Cathay Club, the oldest music club in Chinatown. The group was formed in 1911 by teen-agers as a marching band with a totally Western repertoire. From its beginnings until 1963, when it ceased its band activities, the club provided music for virtually every major holiday and festive occasion in Chinatown. Additionally it was much in demand for the elaborate funeral processions that were a part of the China-town scene. Its performing members were of high-school age, for the most part, and almost all of American birth. After their years of playing with the band, members would typically maintain their ties with the club. Even today, over a decade since the club has existed as a band, the organization has about a hundred "alumni" members who hold meetings from time to time, participate in the club's golf and bowling teams, sponsor social events, and maintain the club's meeting hall. The Cathay Club's headquarters is the largest among Chinatown's music clubs, the only one to have two floors. In the downstairs rehearsal room—now a vacant, cavernous hall empty of chairs or instruments—is the band's library of sheet music, now archived in a large, standing cabinet. Another cabinet holds behind its glass doors an array of trophies from band-com-petition and athletic events. The walls are lined with photographs of the band performing over the years and of such club events as dances, parties, and anniversary banquets.

In its half-century as a performing organization, the club was locally renowned for the splendor and color that its band added to parades and celebrations. With its active music-making days over, the club now functions socially in a manner not unlike that of other older clubs in Chinatown. Members have keys to the spacious quarters and drop in whenever its suits them. The large living room on the ground floor, adjoined by a well-equipped kitchen, contains comfortable chairs and couches, a television set, and plentiful reading material.

The Cathay Club's repertoire was always geared to band mu-sic by Western composers, with marches, overtures, and concert waltzes providing the bulk of its fare. The band made a notable exception to this approach in 1919, when members of the club decided to form a Chinese-instrument ensemble as a novelty attraction. The club brought two yueh-ch'ins, several bamboo transverse flutes, a hu-ch'in, an erh-hu, a san-hsien, and a set of Chinese percussion instruments. The players were taught the use of the instruments by a local merchant who performed Chinese music as a hobby. A handful of Chinese pieces were learned by the boys, for whom one of the club-members made transcriptions from Chinese number-notation into conventional Western staves and symbols. No direct desires for resuscitating Chinese culture motivated these activities. Rather, this band-within-a-band was formed as a novelty group in preparation for a four-month national tour of vaudeville houses on the Orpheum Circuit. The Chinese-instrument group was typically to provide only one or two numbers within a program of the band's more conventional offerings. Twenty of the Cathay youths participated in this tour, which was widely advertised and successful throughout many cities of the Midwest and South. Directed by a United States Navy bandmaster, the group was variously billed as "A Chinese Band," "The Chinese Military Band," and "The Chinese Jazz Band." The last-named title was hardly in keeping with the band's foursquare fare of overtures and marches, interspersed with a Chinese bagatelle, but the youngsters would strive to justify their modish title with an energetic finale of "Trombonium" or another syncopated novelty of the day.

The tour brought a degree of national fame to the Cathay Club and added considerably to the club's treasury. Only on one occasion, however, did the club venture again into show business. In 1922, the band—now gorgeously arrayed in silk Chinese costumes—played a two-week engagement at San Francisco's Golden Gate Theater. Once again, the ensemble of Chinese instruments added flavor to the program. Chinese music and musical instruments were scarcely less exotic to these American-born bandsmen than to their vaudeville-house audiences, however, and the celestial ensemble—abortive precursor of today's instrumental-music societies—did not survive its brief career as a show-business novelty.

For much of its existence, the Cathay Club sponsored a senior band, a junior band, a glee club, and two dance bands—the Cathayans and the Chinatown Knights. The last-named groups were full swing-era dance bands that led a busy professional life during the 1930s and early 1940s. Bowing to coeducational trends, the club sponsored a girls' auxiliary band, which began in 1939 with twenty-one members. The latter unit proved enormously popular in subsequent years, trebling its membership by 1942.

The club was nourished in its beginning years by the Six Companies, which had been content previously in sponsoring a conventional drum corps for parades. The Six Companies supplied the new band with its first instruments and gave the group rehearsal space in the Six Companies headquarters during the first eighteen years of the band's existence. A note in a 1930 commemorative volume published by the club states:

> Ever since our first existence, our headquarters has been located at the Chinese Six Companies building, but on August 3, we established our own headquarters at 1038 Powell Street. There had been rumors that the Chinese Six Companies had been supporting our Club all these years, but only as far as rent and lights are concerned. Nevertheless, we have reciprocated this kindness by the services our Band rendered during all those years for the Chinese Six Companies while residing in their building. The benefits in this case are mutual. However, we would like to emphasize the fact that the Chinese Six Companies has been very kind and helpful to us and as a token of our appreciation the service of our organization has and will continue to be, at the disposal of the Six Companies.[18]

A definite Western flavor has pervaded the Cathay Club's activities, musical and otherwise, throughout its existence, though its membership has been exclusively Chinese. Its by-laws, announcements, newsletters, and other printed material have always been in English, though Cantonese has predominated in speech. Its parties, anniversary banquets, and other social functions have usually been held at well-known Western-style restaurants and hotels in the Bay Area. Assimilation to American life-patterns has been a constant motif throughout the life of the club.

The Chinese Community Chamber Orchestra

In a category of its own is the Chinese Community Chamber Orchestra, an ensemble formed in the summer of 1973 by Sidney Wong, conductor, composer, and cellist. It is the first Western-style chamber orchestra in Chinatown's history. In its first year it grew to about twenty-five members and presented a number of concerts that were well attended by the Chinese community. Entirely Western in instrumentation, the group devotes most of its attention to a Western concert repertoire, but does perform suites of Chinese melodies, arranged by the orchestra's conductor. Increased attention is planned for works by Chinese and Chinese-American composers. The group, which holds weekly rehearsals throughout the year, includes several Caucasians and several Japanese in its membership.[19]

Sources of Instruments, Sheet Music, Records

Most Chinese instruments used by the Chinese community in San Francisco are of Mainland China manufacture. Chinatown has one store, which opened in 1971, that is devoted entirely to Chinese instruments and related musical materials. Though many musicians buy their instruments and such accessories as strings and flute-membranes at this store, others order them direct from Hong Kong. One of the instrumental teachers who has a studio in Chinatown also sells instruments and rents them at monthly rates. Some of the cheaper Chinese instruments such as bamboo flutes and inexpensive hu-ch'ins are found on sale at various souvenir and novelty shops in Chinatown, though one may assume such items are displayed more as potential wall hangings and conversation pieces than for music-making. Bamboo flutes from China are also sold at music stores and import shops in the Bay Area that otherwise do not feature non-Western instruments.

Chinatown's musical-instrument store is owned by a practicing dentist who is also an instrumental teacher and an active musician in one of the intrumental-music clubs. His store, which is open seven days a week, serves as an informal gathering place for Chinese musicians on weekend afternoons. In stock also is a large supply of phonograph records and prerecorded cassettes from Hong Kong and the Mainland, together with various instructional books for instruments and collections of pieces. Though most of the sheet music used by the instrumental-music clubs has been transcribed and arranged by local musicians, some pieces are bought in notation at the Chinatown store or ordered from abroad, then edited and sometimes rearranged by members of the music clubs.

247

There are many sources for phonograph records of Chinese music in Chinatown. Most plentiful is the popular music of Hong Kong and Taiwan, recordings of which can be found at Chinatown's numerous book and stationery stores, sound-equipment shops, and general variety stores. Cantonese-opera records are almost as widely available. All such records are made only at the 33⅓ rpm speed, often in the ten-inch size that has been generally abandoned by United States record companies. Discs and cassettes of post–Cultural Revolution operas, as well as other Mainland instrumental and vocal music, are available at several stores whose inventory is entirely from the Mainland and that also feature publications and small manufactured objects from the People's Republic. Such outlets also carry the scores to operas, ballets, and other musical works whose recordings are distributed by the Mainland government.

Training, Apprenticeship, and Stylistic Continuity

Though texts for singers are written down and there is some use of musical notation, Cantonese opera is essentially an oral-tradition music, as is Peking opera. Opera styles are continued through apprenticeship training. It would appear that there is no other route to real excellence in the art than the training given during the years, from childhood on, spent in full-time apprentice practice and observation by aspirants to the profession. For amateurs, a certain amount can be learned through listening and watching, but ultimately a teacher will be necessary to impart whatever techniques can indeed be learned by an earnest part-time devotee. It is possible to take Chinese-opera lessons in Chinatown without belonging to a music club. However, opera is of course inherently a group experience, and being in a group of like-minded individuals serves to provide a useful milieu for the practice of techniques and a circle of colleagues who can offer help and suggestions.

As mentioned, every opera club has at least one member who has had experience on the professional stage. The teaching in the clubs is often (but not always) done by such professionals. At least one present-day club—Chung Sing—exists specifically because of the influence of a teacher who taught for a period in the Bay Area and left behind an alumni group who organized to carry on his imparted techniques. Another club—Hoy Fung—accepts students from outside its membership, its teacher being the club's current president, who meets with his students at the club headquarters.

The largest club, Nam Chung, does not officially include lessons in its activities but is nonetheless probably the most educationally significant, insofar as it is the most active musically: weekend nights offer continuous singing and playing, which may be participated in by guests and long-time friends of the club as well as by members. Here, the amateur can sing with a good-sized orchestra, always presided over by a knowledgeable drummer-leader, and practice his art in an ambience of good acoustics, excellent sound equipment, and receptive listeners. There is of course also the opportunity to watch other, more seasoned performers in action. One can observe, for instance, the method of signaling by specific hand gestures to the drummer for a change in rhythmic patterns. One can also watch working professionals in action, as performers from Hong Kong, Singapore, and elsewhere who happen to be in San Francisco will often make it a point to sing at Nam Chung. Also, as previously mentioned, individuals who were formerly on the professional stage in China or Hong Kong and have immigrated are performing members or frequent guests of Nam Chung.

The visits of professionals and active amateurs from abroad serve to keep music-club members in current touch with trends and developments in the Cantonese opera. Such contact is also achieved through travels in the opposite direction by club members who make visits to the Far East. One such visitor, a Nam Chung member, has for years also carried on a cassette-tape correspondence with a professional opera performer in Hong Kong. Through this medium they exchange ideas, with impromptu musical demonstrations, and news about musical developments in Cantonese and other regional opera styles.

In various ways, music clubs thus serve a function in keeping Cantonese-opera traditions alive and in reflecting trends from abroad. Other roles in such continuity are played by phonograph records, movies of opera (only rarely supplementing the plethora of martial-arts movies in today's Chinatown theaters), and miscellaneous magazines and newspapers from the Far East that feature stories and pictures dealing with Cantonese opera and its stars.

The educative role of Peking-opera clubs for their members is somewhat similar. As with the Cantonese clubs, formal and informal teaching must take the place of the apprenticeship that has been the traditional route to the professional stage. Former professionals from both Taiwan and the Mainland play important teaching roles in both San Francisco Peking-opera clubs.

Teaching in the instrumental-music clubs is done mainly in the studios of certain members who devote their spare time to such instruction. A principal difference between these clubs and the opera groups is the use of notated music,[20] which provides the student a basis from which to practice. A certain continuity of music traditions within the community is maintained as members of older clubs serve as teachers and informal coaches for the more youthful instrumental groups—such as the Chinese Folk Orchestra, the Chung Sai Band, and the Flowing Stream Ensemble.

Somewhat of a genre in itself is the music-drama that has emanated from the People's Republic since the Great Proletarian Cultural Revolution of 1964–66. Such operas as *The Red Lantern, On the Docks,* and *Taking of Tiger Mountain by Strategy* are readily available in full score, libretto, and phonograph recordings at several of the local stores, together with scores and records for such other productions as the ballets *The White-Haired Girl* and *The Red Detachment of Women.* Though such works have enjoyed a degree of local popularity, particularly among the younger Chinese, there has been no effort to date to mount a production of any of the modern music-dramas from the Mainland. One must take into account here certain inherent problems of logistics and personnel: modern Communist operas and ballets require a large Western-style orchestra in addition to an ensemble of Chinese instruments. Gathering together such a large group of competent musicians—not to speak of actors and dancers—is simply not practicable or even possible in today's Chinatown. Further, the operas are sung in Mandarin, which is not a functional dialect within the San Francisco community, except among the rare North China immigrants. In any case, the existing opera clubs in San Francisco

—both Cantonese and Peking—consist of older Chinese who are well settled into traditions and are not inclined toward change, either in style or in ideology. There is, then, no production of modern Communist music-drama. Smaller-scale vocal music from the Mainland, however, is used by several of the groups (such as the Chinese Progressive Association and the singers in the Chinese Folk Dance group), and recently composed orchestral works—such as the *Yellow River Concerto* (transcribed for small orchestra)—are performed by the Chinese Folk Orchestra. The dissemination of modern Communist music-drama, however, is through the media of records, radio, and film, not through personal participation of members of the local Chinese community.

As a rule, the learning of Chinese instruments by young people is not initially through music clubs but through private lessons and also through group classes for beginners that are sponsored by such organizations as the Community Music Center, the Chinatown YWCA, and the Chinese Recreation Center. A degree of mutual learning is found also in the informal groups of musicians, including beginners, who simply get together for practice in varying numbers. The Chinese Library of America has for some time been a much-used gathering place for such musicians, who congregate there on weekend nights. Courses in playing Chinese instrumental music are also occasionally available at area colleges and universities. Among those who have sponsored such programs are the University of California at Berkeley and the San Francisco Conservatory of Music. Lessons on Chinese instruments have also been offered by the Center for World Music, in Berkeley, which opened in 1974.

Social Integration in Music Clubs

Every type of music club in the Chinese community can be seen as socially integrative in some respects, nonintegrative in others. The Cantonese-opera clubs, for instance, appear to be decidedly nonintegrative, as they are closed and private groups of immigrants, for the most part, rarely communicating except in the Cantonese dialect. Thus, whatever other social considerations may apply, membership is ipso facto extremely unlikely for a Chinese

251

who speaks only Mandarin or English. Yet, such clubs are integrative on another level, as they bring together individuals of different family backgrounds and villages of Kwangtung whose families might lack other occasions to meet, just as do social clubs in the community that are based on, for instance, golf, photography, and chess. The family remains of course the basic social unit in the Chinese community. It should be borne in mind in any case that while such clubs do cut across family and regional lines, any prospective new member must be introduced and sponsored by at least one or two present members, thus narrowing the base somewhat for prospective newcomers to music clubs.

That opera-music clubs do not bring together northern and southern Chinese has been discussed above. Exceptions to this prevailing separation of styles and social factions are negligible. However, in instrumental-music clubs (predominantly Cantonese in membership), one does find northern, Mandarin-speaking Chinese, even as full-fledged club members. Also, one occasionally encounters a Mandarin-speaking guest from abroad performing in one of the instrumental ensembles. The repertoire of such groups is more regionally heterogenous than in the opera clubs; and notated music is used, so that language problems are minimized.

With respect to the integration of different age groups in music clubs, one finds a definite mix of generations in appreciable degree only in the instrumental-music clubs, as few opera-club members are under the age of forty. In the instrumental groups, however, one may find teenagers playing alongside middle-aged and elderly musicians.

One will look in vain for non-Chinese in the music clubs, however, even as guests. Several of the basement clubs do leave their doors open during rehearsals, thus occasionally attracting a curious tourist. Such a visitor rarely stays for long, however, and his presence goes ostensibly unnoticed by the musicians. It has been noted that several of the instrumental ensembles (not clubs as such) do contain non-Chinese members. Generally, however, Caucasians and other non-Chinese are simply not part of the picture in Chinatown's musical activities. Whatever limited degree of social integration is served by music clubs does not include integration outside the ethnic fold.

Outlook for Continuity and Development of Music Clubs

It would seem a safe speculation that the same forces that gradually caused a decline of the professional Cantonese opera in San Francisco will continue to make inroads on the potentials of Cantonese-opera clubs. An argument could be made that the removal of professional opera from the scene has given, at least temporarily, a bit of *increased* life to clubs. One might cite the possibility that an individual's time once spent at the opera theater will be spent instead at his opera club. Additionally, the resident professional performers of Cantonese opera who are perforce in retirement might well be expected to have increased time in which to enliven the meetings of music clubs and to provide instruction for club members.

In some scattered cases it may indeed by true that the former opera-goer will now have more time for his club, but it remains that the same competitive entertainment offerings—notably television and the movies—that hastened the demise of the professional opera might reasonably be expected to monopolize the recreational hours of club members. As to whether former professionals would now channel their energies toward improving opera clubs, one may see some evidence of such activity in present-day clubs, as former professionals give the benefit of their experience to the amateur performers. Such observations apply, however, principally to those performers forced into premature retirement by the decline of the full-time theater in San Francisco. Others who have retired because of age or other factors would presumably be playing a key role in music clubs in any case. The time-exigencies of the younger retirees must be taken into account: in some cases, female performers have left the stage to marry and raise a family, often moving far from the Chinatown milieu and thus the music clubs; male performers typically have taken on other work full-time and, again, may have relocated far from their former professional terrain.

In a sense, Cantonese-opera clubs have been the victims of demographic trends. During the nearly one hundred years in which professional Chinese theater flourished in San Francisco, the character of Chinatown was marked both by its insular position as an ethnic enclave and by its great preponderance of males, either unattached or far from wife and family. In this bachelor society, opera clubs thrived and the opera theater was the Chinese entertainment attraction par excellence. (As one older Chinese stated to this observer: "Where else could you go?") Only since the end of World War II has the balance of sexes—owing to immigration-law revision—changed to allow for patterns of marriage and family life denied earlier residents of Chinatown. The remaining opera clubs now serve as an adjunct to family life, not as a substitute for it; and the continuous exodus of newly middle-class Chinese to more distant neighborhoods narrows the base of the population from which the Cantonese clubs would draw their active membership.

The future destiny of Cantonese-opera clubs is obviously dependent on the tastes and attitudes of the younger Chinese. We have noted earlier that very few Chinese under the age of forty belong to such clubs or indeed show any appreciable interest in Cantonese opera. The young American-born Chinese, in addition to being affected by the cultural currents that create trends for American youth in general, typically grows up away from Chinatown's ghetto milieu and thus the constant exposure to Chinese language, attitudes, and outlooks. In short, the rate of assimilation into the broader American community is accelerated. Cantonese is often no longer the language of choice. Most American-born Chinese do learn Cantonese in infancy and early childhood, but many later cease to use the language, except for communicating with older relatives, and retain only a small functional vocabulary. Many Chinese youths speak no Cantonese at all, this being the case especially with generations beyond the second. Thus, American-born Chinese, to whom the language of the Cantonese opera may be in part or totally incomprehensible, cannot be expected to be attracted to this form or to the clubs that foster its existence.

Nor do youths who are recent immigrants from South China evidence significant interest in traditional opera, though the language is obviously no problem to them. Their dramatic tastes are generally limited to the movies, and if they show interest in Chinese music at all it is likely to be for the present-day Westernized popular music of Hong Kong and (in fewer cases) the vocal and instrumental music of modern Mainland China.[21]

That Cantonese opera does continue to be a living dramatic form should perhaps be emphasized here. Though the traditional genre has ceased to have an official existence in Communist China, there is nonetheless an ongoing, if declining, professional theatrical tradition in other areas dominated by Cantonese, most notably in Hong Kong.[22] The tenacity of this tradition, in the face of both Western and Communist Chinese competitive entertainment forms, is evidenced in San Francisco not only by the sporadic visits of Cantonese-opera troupes and the activities of music clubs, but also by the continuing sales of opera-music recordings and the playing of opera selections over several local radio stations that broadcast in Cantonese.

It remains, however, that the cultural and commercial interest in Cantonese opera in San Francisco is almost exclusively among the middle-aged and older. While an obituary for Cantonese-opera clubs at present would be decidedly premature, one looks in vain for an emerging constituency that would carry on the clubs' traditions twenty or thirty years from now.

The outlook for Peking-opera clubs would appear to be similarly presaged, as the lack of a present youthful membership does not bode well for these groups' ultimate future, however vigorous their activities may be in the present day. As with Cantonese opera, traditional Peking opera has ceased to be a living cultural entity in the People's Republic, though its traditions are continued to some degree in Taiwan under government sponsorship. Thus the Peking-opera clubs have neither a living cultural counterpart on the Mainland nor a generation of younger members who could be expected to keep the clubs' traditions alive in future decades.

One area in which both types of opera clubs may be expected to play an increasing role during the coming years is in explaining and demonstrating their respective musical and dramatic traditions for such institutions as universities and educational television. Factors that might well precipitate increased activities in this direction include the generally increased interest in Chinese culture that has followed in the wake of improved political relations between the United States and the Mainland government. Also, in recent years an upsurge in interest in affirming their Chinese identity can be seen in many Chinese who are American-born and feel a desire to learn about their Chinese cultural heritage.

In line with such interests are the activities of the Chinese Cultural Foundation, established in San Francisco in 1965. The foundation has enlisted the services of music clubs in the past and intends to seek their continuing help. Members of music clubs have been invited to perform at meetings of the foundation, and Cantonese-opera selections were sung by music-club members at opening ceremonies for the foundation's auditorium in the fall of 1973. In the following summer a Cantonese opera—with running explanations in Cantonese and English—was presented by local music-club members in the new auditorium. The foundation plans to present similar programs in the future through the aid of both Cantonese and Peking-opera groups in the local community. In the summer of 1974 it also sponsored an instructional orchestra for children (Western instruments only, but including Chinese melodies in its repertoire) and also scheduled workshops in both Chinese instrumental music and Cantonese opera.

While professional Cantonese opera can still earn its way in Hong Kong and Peking opera's traditions are continued to a degree in Taiwan, the presentation of such performances in full scale by amateurs for a large audience in American cities can be done effectively only with the help and participation of professionals, whether active or retired. As each of these opera genres suffers from the twin menaces of Westernization of tastes and the ceasing of traditional-opera activities in Communist China, however, both the demand for such entertainment and the supply of seasoned performers to provide it continue to diminish year by year. If there is no reversal of this trend, one can envisage someday the virtual impossibility of staging traditional operas except in a most superficial fashion, as neither opera type has an adequate written and notated tradition to allow for staging without the presence of professionals who have been apprenticed at an early age.

The functions served by the Cantonese-opera clubs as social gathering places have similarly declined, as we have seen, as home and family life have changed the social habits of Chinatown's former bachelor society and as families have acquired the means to move away from Chinatown. The removal of discriminatory laws against Orientals has made less necessary the protective nature of the urban ghetto while simultaneously helping facilitate the finding of homes and jobs elsewhere. As both musical and social institutions, the opera clubs may be viewed as a holdover from an earlier time. At present there would appear to be little reason to predict their survival beyond the lives of their present membership.

In contrast to both types of opera clubs, the instrumental-music associations of Chinatown continue to attract youthful members, both immigrant and American-born, who devote much time to the rehearsal of ensemble works, both for the sheer pleasure of playing and to prepare for public performance. An aspiring player in such groups needs neither a command of Cantonese nor an ingrained knowledge of esoteric musical and dramatic customs. Thus the door is open to American-born Chinese whose working language is English and to those Chinese who speak dialects other than Cantonese. With both instruments and instruction readily available in the Chinese community, together with the interest and inspiration provided by recordings and broadcasts of high-quality instrumental music from the Mainland, Taiwan, and Hong Kong, there is both the stimulus and the means for young Chinese to become participants in ensembles. A bright and active future for such groups would seem assured, as both the music itself and the desire thus to perpetuate a proud ethnic identity find wide interest among the community's youth. In the words of one young member of the Chinese Classical Music Club: "Times have changed. Cultural involvement in this community used to be only for the older generation. The young generation had nothing to do with it. We were taught that the white culture was the "correct" culture. But now, the American-born Chinese are not afraid or . . . ashamed of their own cultural heritage. In fact they even want to participate in it."[23]

NOTES

1. The study was carried out during the summer months of 1973 and 1974. I am indebted to the many individuals in the Chinese community who have contributed information and helped provide access to the activities of music clubs and ensembles. Particularly helpful have been the insights and suggestions of Mabel L. Quon, Sherlyn Chew, David Huang, Kenneth Joe, Him Mark Lai, Lim Lai, Lawrence P. L. Liu, Thomas Lym, and Betty Wong.

Errors and misinterpretations are, however, entirely my own. I have been aided in this study by a grant from the University of Illinois Research Board.

2. E.g. Rose Hum Lee, *The Chinese in the United States of America* (Hong Kong: Hong Kong University Press, 1960), p. 181.

3. Victor G. Nee and Brett de Bary Nee, *Longtime Californ'* (New York: Pantheon Books, 1972), p. xxii.

4. In the U.S., only Honolulu, with a reported 10.9% of Chinese, exceeds San Francisco's officially recorded 8.2%. Data derived from U.S. Bureau of the Census, Census of Population: 1970, *Subject Reports: Japanese, Chinese, and Filipinos in the United States* (Washington, D.C., 1973), p. 110.

5. Thomas Chinn, H. Mark Lai, and Philip P. Choy, eds., *A History of the Chinese in California: A Syllabus* (San Francisco: Chinese Historical Society of America, 1969), pp. 2–5; Stanford M. Lyman, *Chinese Americans* (New York: Random House, 1974), pp. 3–7.

6. Richard Springer, "The Migration to the Other Chinatown," *East–West: The Chinese-American Journal,* (Part 1) Mar. 27, 1974, p. 1; (Part 2) Apr. 10, 1974, p. 1. See also Nee and Nee, *Longtime Californ',* p. xxiii.

7. Alien Land Acts prevented the Chinese from owning property until 1947, and restrictive covenants further served to limit their residence to Chinatown. See Betty Lee Sung, *Mountain of Gold: The Story of the Chinese in America* (New York: Macmillan, 1967), pp. 238, 250.

8. See Peter Chu, Lois M. Foster, Nadia Larova, and Steven C. Moy, "Chinese Theatres in America" (n.p.: Bureau of Research, Federal Theatre Project, Division of the Works Progress Administration, typescript, 1936); G. P. MacMinn, *Theater of the Golden Era in California* (Caldwell, Idaho: Caxton, 1941); Ronald Riddle, "The Cantonese Opera: A Chapter in Chinese-American History," in *The Life, Influence and the Role of the Chinese in the United States, 1776–1960* (San Francisco: Chinese Historical Society of America, 1976), pp. 40–47; idem, "Chinatown's Music: A History and Ethnography of Music and Music-Drama in San Francisco's Chinese Community" (Ph.D. diss., University of Illinois, 1976); Lois Rodecape, "Celestial Drama in the Golden Hills," *California Historical Society Quarterly* 23 (1944), 97–116.

9. The organization of American Chinese communities is detailed in Lee, *Chinese in the United States,* pp. 132–41; Lyman, *Chinese Americans,* pp. 29–53; and Sung, *Mountain of Gold,* pp. 134–39. The interrelationship of such organization with the urban organization in traditional China is set forth in Lawrence W. Crissman, "The Segmentary Structure of Urban Overseas Chinese Communities," *Man* 2 (1967), 185–204.

10. They are (with their dates of founding): Nam Chung (1925), Ngi Yeh (1937, 1938), Flying Dragon (1942), Que Gee (1942), Hoy Fung (1943), and Chung Sing (1970). Ngi Yeh represents a merger in 1948 of the Ngi Kun and Jue Yeh clubs, formed respectively in 1937 and 1938.

11. And local amateurs, in turn, were eventually allowed to sit in with the orchestra at professional opera performances. See Alfred Frankenstein, "Flying Dragons and Sounds of Silver and Fine Wood," *This World* (San Francisco *Chronicle* Sunday magazine), Mar. 7, 1943, p. 23.

12. Nam Chung Musical Society, *Nam Chung* (in Chinese) (San Francisco, 1945).

13. The real pioneer in "coeducation" was the Chick Char Club, which admitted women as members from its founding in 1937. Chick Char consisted of youths in their teens and twenties whose musical activities included both Cantonese-opera and more Westernized forms of Chinese music. Additionally, the club was active as a drama group and as a promoter of patriotic drives and rallies during the war years. Many members of today's Cantonese-opera and instrumental-music clubs received musical training in Chick Char, which disbanded in 1947.

14. See Frankenstein, "Flying Dragons."

15. Sung, *Mountain of Gold,* p. 82.

16. "Multi-purpose Theatre-restaurant Debuts," *East–West,* June 13, 1973, p. 5.

17. "Jazz, Chinese Music Featured in Concert," ibid., May 2, 1973.

18. Cathay Music Club, *Cathay Chimes* (San Francisco, 1930), unpaged.

19. "Chamber Orchestra for San Francisco's Chinese Community," *East–West,* Sept. 5, 1973, p. 6.

20. In all cases the notation is in a system, favored in modern Chinese music, based on scale-degree numbers. Western staff notation is familiar to most of the musicians, but it is not used in the local ensembles.

21. Today's Chinatown youth are perceptively described in Stanford M. Lyman, "Red Guard on Grant Avenue: The Rise of Youthful Rebellion in Chinatown," *Trans-Action* 7 (1970), 21–34, reprinted in *Asian-Americans: Psychological Perspectives,* ed. Stanley Sue and Nathaniel N. Wager (Palo Alto: Science & Behavior Books, 1973), pp. 20–44. See also Nee and Nee, *Longtime Californ',* pp. 338–51.

22. Manchester Fu, "Manny, Celestial," *East–West,* Aug. 12, 1970, p. 3; Ken Wong, "The Orient Express," ibid., Aug. 9 (p. 3) and Aug. 23 (p. 3), 1972.

23. Wilma Pang, quoted ibid., Mar. 21, 1973, p. 9.

Jarocho, Tropical, and "Pop":
Aspects of Musical Life in Veracruz, 1971–72

DAVID K. STIGBERG

The city of Veracruz, situated on the tropical Gulf Coast of Mexico, offers considerable potential for studying the general problem of the effect of urbanization upon traditional musical culture. More specifically, it offers opportunities for examining the relationship between the modern mass-communications media (and the music disseminated by them) and the contemporary practice of local musical traditions. With almost a quarter-million inhabitants, Veracruz ranks fifteenth in population among Mexico's cities. Until recently, it has been the principal seaport of the nation, and it remains the agricultural market-center for a large area of the state of Veracruz. At the same time, a variety of modern urban institutions have been established in the city. It has been the site of substantial industrial and commercial development, and it is able today to provide its populace with many of the services associated with contemporary urban centers in the United States.

Among the modern urban institutions found in the city is a large and growing body of commercial mass-communications media. Commercial radio broadcasting, begun in Mexico in 1923,[1] was introduced to Veracruz in 1930; by 1972, the city boasted seven medium-wave and two shortwave commercial AM stations. FM broadcasting, initiated in Veracruz in 1960, was represented by four local stations in 1972, at which time there were plans for further expansion in the near future. Commercial television was

David K. Stigberg is Instructor in Music, University of Illinois at Chicago Circle.

established in Veracruz in 1963, but from as early as 1958 television broadcasts from Mexico City have been received locally via "booster" transmitting facilities.

These media are serving an ever-growing segment of the local populace. According to the national census of 1970, 38,948 of the 46,867 homes in the city of Veracruz contained at least one radio receiver, and 27,435 contained television sets.[2] Private ownership of record players is also becoming widespread in Veracruz. No statistics about this are available, but a subjective impression is that record-playing equipment is owned by people in all but the poorest stratum of local society. There are record stores dotted throughout the commercial sectors of the city, and furniture and department stores feature record players prominently in window displays and in newspaper advertisements. Many families living on a poverty level with otherwise few material possessions own television receivers and radio-phonograph consoles.

Indeed, even apart from private ownership of radio and television receivers and phonographs, the presence of the communications media is palpably felt by everyone in the city. Most record stores broadcast music onto the streets through large speaker-systems throughout their open hours; taped background-music installations are found in the supermarkets and other modern stores that are growing in number; and portable transistor radios are constantly being played on the public buses, in the marketplaces, and on the streets. It would seem impossible for any resident of Veracruz not to be aware of, and influenced by, the musical offerings of the various local media.

In addition, the populace of Veracruz is regularly exposed to nonlocal music and musical culture through the performances of a variety of national and international professional musicians, which are provided by several institutions and organizations in the city. Programs of concert music presented by touring ensembles and solo-recitalists occur with some frequency, as do performances of popular recording artists of Mexico and of other countries. Occasionally, such diverse music as jazz from the United States, flamenco music and dance, and stylized folk music of South America is performed locally by professional musicians on international tour. Citizens of Veracruz, then, have available to them an abundance and variety of music. To a great extent, the musical life of the Veracruzano, like that of his urban counterpart in the United States, is that of a consumer of music that in large part bears little relation to any local musical traditions and is provided for him by a host of modern institutions and media.[3]

At the same time, Veracruz is located in a region where since colonial times there has developed a rich and vital musical tradition, one involving oral poetry and dance as well as music, which has long been esteemed throughout Mexico. Known as *la música jarocha,*[4] this tradition is still to a large extent viable in many communities in the area, and it continues to produce highly skilled musicians to the present day. Also, since at least the turn of the century, Veracruz has sustained the local practice of musical styles originating in Cuba and, secondarily, from elsewhere in the circum-Caribbean area. These adopted styles, collectively referred to as *la música tropical,* have earned something of a traditional status locally and have become identified with the city. Although such Caribbean music can be found elsewhere in Mexico—most prominently in the nation's capital and in other cities along the Gulf Coast—it is most strongly associated with Veracruz.

Both jarocho and tropical musics are represented in the city by professional musicians earning their livelihood there, but these local musicians, along with the visiting performers mentioned above, still account for only a portion of the live musical experiences taking place in the city. Veracruz is able to support other local professional musicians practicing a wide variety of styles. Among these, several major Mexican folk traditions are represented: by marimba ensembles (native to southern Mexico and Guatemala); *conjuntos norteños* (small ensembles of singer-instrumentalists with six- and twelve-string guitars, string bass, and accordion—typical of the northern region of the country); and *mariachis* (ensembles traditionally associated with west-central Mexico and especially the state of Jalisco, characterized today by the use of violins and trumpets as well as guitars and guitar-related instruments). Also present and performing in a variety of national and Caribbean-derived styles are other soloists and small ensembles, with the guitar as instrumental foundation but often including such related instruments as the *requinto* (or *guitarra requinto,* a smaller six-string guitar) and the Cuban *tres* (a guitar with three pairs of metal strings, known locally as a *tresillo*), occasionally a trumpet, and with such accompanying instruments as maracas, bongos, and congas. Finally, there are many local professional musicians whose music bears only an incidental and occasional relation to specific Mexican or Latin American traditions. These include nightclub trios; large, conventional dance-music orchestras; and—in growing number—small ensembles with electrified instruments whose music is primarily oriented to the youth of the city. It is these latter youth-oriented musicians who are chiefly responsible for the local performance of the recent varieties of popular music of Mexico and of several other countries, including the United States, which increasingly are being disseminated by the local commercial media.

The activities of all local professional musicians are in different ways reflective of their contemporary urban environment, and it is the primary task of this paper to describe the practices of these musicians that point up their distinctive relationships to this environment. Rather than attempt to discuss the full spectrum of professional music-making in Veracruz, I shall focus on the three distinct styles or style-complexes that are probably most important in the musical life of the city today. These are: (*a*) the contemporary representatives of la música jarocha; (*b*) the carriers of the tradition of la música tropical; and (*c*) the players of current popular styles having little to do with local or regional traditions, such styles commonly referred to collectively by Veracruzanos as *la música moderna* or *la música "pop."*[5]

The principal focal points of the following discussion will be, first, the characteristic practices of these professional musicians; second, the attitudes of these musicians and of their audiences that seem most relevant to these practices; and third, aspects of the relationships among practitioners of different styles, and particularly between these musicians and the activities of the commercial media of the city. It is hoped that the picture that emerges from this discussion will have some comparative value for the study of other areas of Mexico and Latin America and of other societies whose traditional musical life is becoming increasingly affected by the introduction and growth of modern urban institutions. Finally, although prediction in this situation is virtually impossible, this study endeavors to provide at least some of the background necessary to assess future changes in the musical life of Veracruz and of Mexico.[6]

La Música Jarocha

In distinction to professional musicians associated with other styles in Veracruz, a majority of the jarocho musicians performing professionally in and around Veracruz are not native to the city itself. Many make their homes in the rural communities of the immediate area, while others who have established residence in the city often have come there from more distant communities in the coastal region to the south, which is regarded as the seat of jarocho music and culture. Most local musicians are of rural background, many of them having earned their livelihood as farmers and fishermen before turning to music as a profession. Although the city provides the principal economic base for the professional jarocho musicians of the immediate area, and although some jarocho musicians are in fact natives of the city and have learned their styles there, recruitment of local musicians continues to be primarily from outside the city.

The principal form of musical employment for jarocho musicians in and around the city today is that of the *ambulante,* or strolling musician. The ambulante's income is obtained from clients in bars and restaurants, who request music of him, paying a fee for each item requested. The jarocho musician shares this mode of work with other musicians; mariachis, marimberos, conjuntos norteños, and other soloists and small ensembles earn a substantial portion of their income as ambulantes. On the other hand, many musicians in Veracruz, including the performers of tropical and popular music, do not participate in this activity.

Bars and restaurants in which ambulantes find regular employment in Veracruz are restricted largely to the central blocks of the city. These establishments are the most heavily patronized, and most musicians choose to concentrate their activities there with only occasional forays into more peripheral areas; less centrally located bars and restaurants, and establishments in residential neighborhoods, often have jukeboxes to provide music for their customers. Although ambulantes will move into such areas when business in the center is slow or when competition from other musicians is particularly acute, few rely heavily on this practice.

In the center of the city, two adjacent complexes of bars and restaurants are especially important for the support of the city's ambulantes. Facing the central Plaza de Armas is a string of open-air establishments sharing a common architectural facade, from which derives their collective name of Los Portales. Near Los Portales is a second group of restaurants that face the Paseo del Malecón, which borders the harbor of Veracruz and is a principal gathering place for tourists. It is in these two areas, and in bars and restaurants between them and in the city blocks in the immediate periphery, that ambulante musical activity is concentrated.

These establishments serve a variety of people. Members of most economic classes frequent them, as do virtually all visitors to the city, including both Mexican and foreign businessmen, tourists, and seamen of many nationalities. The clientele in any one bar or restaurant is always extremely heterogeneous, but some general distinctions can be made among the various establishments and their clientele that have relevance to the activities of musicians working there. The establishments of Los Portales are primarily bars and secondarily restaurants; they typically remain open until the early morning, and while they derive substantial income from tourists, they also function as social gathering-places for many local citizens. The establishments along the Paseo del Malecón, by contrast, are restaurants in the strict sense, heavily dependent on a mealtime tourist trade and closing by mid-evening. A further distinction can be made among the establishments of Los Portales. Although all of these serve a mixed clientele, some are more sumptuously outfitted, charge higher prices, and enjoy substantial patronage from tourists, other visitors, and wealthy local residents.

Musicians spend their working hours moving back and forth among the bar-restaurants of Los Portales and the restaurants of the Paseo del Malecón in search of prospective clients. The situation is one of open competition among all ambulantes, with only occasional and temporary delineation of territory among groups of musicians by mutual consent. In the hours of the most heavy activity, it is not uncommon for several groups of musicians to find themselves soliciting clients more or less aggressively. Sometimes they will attempt to perform pieces requested by their respective clients while only a few feet apart from one another. In this situation, the jarocho musician has carved out a working pattern that separates him from other ambulantes. First, while many ambulantes find the mid-evening hours of intense activity in Los Portales potentially most profitable and will work until the early-morning closing time if there are available clients, the jarocho musician typically confines his work to the daytime and early evening. Second, the jarocho musician concentrates his activities in the restaurants bordering the Paseo del Malecón, where his principal, though not exclusive, clients are Mexican and foreign tourists. Although he does seek out clients in other establishments, he does not compete well with the other ambulantes; and when there are many musicians present, the jarocho musician often is forced to work in the less-expensive bars where there are fewer potential clients, among whom requests for extended playing tend to be economically prohibitive. Jarocho musicians working in the center of Veracruz often complain about the stiff competition from other ambulantes; an explanation for the jarocho musician's relative lack of success in this context will be suggested below.

Whereas the bar and restaurant activities of most other musicians are restricted largely to the city, and to the city's center, many jarocho ambulantes do work elsewhere. The most important alternative work-sites for jarocho musicians are the town of Boca del Río, and the small fishing village of Mandinga, respectively eight and eleven kilometers south of Veracruz. In both of these communities, restaurants have been established that are dependent upon the city, serving an essentially nonlocal clientele. Such patrons consist principally of Veracruz residents, together with tourists and vacationers from other parts of Mexico, especially Mexico City, who are sojourning in Veracruz. In these establishments, in marked contrast to those in the city, ambulante musical activity is dominated by jarocho musicians, with only a small number of other ambulantes competing with them for clients.

The preponderance of jarocho musicians in the restaurants in these rural communities, while partly related to the musicians' residential base, also seems to be a function of the specific rural associations of the jarocho tradition itself.[7] There is a feeling on the part of many Veracruzanos that jarocho music is most appropriate in a rural context. This attitude, while favoring jarocho musicians working in the restaurants of Boca del Río and Mandinga, may be a factor militating against jarocho success in the urban ambience of Veracruz, especially in the bar-restaurants of Los Portales. The difference between rural and urban context could be crucial in determining a prospective client's response to professional jarocho musicians; several residents of the city asserted that while patronizing an establishment in the center of Veracruz they would never request music of a jarocho ensemble, but would be much more likely to do so while on a Sunday outing in Boca del Río or Mandinga.

Apart from work in bars and restaurants, there are only a few additional possibilities for musical employment available to the professional jarocho musician. Private serenades and parties of various kinds provide at least occasional employment for many ambulantes; for some, this activity is lucrative enough to enable them to avoid bar and restaurant work almost entirely. As an economically significant activity, however, performance at such private affairs is limited primarily to the city itself; and in the city, jarocho musicians are contracted for parties and serenades less often than are other ambulantes. Another possibility for musical employment is in connection with official celebrations and festivals, in which jarocho musicians along with other professional musicians are hired to provide public entertainment. Such events, in which the jarocho musician typically is explicitly presented as an example of the folklore of Veracruz, provide only occasional employment for a few jarocho musicians. A final opportunity for musical employment, also marginal to the jarocho musician's primary economic activities, is as an accompanist at one of the three small private academies of jarocho dance found in the city. In at least one of these, the services of jarocho musicians often are dispensed with, and recordings used instead.

Although there is a range of income derived from musical activities among the different types of ambulante musicians in Veracruz, and economic success varies considerably among individual musicians and ensembles, ambulante musicians receive the lowest income from music of any professional musicians in Veracruz. Moreover, most ambulantes, especially those who rely heavily on bar and restaurant work, must work long hours to achieve their modest income in a situation where day-to-day earnings fluctuate widely and unpredictably, and in which little time is allowed for the extramusical employment with which other professional musicians are able to supplement their musical incomes. Jarocho musicians are perhaps the least economically advantaged of ambulante musicians. Their income from music tends to be somewhat lower than that of most ambulantes; and while they typically supplement their income through various kinds of part-time work, few of them possess the skills necessary for all but the lowest-paying employment.

Most jarocho musicians attempt to improve their economic situation from time to time, most often by simply moving from one work-site to another within the Veracruz–Boca del Rio–Mandinga area, but occasionally by seeking work elsewhere. Frequently, individual musicians relinquish membership in one ensemble to take up work with other musicians; and occasionally a musician will abandon professional musical activities altogether, at least temporarily, to pursue other full-time work. As a result, jarocho ensembles in and around Veracruz tend to be short-lived, and it is unusual for the personnel of an ensemble to remain intact for more than one or two years.

The typical jarocho ensemble consists of from three to five musicians performing on a harp, a *requinto* (a small guitar with four strings, unrelated to the *guitarra requinto*), and one or more *jaranas* (instruments similar to the requinto but with eight strings in single and double courses). Such groups retain in their contemporary performance of *sones jarochos* many of the features of the jarocho tradition as it has been described in the scholarly literature and by older informants in the Veracruz area.[8] There are, however, several respects in which the practice of the tradition shows changes from the past; and certain aspects of contemporary practice would seem to have implications for further changes in the future.

First, the traditional jarocho dance is all but absent in most situations in which professional musicians perform today. Clients requesting music from jarocho ambulantes do not dance; nor does jarocho dancing take place except incidentally during the ceremonial affairs for which jarocho musicians are hired—such as banquets, reunions, weddings, and birthday celebrations. Jarocho dancing does occur in the city in connection with publicly sponsored events of the kind mentioned above; here, dancers from the private academies, with elaborate choreography and costumes, are employed to enhance what is essentially a folkloristic spectacle.

Also, the traditional repertory of sones jarochos, as practiced by local professional musicans today, may be diminishing. Older musicians in the area are able to perform some fifty to sixty different sones. These musicians assert that within their memory, these pieces constituted a shared repertory that any competent musician would have been expected to perform. However, the clientele of professional jarocho musicians in Veracruz today typically do not possess intimate knowledge of the jarocho musical tradition or a familiarity with the scope of its repertory. Consequently, most musicians are called upon to perform a much smaller number of sones than were their earlier counterparts. Only four or five sones familiar to everyone are regularly requested, and perhaps fifteen more are requested with some frequency. This reduction in the material demanded of jarocho musicians today may be contributing to a real loss of the jarocho repertory itself. I have observed that many active jarocho musicians today are unable to perform many of the sones formerly in the repertory. On several occasions, in ensembles of mixed ages, I have heard older musicians complain that their younger colleagues did not know the texts of various sones; and even older musicians will admit to only partial recollection of sones that they formerly played but that are no longer demanded of them.[9]

Of equal importance is the fact that, while the older repertory of sones may in effect be diminishing, it is not being replenished in any substantial way, either through the creation and incorporation of new sones or through the adaptation of other music to the jarocho ensemble. With regard to the first point, the jarocho repertory is a mixture of pieces of both known and unknown authorship, and while the existence of some sones has been traced to at least the beginning of the nineteenth century,[10] others are the work of performer-composers of the present century, such as Lorenzo Barcelata, Andres Huesca, and Lino Chávez, the last of whom is still active in the style today. However, although new sones jarochos occasionally appear on the commercial recordings of various jarocho ensembles, apparently there has been little interest in this new material on the part of contemporary local performers;

nor is there evidence of the local composition of new sones. Jarocho musicians in Veracruz with whom I have been familiar regard themselves as performers only of traditional sones; none would admit to the composition of new pieces.

Although local jarocho musicians are not incorporating the new sones jarochos that appear on commercial recordings into their performing repertories, this is not to say that they are not aware of such recordings or influenced by them. Commercially successful ensembles such as the Conjunto Medellín of Lino Chávez are comprised of musicians who have a background in the jarocho region and are known personally by musicians still active there, but who today center their professional activities in Mexico City and retain little contact with the ongoing local tradition. Typically, these musicians are regarded with great esteem by local jarocho musicians. There is substantial evidence that many local musicians look to these commercially successful musicians as stylistic models for their own performances of the traditional sones, though not as potential sources of new material.

It would also seem that the repertory of local jarocho musicians is not being affected significantly by the incorporation of items originating in other styles; nor are local jarocho musicians attempting to assimilate elements of the other styles within their purview. In my experience, jarocho musicians in the city itself rarely performed pieces that were not specifically identified with the jarocho tradition.[11] Other musicians, including other ambulantes, were much more likely to have at least a few items in their working repertories that were not specifically related to their respective styles, and were able to use these pieces professionally.

A view of jarocho music as a kind of *folklore musical* is widespread among the citizens of Veracruz. This designation has been promoted by the local media and on commercial recordings of jarocho music; and it is used by members of virtually all strata of Veracruz society in reference to jarocho music. The designation also is used freely by the professional jarocho musicians themselves. Indeed, it has been incorporated into the name of their professional organization: La Unión de la Música Folklórica del Municipio de Boca del Río.[12] Musicians have been quite aware of this attribute of their music, and they have accordingly exploited their status as carriers of a valued tradition. This self-conception may have a significant influence on the way the jarocho musician in Veracruz today handles the tradition he represents. It may help prevent him from making use of the other musical styles around him, and it also may promote his reliance on a handful of traditional sones that are widely known and readily identifiable to his audience. Consistent with this idea is the fact that, of all musicians with whom I had personal contact in Veracruz, jarocho musicians seemed least interested in musical developments outside their tradition; they were also the musicians with whom it was most difficult to bridge the gap between themselves as performers of folk music for money and myself as prospective client.

Veracruzanos are quick to inform outsiders of the identification of their city and region with the jarocho musical tradition, but although many of them regard jarocho music with great pride, they do not demonstrate an active interest in it. No citizen spoke of jarocho music as being among his favorite musics. No one claimed to spend much time listening to it, and none attempted to play or sing sones jarochos in an amateur capacity. In general, local citizens revealed only superficial knowledge of the tradition and of its practitioners. Various explanations were given by individuals for their lack of interest in jarocho music. The most important and prevalent are the following: (a) Jarocho music is music for dancing, and the traditional jarocho dance is unfamiliar and too difficult. At the same time, other dance styles currently popular cannot be adapted to fit the jarocho musical style. (b) Local musicians are not very good. The better musicians are located, in order of ascending quality, in Boca del Río and Mandinga, in communities further to the south, such as Alvarado and Tlacotalpan, and, finally, in Mexico City. (Although statements along these lines were commonly made, few individuals were able to identify specific local or nonlocal jarocho musicians or ensembles.) (c) Jarocho music does not belong in the city. The texts of sones jarochos have nothing to do with urban life, and the practitioners of jarocho music are associated with the country. (Jarocho musicians are typically ascribed the same social status given to farmers and fishermen.) (d) Jarocho music is monotonous. The musicians play the same pieces over and over, and the style itself has not changed for years. It is essentially a music of the past.

These explanations for the limited interest in jarocho music seem consistent with the overriding conception of this music as folklore musical; and the contexts in which jarocho music is favored over other music also support the notion that jarocho music retains for many Veracruzanos an essentially symbolic value as a piece of local and regional heritage. It is for special affairs with some ceremonial or commemorative content, not for parties and gatherings of a more strictly recreational nature, that jarocho musicians are most often employed in the city; similarly, citizens of Veracruz who own record players often possess one or two recordings of jarocho music, which are played on special occasions and rarely at other times. Urban residents dining in the country will request music of jarocho musicians working in the rural restaurants, but tend to ignore their counterparts in the city; and Veracruzanos visiting Mexico City admit to requesting sones jarochos from professional groups there, as a reminder of home.

A word should be said about the jarocho music offered by the local communications media. In 1971–72, the only relatively sustained attention to jarocho music was given by two local AM radio stations, and the jarocho music programming of these stations accounted for only a small portion of their total broadcasts. One station had a half-hour program on Saturdays at midday that featured a local jarocho ensemble, while the other broadcast a daily half-hour program of recorded jarocho music, beginning at 6:30 A.M. Snatches of jarocho music were used in radio commercials for various local and regional products, but jarocho musical items per se did not occur in the course of other music programming. The limited participation of the jarocho musician in the musical life of the city thus was reinforced by the treatment given jarocho music by the local media.

Jarocho music today would seem to be largely peripheral to the musical interests of the populace of Veracruz, and although it may hold considerable symbolic importance, jarocho music actually is used only in a restricted set of contexts. Moreover, the contemporary audience of jarocho music participates only minimally, lacking expertise in both the musical style and the dance that it traditionally accompanies, and possessing little familiarity with its repertory of sones. The economic situation of its practitioners is precarious, and they do not enjoy any measure of social regard on the part of their audiences. The performance situation itself is unstable enough and possesses sufficient negative features to hinder the formation of productive musical bonds among performers, and may have socially destructive consequences as well. Finally, the conception of jarocho musicians as the carriers of folklore, a notion held by musicians and audiences alike, may be promoting the reliance on a static repertory and style, inhibiting innovations that might otherwise help secure a more substantial place for jarocho music in contemporary Veracruz society.

La Música Tropical

In several respects, the background of the professional practitioners of la música tropical in Veracruz today differs from that of their jarocho counterparts. The majority of tropical musicians working in Veracruz are residents of the city, and recruitment into the ranks of professional tropical musicians comes primarily from the city's population and only secondarily from communities in the surrounding rural area. Although tropical musicians tend to be drawn from the lower economic strata of the city, there is a significant number of musicians who come from more advantaged backgrounds. All tropical musicians with whom I was familiar were fully literate, and many had undergone at least rudimentary formal training in music.

Probably the most important contemporary exponents of tropical music in Veracruz are large *conjuntos tropicales* made up of from eight to eleven instrumentalists and vocalists. Such ensembles are employed almost exclusively to provide music for dancing, and their principal work is found in two large open-air dance halls situated along the beach inside the city, which hold dances on weekend afternoons and evenings. Two ensembles have contracts for regular weekly engagements at these halls, and the other local groups are employed there with frequency. Typically, an evening's dance will feature a local group along with another brought from outside, most often from Mexico City.

Ensembles are able to supplement this employment in the following ways. Frequently, ensembles secure single-evening engagements for dances held in various of the communities in the area surrounding Veracruz, and some groups occasionally receive contracts for more sustained employment in dance halls in Mexico City and other cities. Another source of musical income is employment at private parties and dances in the city, but this practice, at one time fairly frequent, has diminished in the face of competition from ensembles specializing in the performance of la música moderna. Tropical groups are also occasionally employed to perform in the kinds of publicly sponsored events described in connection with jarocho musicians; however, income from such employment is of incidental importance to local groups, as is that derived from the commercial recordings that some local ensembles have made. More important for many tropical musicians is income obtained from various kinds of extramusical work, which the relatively modest demands made on their time by musical obligations allows them to pursue.

Two points with regard to professional activities sharply differentiate the tropical musician from the jarocho musician in Veracruz. First, the large conjuntos tropicales are part of a larger network of performing ensembles in which tropical musicians may find employment. Among these are a variety of ensembles that fall under the tropical rubric. In addition to the large ensembles of primary importance, there are several smaller but similar ensembles that typically perform in various *centros nocturnos* and smaller dance halls found in the city; there are specialized ensembles known as *danzoneras,* which are dedicated to the performance of the older Cuban *danzón*,[13] and which share performance contexts with the large tropical conjuntos; and there are finally a number of small ambulante ensembles with a tropical orientation. But the tropical musician may also play in one of several ensembles essentially outside the tropical sphere: in nightclub combos, in nontropical dance orchestras, and even in the rock ensembles that are growing in number in Veracruz. At the same time, recruitment into the various tropical ensembles may come from any of these other groups. Similar, if less extensive, channels would seem to be open to jarocho musicians, but only rarely is there such interaction between jarocho and nonjarocho ensembles.

A second point of differentiation is that tropical musicians, both as individuals and as members of ensembles, have the possibility open to them of leaving the city for more lucative musical pastures, especially in the entertainment market of Mexico City. Not infrequently, a musician will leave Veracruz to seek work in the capital; sometimes contacts for jobs there can be made by individuals temporarily working in the city with Veracruz-based ensembles. Less commonly, a whole group will try to establish itself in Mexico City on a permanent basis. Such attempts are generally unsuccessful, but it occasionally happens that a local group will achieve this goal, as did the Sonora Veracruz, a formerly local tropical ensemble that now operates in and tours from Mexico City. Again, very seldom are such opportunities explored by jarocho musicians in Veracruz.

The history of the tradition of la música tropical in Veracruz, which took root in the city at least as early as the turn of the century, cannot be reconstructed in any detail at the present time.[14] From at least the early 1940s, however, there is evidence for a high degree of continuity in the local practice of tropical music. The *bolero,* the *guaracha,* and other Cuban *ritmos*[15] have remained the staples of the tropical repertory; the instrumental and vocal complement of the tropical ensemble, although having undergone certain changes, has retained the essential features of early ensembles; and the tropical style itself has been maintained in considerable detail by contemporary ensembles in Veracruz. What is significant is not merely that these ensembles have been able to maintain such continuity with the past, but also that they, unlike jarocho musicians, have done so while being able to accommodate changes of various kinds.

In current practice, tropical music does not consist of a fixed repertory; instead, this repertory is constantly changing. A large ensemble may have a working repertory of some one hundred pieces, to which additions and deletions are continually being made, with individual items having a performance life of as little as four or five months before being set aside for possible future use. Additions to local repertories come from a variety of sources. Many new pieces are original compositions by the local groups themselves. Others are the products of amateur composers in the city. But more important in most repertories are local arrangements of borrowed material, most of which is taken from recent commercial recordings. The adoption of music found on commercial recordings takes essentially two forms: first, local bandleaders seek out recorded material of musicians regarded as exponents of tropical style outside Mexico—most importantly today, of Cuban and especially Puerto Rican ensembles working and recording in the United States—selecting pieces that have yet to become familiar to local audiences; second, and to a lesser extent, local groups draw on the music of both tropical and nontropical styles that currently is receiving the greatest amount of attention from local radio stations, and is judged to be most popular with local audiences.

It must be stressed that these ensembles have been able to incorporate such new material into their repertories without apparently endangering their identification with tropical music; at least by mid-1972 there remained a clear distinction in Veracruz between tropical and nontropical ensembles. The majority of new items adopted by local groups that were not the product of local tropically oriented musicians were taken from recordings of other tropical musicians. Only the biggest hits from the domain of nontropical popular music disseminated by the local media were performed by local tropical groups, and the performances of these borrowed items, typically modified to conform to tropical stylistic criteria,[16] were regarded essentially as novelties by both tropical musicians and their audiences. Similarly, the indirect influence of popular music on local tropical ensembles, which can be seen in their incorporation of pieces in the ritmo of the "tropicalized" boogaloo along with other developments associated primarily with Puerto Rican ensembles in New York, has been relatively minor; local tropical musicians continued to concentrate on the performance of the older Cuban forms according to more or less traditional stylistic procedures.

Probably the most substantial changes that have taken place among local tropical ensembles, and that reflect the growing popular music culture of the city, have been in the realm of instrumentation. The traditional string bass, the Cuban tres, and the six-string guitar have been replaced with electrified instruments, and in some instances, the piano has been replaced by the portable electronic organ. A bass drum and cymbal have been added to some timbale-players' equipment.[17] But for the most part, the musical styles of recent popular music have not accompanied these borrowings, and the new instruments perform the roles and in the idioms of those they have replaced. In 1971–72, there were no groups in Veracruz whose style could be said to represent any real synthesis of tropical and popular music, and although occasionally local tropical musicians would talk of moving their ensembles in the direction of la música moderna, there had been up to that time little real effort to do so.[18]

Members of all classes in Veracruz expressed and demonstrated their positive regard for la música tropical, although the degree and nature of their enthusiasm for it varied considerably. The greatest interest in this music was probably concentrated in the lower economic strata of the city, among all age groups, although it was by no means exclusive to these strata. Conversely, the least interest in tropical music was demonstrated by members of the most educated and affluent segments of Veracruz society. Apparently cutting across class lines, negative attitudes toward la música tropical were also found among those young people in the city for whom recent developments in the music of rock from the United States and England held the greatest attraction.[19]

La música tropical was music that was listened to for its own sake in a variety of contexts, although much of its appeal for many was as music for dancing. People who did not indicate any strong interest in the music itself were often enthusiastic participants in the dances that featured tropical music. The ability to dance in tropical style was regarded as virtually instinctual among Veracruzanos (an ability that typically North Americans were not regarded as sharing). The favorable regard in which tropical music is held doubtless derives in part from the sheer love of dancing and bodily movement, together with the fact that the tropical dance-halls provided a somewhat unique vehicle for establishing male-female relationships.

Individuals discussing tropical music would often emphasize its identification with the city of Veracruz. In response to queries about the possible decline in interest in this music in the face of new musical developments, I was almost always assured that la música tropical could not die in Veracruz—that it was "rooted in the blood" of the Veracruzano and belonged in the city. There is a crucial distinction between attitudes held toward la música jarocha and la música tropical in this regard. In contrast with jarocho music, tropical music was never referred to as being in any way a folklore of the city or area. It was regarded as a local tradition by virtue of its sustained practice over a substantial period of time, but it was also explicitly recognized as a music that had originated elsewhere. Moreover, most Veracruzanos did not feel that contemporary local tropical ensembles were making unique contributions to tropical style; as in the past, Veracruz was seen basically as an assimilator of external developments.[20]

Favorable attitudes toward tropical music in Veracruz did often take the form of intense interest in local groups, and there was a good amount of partisanship among tropical music devotees. Individuals with varying degrees of interest in this music would express preferences for one local group over another. They were often able to discuss in general terms the qualities of individual vocalists and instrumentalists, the characteristic handling of a particular ritmo by respective ensembles, and other attributes of the various local groups. For the most part, however, these groups were regarded collectively as inferior to nonlocal tropical ensembles with national and international reputations.

The position of la música tropical in Veracruz was apparently enhanced by its cosmopolitan image. Not only was it a local tradition, but it was also seen as being international in scope and evidently of substantial value for vast numbers of people outside the local context. At the same time, any positive esteem for local tropical music stemming from these perceptions was tempered by the notion that Veracruz was no more than one of many repositories of a widespread style whose innovative centers were elsewhere. It would seem that this complex of ideas has some relevance for the attitudes of professional tropical musicians in Veracruz. As a group, they were enthusiastic and optimistic about their work, expressing pride in their importance to Veracruz life and their connection with national and international musical developments.[21] However, they also recognized the relatively low status that they held in comparison with outside tropical musicians, and they complained that their economic and social lot in Veracruz was not what it might be.

These considerations suggest an explanation for differences in the flexibility with which the styles and repertories of tropical and jarocho musics are handled by their practitioners in Veracruz. Jarocho musicians represent an effectively isolated musical style,

distinct from the other music around them and—of special importance today—having little in common with the musical styles most
heavily disseminated by the commercial media of the city. There
are no examples available to local jarocho musicians that would
show how an assimilation of elements of any of these styles might
be effected. On the contrary, as we have seen, the conception of
the specialized role of jarocho music and musicians in Veracruz
held by the local populace probably serves to reinforce the musical strategies the jarocho musician currently employs, and it militates against any such attempt at innovation. Tropical musicians,
on the other hand, not only have a relative multitude of resources
available to them for both repertorial additions and stylistic innovations, but also have perceived their situation as requiring them
to be aware of such resources and to make use of them, within the
boundaries of tropical style.

Local commercial media support for tropical music during 1971–
72 was confined for the most part to AM radio. Programming of
this music by several stations was considerable. One station, which
called itself "Radio Trópico," devoted at least 90 percent of its
broadcast day to it. Tropical-music programming was varied in
its presentation. Most prominent were programs of recorded music, which typically presented a mixture of items more or less long-
standing in the repertory, along with more recent tropical hits.
Much as in "top-40" radio in the United States, several pieces
would receive repeated air play during a given period. Programs
differed from a conventional "top-40" format, however (and from
other Veracruz programming as well), in that a relatively large
number of tropical items would be rotated in daily programming.
Also, individual tropical items tended to have greater longevity
than their counterparts in nontropical popular-music programming.

In addition, there were programs devoted to the recorded music of specific tropical ensembles of current popularity. Other programs featured the older tropical style of the danzón. Live studio
performances of a few local ensembles were regularly programmed.
Dances in the large beach-front halls were also broadcast, although, as a rule, only when a nationally prominent ensemble

was performing along with a local group. Through all of this programming, the populace of Veracruz was exposed continuously to a wide variety of local and other tropical music.

It has already been noted that local radio provides one source for additions to the repertories of tropical musicians in Veracruz. More importantly, it would seem that the amount and kinds of radio attention given to tropical music substantially reinforce the urban identification of the local tradition, as well as its association with modern, international musical developments in the minds of musicians and audiences in Veracruz. Both of these factors contribute to the support of tropical music in the city. At the same time, it is clear that the quantity of tropical music programmed by local radio reflects the interest in this music on the part of the populace of Veracruz. Tropical musicians do continue to thrive in the city, and their music still enjoys substantial support from a large segment of local society. Both musicians and nonmusicians feel that tropical music will endure as a central part of the city's musical life.

La Música Moderna

I would now like to discuss the nontropical popular music, which, available to the populace primarily via the local media of radio and television, has been attracting an increasing number of adherents in the city. Collectively designated locally as música moderna or música "pop," this music is further perceived as falling into two categories, based on the language that prevails in each.

Spanish-language popular music

The first música "pop" category may be regarded as a kind of "mainstream" popular music in terms of its acceptance by the youth of Veracruz. Becoming locally important in the early 1960s, this music seems to have received its initial impetus from the emergence of rock 'n' roll, and the increasing international dissemination of youth-dominated music from the United States since the late 1950s. At least by mid-1972, this mainstream music continued to reflect contemporary popular music developments of the United States and England. It has consisted primarily of popular music available on 45 rpm records, sung primarily by recording artists from Mexico, other Latin American countries, and Spain. Other European countries in addition to Spain, especially Italy and France, are occasionally represented by especially popular recordings that appear in both Spanish and original-language versions. An important segment of this mainstream popular music consists of pieces from the United States and England, especially of the varieties associated with "top-40" AM radio, which are heard in Veracruz in both the original and in Spanish-language cover-versions. Although there is some variation among these bodies of music, they share general features of musical style and textual content, and they have tended to be regarded as a single unit in Veracruz.[22]

English-language rock

Recent North American and British rock was often distinguished locally from the mainstream styles by such designations as *música a go-gó, música pesada* ("heavy" music), *música de la onda* (music of the [new] wave), or, simply, "rock." Original recordings of this music, and not Spanish-language cover versions, were most commonly heard in Veracruz, and increasingly such music was being performed by local musicians in the original language of English. Since early 1971, a growing number of Mexican groups have been performing and recording original compositions in rock style with English lyrics.

Popular music of both categories occupied the major portion of air time of AM radio in Veracruz, with the daily programming of three of the local AM stations devoted to this music in 1971–72. Apart from special programs of *complacencias,* in which individual items to be aired were based upon listeners' requests, the selection of items to be broadcast and program format were closely modeled after those techniques developed by AM radio in the United States. A relatively small number of current hits would be rotated throughout the broadcast day, along with a smaller number of older items and new releases. As with commercial radio in the United States, the program formats featured disc-jockey patter, electronically enhanced program and station rubrics, and the dovetailing of music, announcements, and commercials.[23] With regard to the actual musical offerings of these stations, Spanish-language popular music occupied the major portion of broadcasts, but an increasing amount of time was being devoted to English-language rock, and some station managers anticipated giving greater weight to such music in the future. Popular music was also programmed by local FM stations, but the extent and nature of this programming were not determined.[24]

A substantial amount of popular music, along with other kinds of music, was also available to Veracruzanos from television. Several national programs broadcast in the city consisted largely of presentations of national and international popular musicians. Variety programs from the United States oriented around music, such as *The Tom Jones Show,* have also been programmed by national television and have been extremely popular locally. Both national and imported recordings were available in the record stores of the city, and recordings of popular music and rock formed the biggest part of the stock of several stores; this was the music most likely to be broadcast onto the street from record-store sound-systems.

Veracruz is of course not unique in its devotion to popular music, and these statements would probably apply to most larger Mexican cities. There can be no question that popular music and rock have been flourishing throughout Mexico. A large segment of the national recording industry is devoted to national and international performers of youth-oriented popular music, and such music has increasingly dominated record sales in Mexico.[25] In September of 1971, an open-air concert modeled after extravaganzas like that of Woodstock was held at Avándaro, about a hundred miles from Mexico City in the State of Mexico. This attracted an estimated one hundred fifty thousand spectators and became something of a cause célèbre among enthusiasts of rock and of rock culture. A substantial popular literature devoted to rock has appeared;[26] and the hair, clothing, and drug fashions associated with youth culture in the United States have accompanied the importations of music from this country. That popular music and rock culture have been playing an increasing role in Mexican urban society seems apparent. In the following pages I wish to discuss the relevance of this phenomenon to musical life in Veracruz.

There were several ensembles of professional musicians in Veracruz dedicated to the performance of popular music. Both Spanish-

and English-language varieties were represented, with the latter showing an increase in the number of groups. Musicians were typically young, in their late teens or twenties. Popular-music performers show a greater variety of socioeconomic background than is the case with other styles, with members of a single ensemble often coming from different strata of local society. There was a greater possibility with popular music than with other styles in Veracruz that its practitioners would not be lifelong professional musicians. Most popular musicians were only part-time professionals. Among these were many students who had little intention of pursuing a career in music; most other popular musicians maintained other part- or full-time employment. Some also spent part of their time working professionally in other musical styles, particularly in that of tropical music; it is likely that some of these would have entered the career ranks of tropical musicians in the city, had not rock and popular music offered an alternative. It remains to be seen whether these musicians will eventually turn to tropical music full time, or remain in music at all. Although many popular musicians expressed career ambitions in their field, the attrition rate among them has been very high.

Engagement for work in private parties and dances represented practically the sole employment opportunity for popular musicians in Veracruz. Such jobs were of several kinds; by far the most frequent and lucrative were the dances sponsored by the various business and social clubs in the city for their members' sons and daughters.[27] Occasionally a restaurant will contract a popular group for a short period of time, but during 1971–72 only one restaurant was doing this on a regular basis. Occasionally local groups would be hired for dances in other communities in the Veracruz area. Finally, the municipal government from time to time has hired a popular group along with other ensembles for public performances directed primarily at tourists.

In this variegated job situation, only two or three groups enjoyed regular employment during any given period. Except at certain times of the year—especially during the Christmas and New Year season and during the pre-Lenten festival of Carnaval—employment was sporadic and undependable for most popular musicians. As late as mid-1972, the city had developed no such institutions as existed for tropical and jarocho musicians, in which more than a handful of popular musicians could earn a dependable income.

The repertory of popular musicians in Veracruz derived almost entirely from commercial recordings, often with only minimal alteration of adopted pieces. There is, however, an important distinction to be made in this regard between the practices of musicians oriented to Spanish-language popular music and those involved principally with English-language rock. The former groups' repertories were much more directly tied to the music heard on the local AM radio stations than were those of the latter. Performances by the Spanish-language groups tended to emphasize current hits, and thus paralleled the offerings of AM radio. Groups concentrating on English-language rock, on the other hand, showed more independence from local radio, and they more often obtained their material from privately purchased LP recordings that had yet to be widely heard in the city. These musicians were responsible to a significant extent for the introduction of new music to their audiences, and as such, they can be seen as important cultural agents who supplemented, rather than merely reinforced, the role of the media as a disseminator of new music.

Another point concerning groups oriented to English-language rock should be stressed, and that is the degree to which these musicians have embraced and been able to assimilate the musical idioms of the British and North American ensembles they imitate. This is seen most dramatically in the area of vocal style, and particularly in the success with which the characteristic manipulations of the English language associated with rock have been duplicated by rock vocalists in Veracruz. The use of English is generally regarded by local musicians (and by many nonmusicians) as essential to rock vocal style. Accordingly, local vocalists sing in English, consciously sacrificing virtually all concern for the specific meanings of the texts they sing. The English texts of rock performed locally were in all probability understood only in a very general sense by most musicians and audiences in Veracruz. None of the rock singers with whom I was familiar possessed more than the most fragmentary knowledge of English; nor, apparently, did the majority of their listeners.

Of all varieties of music represented in Veracruz, Spanish-language popular music was probably that heard most widely and frequently in the city in 1971–72. It provided an accompaniment for the daily activities of many; and current hits were recognized, sung, and hummed by people of all ages and classes. Guitar-playing amateurs were as likely to play and sing Spanish-language popular music as they were music of any other style, including that of Mexican tradition. Popular songs found at least a small place in the repertories of almost all local professional musicians; only the jarocho musician seemed not to take part in this activity.

Notwithstanding the ubiquity and popularity of this music, however, there was relatively little verbalization about it on the part of Veracruzanos in general. Responses to questioning on the subject almost invariably minimized its importance or value. The words and music of individual songs were often referred to with outright derision, as were the music's performers. It was only among teenagers and younger children that unqualified enthusiasm for the music was commonly expressed, and it was this segment of society that took the most active part in the radio programs of popular-music complacencias. The most hostile attitudes toward Spanish-language popular music existed among adherents of recent English-language rock. For them, such music was typically regarded as *música fresa* ("strawberry" music), a designation that directly parallels in connotation the familiar perjoratives of North American parlance: "bubble-gum" and "teenybopper" music.

There was much more verbalization on the subject of English-language rock and its practitioners. Although many of its stylistic features have been duplicated successfully by musicians in Veracruz, the phenomenon of rock itself remained only partially assimilated by local musicians and audiences. It clearly was not taken for granted, as Spanish-language popular music often seemed to be; instead, it represented a center of controversy, with statements about it tending to be either strongly positive or negative. Criticisms of rock seemed to echo those familiarly heard in the United States: it was regarded as being too loud, as representing a departure from real musical values, or simply as noise. Similarly, criticisms of the music were often inseparable from complaints about what was perceived as associated behavior: bizarre hair and clothing styles, the use of drugs, irresponsibility and even criminality among local youth.

It was naturally with youth that the most enthusiastic attitudes toward rock were seen, and there was a good deal of excitement and curiosity about it among them. But by no means had rock been completely accepted by even young Veracruzanos. Performers oriented to a repertory of rock often complained of having to "dilute" their programs with música fresa in order to ensure employment at parties and dances. There was a difference in behavior exhibited at such social events according to which of the two kinds of music was being performed: Spanish-language items were typically received with overt displays of recognition and approval, and dancing tended to be spontaneous and general; rock items provoked a more mixed response in its listeners, with some of them listening avidly, and others standing immobile with expressions of what could be interpreted variously as curiosity, bewilderment, or consternation. These impressions were supported by statements of individuals among audiences and musicians alike.

Rock musicians themselves exhibited a set of attitudes that distinguished them sharply from other musicians in Veracruz. Perhaps most important, they possessed a manifest enthusiasm for what they were doing. The imported style of rock tended to be embraced unabashedly, with apparently few qualms about "cultural imperialism." When questioned about this point, most musicians felt that the presence of rock in Mexico represented no real threat to the survival of more indigenous traditions, some of which were held in considerable pride and affection by the musicians in question.[28] Any problems presented by the practice of singing in English were dismissed, though neither the performers nor their audiences really understood the language. The use of English was justified on the ground that it is essential to the style of rock, that rock sung in Spanish "just doesn't sound right."

There was intense interest among these musicians concerning new releases of favorite recording groups. Also, they were not content with the rock offerings of the local media or with what was available in local record stores, and were anxious to obtain LPs that they had heard about but that were unavailable locally or in Mexico City. This was more than a practical concern, as most of these musicians did *not* feel that the introduction of new material to their audiences would encourage their acceptance as performers.

The rock musicians generally felt that what they were doing was important. More than with any other group, these musicians tended to view themselves as creative artists, and they expressed this view at times with aggressive conviction. In line with their "creative" self-image, rock musicians tended to be critical of other music and related phenomena in the city. Tropical music was often regarded as being overly conservative; much of Spanish-language popular music was scornfully dismissed as música fresa; and within the domain of English-language rock, strong feelings were expressed about the relative merits of various groups. Above all, rock musicians tended to be critical of prevailing tastes and attitudes in Veracruz. They saw the city in general as backward and provincial in its musical tastes, and regarded the local media as simply pandering to that taste and not as reliable sources of new music. Rock musicians were equally critical of the tastes of the youth that formed their principal clientele. Notwithstanding their enthusiasm for the music, Veracruz's young people, in most rock musicians' opinion, were not ready to accept a full diet of the music that was really worthwhile. Rock musicians felt, with some justification, that they represented a vanguard of taste in the city, and the more sanguine among them predicted that their present shaky economic position would improve when the public caught up with them.

Rock musicians in Veracruz also have been leaders in the adoption of certain of the cultural trappings of English-language rock, such as hair and clothing styles, a new vocabulary of slang, and to some extent the use of drugs. Such attributes had not been adopted or accepted by the young population at large, and apparently for all but a minority of youth in Veracruz they were looked upon with suspicion. There was a growing subculture among youth that did focus on rock and its associated lifestyles, but there was evidence that a large segment of the youth of Veracruz shared with their parents a view of "hippies" (*jipis*), whether North American or Mexican, as irresponsible, unproductive, and potentially harmful elements of society. Such behavior among rock musicians was within limits accepted by the public as appropriate

to their occupation; nevertheless, rock musicians were on the bor-
derline of social respectability and were aware of the delicacy of
their position.

Many of the attitudes and behavior of local rock musicians outlined here can be seen as deriving directly from the cultural materials associated with rock: artistic self-consciousness; a tendency
toward a categorically negative regard for other musical styles
and especially for popular music that has gained mass acceptance;
a perception of the media as "commercial"; and the adoption of
certain extramusical modes of appearance and behavior. However,
not all elements of rock culture have been adopted by local rock
musicians. In particular, little of the political and social content
of rock of the late 1960s has had an impact locally. On being questioned about this, musicians and other individuals in Veracruz
typically stated that realities in the United States and Mexico
were too different for this ideological material to be transferred.
Notions that rock and rock culture have the power to transform
society were not taken seriously by rock musicians in Veracruz.

Rock musicians in Veracruz were of course fully aware that
they were simply copying a foreign musical style. Their general
reaction to commercially recorded Mexican rock groups reflected
this feeling: they were cognizant of the fact that there was relatively little local or national interest in Mexican rock groups in
comparison with that shown for music from England and the
United States. They tended to feel that Mexican musicians would
inevitably be second-rate as long as they remained imitative of
these styles. Nevertheless, most musicians in Veracruz did not try
to do otherwise. Several musicians did express the desire or need
to be "original," but this rarely motivated them to write new
pieces, and even these were conceived totally in the borrowed
idiom. Interestingly, although a group like Santana was often
singled out for praise because it incorporated elements of Latin
music into rock, as was the tropical-flavored "Latin Feeling" by
the Mexican rock group Peace and Love, no ensembles in Veracruz were attempting to incorporate tropical music or any other
Mexican or Latin styles into their rock repertories. Perhaps such
a development was to come in time, but in 1971–72 it seemed that
rock musicians in Veracruz were too involved with perfecting their

performance of rock in its existing style to be able to treat the music with more flexibility.

In 1971–72, rock in Veracruz was still in its infancy. Performers and devotees of rock were still a minority even among youth, although this minority exhibited a great deal of enthusiasm and conviction towards its music. A clear discrepancy existed between these participants and the majority of youth in Veracruz—to say nothing of the general populace—regarding rock knowledge and interest. Among popular musics, it was those varieties sung in Spanish, along with foreign-language music of similar style, with which most Veracruzanos were familiar and felt most comfortable, although verbalizations about this music were typically directed at diminishing its value or importance. Finally, even among devotees of rock, interest in local groups fell a poor third, after British and North American groups and a handful of commercially recorded Mexican ensembles.

But there were indications that English-language rock would have a more substantial role in Veracruz's future musical life. On radio stations devoted to various kinds of popular music, the amount of attention given to English-language rock was increasing, and some station managers expressed the conviction that rock represented the mainstream taste of the future in Veracruz. Commercially recorded Mexican rock groups were increasing in number and were beginning to receive some attention from the local media. In the spring of 1972, at least two pieces by Mexican groups singing in English enjoyed a frequency of air play equal to the biggest Spanish-language hits of the season. During 1971–72, there seemed to be a shift in the response to local groups dedicated to English-language rock, with such groups increasingly hired for society dances normally the province of Spanish-language popular groups. An isolated, but nevertheless significant portent of rock's increased acceptance lay in the redistribution of some well-known local musicians in the spring of 1972. Several members of what was by far the most successful local ensemble specializing in mainstream popular music left to form an English-language group that, by early summer, was capturing some of the clientele of the former ensemble.

In mid-1972, a larger place for rock in Veracruz seemed assured. One might have predicted that, for a time, Spanish-language and English-language performing groups would remain relative separate entities, with Spanish-language popular music suffering some loss of popularity relative to that of English-language rock. However, it seems accurate to say that the rock styles of most recent introduction to Veracruz represent a more radical departure from the prevailing musical styles than did those popular styles introduced earlier to the city, which had gained widespread local acceptance by 1971–72. It is questionable whether the newer imported styles would eventually achieve an equivalent measure of local support. More reasonably, one might expect a merger of the newer styles with those already established in Veracruz. It seems especially unlikely that the practice of singing in English would achieve widespread and sustained local support. Recent correspondence with rock musicians in Veracruz suggests an apparent tempering of the initial enthusiasm for rock. In any case, the practice of singing in English is being abandoned.

More important to this paper is the destiny of Veracruz's more traditional musical practices—specifically, the future role of la música jarocha and la música tropical, in light of a large and growing body of extralocal popular music and musical culture. Of all the factors that would determine the future of these styles, none would seem more critical than the continuing activities of the local communications media. The local impact of international popular-music styles and musical culture offers striking evidence of the influence that the mass-communications media can have on the musical life of a city such as Veracruz. We have also seen that certain local media, especially AM radio, have reflected the interests of the urban populace in the traditional styles of jarocho and tropical music and that the different treatment given each of these musics parallels the interests in these musics demonstrated by local citizens in other contexts. It is likely, however, that the commercial media do not merely reflect local interest in jarocho or tropical musics, but probably play a major part in determining their maintenance, just as they have helped shape interest in popular-music styles of extralocal origin.

In 1971–72 jarocho music, with its strong rural associations, was seen to be essentially peripheral to the interests of the local urban populace, appropriate in only a small number of specialized contexts. It also received only limited attention from the local media, and there were no plans for increasing this attention in the future. Tropical music, on the other hand, has not only enjoyed traditional associations with the city of Veracruz, but has also been associated with specifically modern, urban, and international musical developments. A large part of the responsibility for the maintenance of these latter associations must rest with the city's media, which have given significant attention to tropical music. Ultimately, the associations of tropical music with contemporary developments and—above all—the participation of tropical music in the dynamics of popularity peculiar to the modern commercial media probably provide the best insurance for the survival of this traditional music as a vital part of the life of Veracruz.

NOTES

1. Marvin Alisky, "Early Mexican Broadcasting," *Hispanic American Historical Review* 34 (1954), 516–18.

2. México, Dirección General de Estadística, *IX censo general de población 1970, Estado de Veracruz* (Mexico, 1971), p. 1081.

3. Two other important sources of nonlocal musical information are (a) commercial films and (b) magazines devoted to musical subjects. There are six theaters in Veracruz offering both national and international films, and the admission prices at these theaters, ranging from one to five pesos (eight to forty cents), are within the range of everyone in the city. There are several magazines that primarily cover national and international developments in the area of popular music, available at newsstands throughout the city.

4. The term *jarocho* was apparently originally a pejorative applied to the African slaves who, brought into Mexico through the port of Veracruz, have substantially contributed to the ethnic mixture of the coastal population. Today the term, without negative connotation, refers most commonly to the people and culture of the Sotavento Veracruzano, the coastal plain extending from just north of Veracruz to the area of the Tuxtlas some 140 kilometers to the south. It is also sometimes used more loosely in reference to the entire state of Veracruz. See Leonardo Pasquel, "Qué significa lo jarocho?," in *Biografía Integral de la Ciudad de Veracruz: 1519–1969* (Mexico: Editorial "Citaltépetl," 1969), pp. 204–8, and Gonzalo Aguirre Beltrán, *La Población negra de México*, 2d ed. (Mexico: Fondo de Cultura Económica, 1972), p. 179.

5. This expression is not to be confused with the term *música popular*, which typically refers to folk or traditional music.

6. Most of the data upon which this paper is based were obtained in Veracruz from October, 1971, to July, 1972, when I was engaged in research for a doctoral dissertation in musicology on the contemporary musical life

of the city of Veracruz. I would like to express my gratitude for the financial support I received for this research as a National Defense Foreign Language Fellow, as well as my deep appreciation of the generous help received from Gerard Béhague (my principal advisor at the University of Illinois) and Bruno Nettl throughout my research and in the preparation of the present study.

Fieldwork in Veracruz included a survey of institutions in and around the city involved with local musical life, with special attention to the activities of the local broadcast media; a sampling of the musical attitudes of as broad a spectrum of the local populace as possible; and an eventual concentration on intensive work with a small number of local professional musicians, especially with those responsible for the local practice of jarocho, tropical, and popular music. The concentration on these three varieties of musicians was based not only on their apparent importance for the local populace of Veracruz but also on the fact that around each there seemed to be clustered a distinctive set of attitudes and behavior, which, taken together, held the greatest promise for elucidating contemporary musical trends in the city.

7. Nonjarocho ambulantes working in Veracruz tend to be urbanites to a greater extent than are jarocho musicians. However, among jarocho musicians, no simple correspondence exists between place of residence and place of employment. Although musicians tend to confine their activities to one of the three principal locales, they also move from one locale to another over a period of time. Proximity to one's residence is but one reason for the choice of work-location; evaluations of the competition, compatibility with fellow musicians, and various personal considerations are equally important factors.

8. Gerónimo Baqueiro Foster has done the most detailed work on jarocho music; see e.g. "El Huapango," *Revista Musical Mexicana* 1:8 (Apr., 1942), 174–83; "La Música Popular de Arpa y Jarana en el Sotavento Veracruzano," *Revista Trimestral de la Universidad Veracruzana* 1:1 (Jan.–Mar., 1952), 31–38; and "La Musica Popular de Veracruz," *Revista Jarocha* 6:33 (Oct., 1964), 12–13. See also José de J. Nuñez y Domínguez, "Los Huapangos," *Mexican Folkways* 7:4 (1932), 185–97; Paul Bowles, "On Mexico's Popular Music," *Modern Music* 18:4 (May–June, 1941), 225–30; and Vicente T. Mendoza, *Panorama de la Música Tradicional de México* (Mexico: Imprenta Universitaria, 1956), pp. 83–90 passim.

The term *huapango*, the precise origin and application of which have been subjects of debate, is applied generally to the related tradition of the Huasteca region of northern Veracruz and adjacent states, as well as to that of the jarocho area; it refers primarily to the dance proper, and secondarily to the music that accompanies it. Individual pieces from the two areas, although often called huapangos (perhaps most appropriately in the Huasteca area), are distinguished respectively as *sones huastecos* and *sones jarochos*. The term *son*, although having other meanings, is widely used as a generic term for individual items accompanying traditional dances of various regions of Mexico, each of which has developed its own distinctive repertory of sones. See E. Thomas Stanford, "The Mexican *Son*," *Yearbook of the International Folk Music Council* 4 (1972), 66–86.

9. In the rural communities, both in bar and restaurant contexts and in private parties in *casas familiares,* jarocho musicians do occasionally play

for audiences that share with the musicians a more or less intimate knowledge of the tradition, and make demands on the musicians accordingly. However, this practice is largely incidental to the jarocho musician's principal activities; rural musicians must depend on a clientele that is prepared to pay them more than their peers can afford.

10. Evidence for the early existence of several sones of Veracruz is given by Gabriel Saldívar and Elisa Osorio Bolio, *Historia de la Música en México* (*épocas pre-cortesiana y colonial*) (Mexico: Editorial "Cultura," 1934), pp. 290 ff. There is some justification for placing the origin of at least one son in the current repertory, that of "La Bamba," as early as 1683; see Vicente Ruiz Maza, "Como Nació La Bamba," *Revista Jarocha* 6:33 (Oct., 1964), 18. Baqueiro Foster ("La Música Popular de Arpa y Jarana," p. 37 and passim) speculates that other sones still performed today may have originated in the seventeenth century as well.

11. Musicians active in Boca del Río and Mandinga did do so with greater frequency, probably because in the city other types of ensembles were more readily available than in either of the rural localities to clients interested in hearing nonjarocho music. For the most part, in all contexts, nonjarocho music would be requested of jarocho musicians only when alternatives were unavailable.

12. The union, an affiliate of the national Confederación Revolucionaria de Obreros y Campesinos, has a membership of jarocho musicians residing and working in each of the localities discussed here. It was founded in 1964 by Mario Cabrera, a native of Boca del Río, who also heads one of the dance academies in Veracruz. He, along with his sister Iseta, is a professional jarocho dancer of national reputation.

13. The danzón, introduced to Veracruz toward the end of the nineteenth century by Cuban musicians, has retained a limited measure of popularity to the present. The danzonera in Veracruz today preserves the basic instrumentation of its Cuban antecedents: a rhythm section of piano, string bass, timpani (for which timbales are often substituted), conga, claves, and güiro, to which are added two musicians doubling on clarinets and alto saxophones, a tenor or baritone saxophone, trombone, and trumpet or cornet. See Emilio Grenet, *Popular Cuban Music* (Havana: Carasa & Companía, 1939), pp. xxxiii–xxxiv.

14. The practice of this music has been virtually ignored by writers on music in Mexico, and even the most preliminary serious research into its early history has yet to be undertaken. Some indications of the importance of Cuban musicians, and of the practice of such Cuban forms as the danzón, the son, and the rumba in the first decades of the century are given in the reminiscences of Veracruz of Anselmo Mancisidor Ortiz, *Jarochilandia* (Mexico: Talleres Gráficos de la Nación, 1971), passim; some specific details about the early performance of the danzón are found in Francisco Rivera Avila, "Algo sobre El Danzón," *El Dictamen* (Veracruz), June 20, 1971, sec. C, pp. 1, 4.

15. This designation would seem to derive from the fact that, although other factors distinguish at least some of the many genres of dance music that form the repertories of la música tropical in Veracruz, they are most clearly differentiated from one another in current practice in the areas of tempo, meter, and accompanimental rhythmic patterns associated with different genres.

293

16. Such "tropicalization," whether of a piece of Mexican folk music or a current popular hit, generally involves at a minimum the application of the complex accompanimental patterns of tropical music to the borrowed item. Further alterations include the addition of characteristic brass riffs and other figuration, of vocal solo-chorus call-and-response passages often involving improvisation by the vocal soloist, and of tropical-style solo instrumental improvisations.

17. The tropical ensemble in Veracruz today, basically unchanged since the 1940s, generally consists of a brass section of two or three trumpets and sometimes a trombone; a piano (or organ), guitar, or tres, or a combination of two or three of these instruments; a string bass; and a percussion battery consisting of a pair of congas and timbales, along with maracas, claves, güiro, *cencerro* (cowbell), and occasionally a tambourine. These latter hand-held instruments are normally played by the two or three principal vocalists in the ensemble.

18. One local group did recently work up a small repertory of nontropical material, and performed it in a commercially sponsored competition with other bona fide rock groups. It is significant that the leader changed the group's name for the occasion. His tropical ensemble still exists under his directorship and with the original name.

19. These statements, based on my limited personal contacts and observations, were generally corroborated by the assessments, sometimes based on private market research, of radio-station personnel in Veracruz.

20. Significantly, those individuals in the city who did especially value jarocho music tended to denigrate tropical music, and they would advance this argument in support of their preference.

21. Most of the tropical musicians and devotees of tropical style in Veracruz thought the principal audience for such music in the United States to be a general one, and they were invariably surprised to learn that non-Latins in the United States were not necessarily very familiar with or interested in the Latin ensembles active there. It should be noted that since 1971–72 much of the music referred to here as música tropical has come to enjoy more widespread attention in the United States, under the label *salsa*.

22. Although occasionally pieces of current popular music of Mexican origin will display stylistic features that connect them with specifically Mexican traditional or popular antecedents, for the most part there is little that betrays the nationality of Mexican exponents of this mainstream popular music. For example, there is very little apparent difference in the stylistic characteristics (or in the reception by local audiences) of Roberto Jordán's recording of "No se ha dado cuenta," by the Mexican singer-composer Juan Gabriel, and Jordán's "Rosa Marchita," a cover version of Neil Diamond's "Cracklin' Rose."

23. These devices were used for all kinds of programming on AM radio in Veracruz, but with special intensity for popular music broadcasts.

24. Local FM stations, while offering some popular- and classical-music programming, appeared to devote little if any air time to jarocho or tropical music. They seemed to concentrate on an "easy-listening" broadcast format, relying heavily on North American recordings. At least one FM station based its entire music programming on prerecorded tapes obtained from a company in the United States.

25. A dramatic idea of the changes that have taken place can be obtained

from *Billboard*'s weekly "Hits of the World" charts and from the annual compilations of this information found in the international supplements (*Who's Who in the World of Music*, and other titles) published by *Billboard* in December of each year since 1961. In the charts of 1961 and 1962, several Mexican musicians representing a variety of national and regional styles share positions of popularity with the exponents of the newer youth-oriented styles, but by 1971 these former musicians rarely appear on the best-selling lists.

26. Examples are the popular music magazines *Dimensión*, *Pop*, *México Canta*, and *Piedra Rodante*, all published in Mexico City. These and other similar magazines were sold at newsstands in Veracruz.

27. These jobs, until the late 1960s, were dominated by tropical ensembles and by nontropical dance bands and orchestras. Gradually, this employment has been usurped by small popular-music ensembles made up of younger musicians.

28. Others have had such qualms. Local and national expressions of this are, respectively, Procoro Vega, "Imperialismo Cultural," *El Dictamen* (Veracruz), Feb. 6, 1972, p. 2; and "Rock: disidencia o colonización?," *Diorama de la Cultura* (Sunday supplement to *Excelsior*), Mar. 5, 1972, p. 14. For another discussion of this problem, see the treatment of the September, 1971, rock concert (mentioned above) by Luis Carrión and Graciela Iturbide, *Avándaro* (Mexico: Editorial "Diógenes," 1971).

Popular Music and African Identity in Freetown, Sierra Leone

NAOMI WARE

No area outside North America and Western Europe conjures up more musical images than Africa. Decades of experience with African-derived music in the Americas and of exposure to the Hollywood concept of Africa have helped create and reinforce stereotypical views of Africans and their music. This has continued to the present even among more informed people with regard to African urban music. Even those who recognize regional differences tend to think of West African music as "high-life"—assuming it to be a monolithic style. This is attributable to the scarcity of data available. Both Ghanaian and Nigerian bands have made European tours and have recordings released at home and abroad; likewise, in the West and Central African Franco-phone countries French recording companies released discs by local bands, which tended to be in rumba, *pachanga, kiri-kiri,* or other styles known collectively as "Congolese" (although not all was from either of the then Congoes). Other than this, outside exposure for West African popular music has been limited, and virtually nothing was known about the musicians who produced it.

I was drawn to the port city of Freetown, capital of Sierra Leone, precisely because of this: nothing whatsoever was known of its popular music, and yet it is one of the most thoroughly studied cities in Africa. What I discovered there was a combination of the various styles to be found in West Africa, together

Naomi Ware has done research in West and Central Africa and the Carib-bean; she now lives in Ripon, Wisconsin.

with imported forms such as United States soul music and West Indian reggae and "blue beat." The musicians were no more or less valued or respected than are popular musicians anywhere, and they occupy the ambivalent status of such performers everywhere. In this essay I will outline the major features of Freetown's popular music, past and present, and discuss the social position of the commercial popular musician at more length than I have done previously.[1] The data base is the period 1968–70; some things have undoubtedly changed since then—but such is the ephemeral nature of popular music. Because of the complexity of the urban situation and the limitations of space, I have chosen to give a broad overview, especially since many readers will come fresh to a West African setting.

Generally, an understanding of Freetown's popular-music subculture contributes to an understanding of the city itself, and concurrently it leads to a better understanding of the larger phenomenon of urban music. More specifically, the new Westernized forms of African popular music and the performers themselves represent a less self-conscious Afro-European synthesis than do the European-style African-composed orchestral/choral compositions and the European-trained musicians who produce them. Like commercial musicians everywhere, those of Freetown must please their audiences to survive, and their repertoire must change with demand. Demand is created in several ways: foreign and domestic broadcasts, commercial recordings, foreign movies, and the preference of the bands themselves that is absorbed by the listeners. An examination of this subculture may help indicate the direction of change in contemporary West Africa, especially with respect to black Africans' increasing identity and relationship with black populations in the Americas. While this sense of solidarity is hardly new, it continues to grow in strength and is clearly illustrated by developments in popular music.

Cultural and Historical Background

Freetown, capital of Sierra Leone, is a port city of somewhat over two hundred thousand inhabitants founded as a haven colony for former slaves from various parts of the British Empire; it was also an unloading point for thousands of West Africans originally destined to be slaves who got no farther from Africa than the ship. From this cultural and linguistic conglomerate emerged a new group, known collectively as "Creoles." The complicated history of their development has been dealt with by many writers, notably Banton,[2] Fyfe,[3] Porter,[4] Peterson,[5] and Spitzer;[6] no attempt is made here to review it. The city was dominated by the Creoles until the early 1920s. Since then, an ever-increasing amount of immigration from up-country (the former Protectorate) has swung the city's population-balance heavily in favor of the indigenous, non-Creole population, much to the dismay of the Creole community. Political and economic power has long since been gained by non-Creoles: in fact, no Creole has headed the country since Independence (1961).

Religiously, as well as ethnically, Freetown is a divided city. Although precise figures are unavailable, a recent estimate puts the religious affiliation of Freetonians at fifty thousand Muslim and forty thousand Christian, the remainder being followers of various indigenous religions or none at all.[7] Both Christian and Muslim festivals are accorded the status of public holiday; indeed, the lantern parade on Eid-Ul-Fitri (the end of Ramadan, the month of fasting) is undoubtedly the greatest public spectacle of the year, since Christmas tends to be more of a private celebration.

It is important to realize that the ethnic and religious divisions in Freetown by no means coincide. There is a strong and viable Muslim Creole tradition;[8] likewise, there are significant numbers of up-country Christians and Muslims. Thus one may be Creole and Christian, Creole and Muslim, non-Creole and Christian, non-Creole and Muslim, or non-Creole and neither, with the latter group the largest.

Religious musical activity in the city reflects this situation, as one would expect. Formal religious music in Islam is limited to Koranic chant and the call of the muezzin; formal Christian music includes church choirs, soloists, and organists or pianists, depending somewhat upon denomination. Outside the mosque or church, however, much informal music appears on religious holidays. A great deal of this is of a semireligious or outright secular nature, reflecting pre-Christian or Muslim practices; mask dancers invariably appear in the streets on such occasions, accompanied by a small rhythm band and by groups of unmasked dancers circulat-

ing loosely in the area and interacting with spectators. Music outside the church or mosque that is associated with one of the rites
of passage—birth, death, marriage—tends to be distinctly African-
derived and differs according to the ethnic group performing it.

Strictly secular music can be divided along ethnic lines. There
is a strong tradition of Creole secular music for dancing and general entertainment; likewise, as other writers have demonstrated,
there are ongoing non-Creole secular musical forms in Freetown,
many of them a direct response to the urban situation. The "dancing compins" described by Banton are a prime example.[9] Since the
roots of contemporary urban popular music lie in the Creole community, however, non-Creole secular music will not be examined
here.

While the literature on the Sierra Leone colony from its founding is voluminous, nowhere is the subject of secular music among
the colonists broached. The Sierra Leone Government Archives
contains many Krio texts, but these lack musical transcriptions or
information about the circumstances of collection.[10] In addition,
several of the newspapers were church influenced or controlled,
which virtually ensured minimal coverage of secular musical
events. This scarcity of printed evidence has continued to the
present, so that one can obtain historical data only through glean-
ing occasional dance advertisements or rare feature pieces from
the popular press, together with music and record store advertisements and broadcast schedules. The following summary is based
on these meager sources, which usually neglect to mention the
type of music being played.

Despite such limitations, one can find evidence of Western-type
popular-music occasions in the press back to the late nineteenth
century: the "grand ball" is clearly non-African. From subsequent
newspapers of the period between the world wars, it is clear that
there was already a strong tradition of public dances and of musicians to service them. The following advertisement is an example:

> COMMITTEE OF GENTLEMEN
> Under the patronage of His Excellency, Dr. J. C.
> MAXWELL, C.M.G. Acting Governor and other
> Distinguished Patrons and Vice Patrons there will
> be A SPECIAL ENTERTAINMENT AND DANCE at the

Wilberforce Memorial Hall on Friday 7th October
1921.[11]

Throughout 1921 advertisements regularly appeared in the *Aurora*
for "W. Lionel Branche—The Music Man," advertising all manner
of Western instruments and sheet music.

Between World War I and World War II, the Royal West African Frontier Force Band was extremely active in providing music
for band concerts and dances. However, the *Sierra Leone Guardian* noted that "two other" (unnamed) bands were to play for the
Portrait Society dance on June 3, 1930.[12] While the exact composition of these bands remains a mystery, it is worth pointing out that
many members of the Royal West African Frontier Force were
black West Indians—an unexplored and intriguing possible factor
in the development of West African popular music.

Wartime brought people and money to Freetown, as it did to
so many other port cities.[13] This was reflected in the increased
night life. In 1941 the *Daily Mail* carried the following notice:
"Grand Carnival Dance. The East End Games Club will give the
First Fancy Dress Dance of the year in the Wilberforce Memorial
Hall on Friday, 7th February from 6 P.M. The Mayfair Jazz Band
will play."[14] Tickets were to be five shillings apiece, a substantial
sum in those days. Other bands active included the Blue Rhythm
Band,[15] Ralph Wright and His Melody Swingers,[16] Charles Mann
and His Band,[17] the R.W.A.F.F. Band, and, in the Protectorate,
the Njala Symphonic Orchestra, which played for the Christmas
Eve dance of the Protectorate Descendants Association (a non-
Creole organization).[18] As far as one can tell from the dance notices, the repertoire of most of these bands was Western European: waltzes, fox-trots, and what could be called "novelty pop"
music. One advertisement specified that "the Blue Rhythm Jazz
Band will render SWING MUSIC."[19]

By the late 1940s and early 1950s the "Latin" music so popular
in the United States and Britain had spread to Freetown. One of
the most popular bands of the period was called the "Cuban Swing
Band." Even the *Sierra Leone Weekly News*, which normally devoted little space to coverage of entertainment, noted dances at
which this group was scheduled to appear.[20]

Hitherto, Freetown had had to rely upon the overseas service of the British Broadcasting Corporation (BBC) and such other sources as the United States armed forces–built Radio Brazzaville for broadcast music. Although as early as 1930 recordings of West African music were being sold in Freetown,[21] these were solo songs in Mende and Temne, with occasional imports by such groups as the Gold Coast Quartet. In 1951 Freetown had a re-diffusion broadcast service, for which the weekly schedule for June 24–30 showed only three popular-music programs: BBC "Listeners' Choice for West Africa" on Tuesday and Saturday evenings, and a Saturday-evening program entitled "It's Time for Music."[22]

By 1961, the year of Independence, the scene had changed dramatically. On October 18, 1955, the Sierra Leone Broadcasting Service had inaugurated direct broadcast in Sierra Leone.[23] Now, in one day alone, there were seven musical programs: one record request; one locally taped production, "Chris During's Maringa Group"; a disc-jockey show, "My Kind of Music," patterned after a similar BBC offering; a program entitled "Music and the Film"; "Mantovani and His Orchestra"; "Forces Favourites"; and "Let the Music Play," a continuous show of recordings.[24] Although European influence and format were still strong, clearly Sierra Leonean music was beginning to be broadcast. The dance notices for 1961 reflect the growing impact of commercial recordings, particularly of African popular music, in the advertisement of a new phenomenon: the "amplifier."

"Amplifiers," which were still very much in evidence during 1968–69, are complete sets of equipment for playing records at a public dance—turntable, amplifier, and speaker—plus a collection of the latest popular records. These are financed by a group of young men who then hire the outfit out to social clubs or individuals for a dance. Each has a distinctive name; "Man-Mart," "Baborton," "Riky's" [sic], "Melodies," and "Zodiac" were among those mentioned in the 1961 press.[25] That they were so prevalent is a sure sign that a wide variety of commercial dance music was available on record; since many of the advertisements specified highlife as the dance form, it is evident that African popular music was finally being recorded. This is supported by the record-shop notices during the year that singled out Nigerian highlife titles and performers (Victor Olaiya, "Mumude," etc.) as well as

301

Congolese rumbas and kiri-kiri. Although few references were made to live bands of Freetown origin before the end of the year, at least three different bands—two from Liberia and one from a French territory—toured the city in 1961.[26]

By the second half of 1961, popular music in Freetown was beginning to assume the character it would maintain for most of the 1960s, featuring the same personnel. An advertisement in the *Daily Mail* for August 23 ran thus:

> The Flamingo Jazz Club hit Freetown with a Bang just a year ago. Every Saturday Since, Flamingo Has Been the Place To Spend Your Saturday Night.
>
> TONIGHT
>
> Start the holiday tomorrow with a Bigger Bang!!! The African Rhythm Brothers Our Resident Band Will Make Tonight a Night to Remember. Rich High Life . . . Cool Jazz . . . Hot Rocks . . . Rhythmic Cha-Cha . . . Really Everything . . .[27]

On August 26, an article on a member of the above band reported that it was "incorporating the Heartbeats,"[28] a band that emerged later to succeed, record, and eventually embark upon a prolonged West African tour. A September 27 dance notice advertised the Ticklers Band, another that survived to 1969, although much reduced in popularity.[29]

In 1961 Freetonians were beginning to express in their popular music the independence they had just attained in the political sphere. A dance form known as "rainbow" (a type of highlife) evoked these nationalistic sentiments quoted by Clarence Labor from a reader's letter; Labor's article was entitled "Stoop Down!"

> What's the use of being pedantic about ballroom dancing when you are energetic enough to stoop down well and dance to the rhythm of rainbow.
>
> In many dances since the advent of rainbow I have seen many people standing erect and pretending to be dancing to this popular music. It is wrong to do this fellows because the rainbow which is our "national" dance has its set movements of the body just as the waltz, ballet and bajan.[30]

Record shops in 1961 consistently advertised popular-music hits by African groups, as indicated above. As before, they continued to sell European and American popular records by such performers as Elvis Presley, Marty Robbins, and Cliff Richards. Adenuga's record shop urged customers: "Even if you have nothing to buy, you can at least come round to hear the latest hits in Western Music, Congo rainbows, West African high life, and Celestial melodies."[31]

This mixture of taste in popular music has continued to the present; in fact, despite the nationalistic aspects of indigenous popular music, it was an American band that inspired the first of the 1960s electrified bands to form. A young Creole lawyer and ex-member of the Heartbeats recalled that seeing the film *Rock around the Clock* solidified Gerald Pine's idea of forming a rock band. This initial conception quickly expanded to feature Afro-Latin forms such as cha-cha, merengue, and rumba.[32]

So strong was the Latin influence still that Pine saw fit to adopt the name "Geraldo Pino" for professional purposes, and it is this name that appears on all discs issued by his band.[33] A 1965 release of theirs, entitled "Oh Ye Charanga" and labeled "Spanish," is a nonsense lyric consisting of "words" that sound like Spanish but are not and mean nothing.[34]

Music in the Creole Community

Before concentrating on Western-style popular musicians, let us examine the 1968–69 Creole music situation in more detail.

Large numbers of adults and children are involved in Christian church choirs, and each of the major churches in Freetown and the surrounding Creole villages has a full-time organist and full- or part-time choir director, often trained abroad. These specialists are always male and Creole—the latter undoubtedly because these churches were Creole-founded and are still Creole-dominated. Most belong to the National College of Music and Arts Association, whose secretary, Mr. G. Hamilton, is an organist.

Although not directly associated with any particular church, several organizations exist that perform religious music at concerts that are often held in churches. Unlike similar groups in the United States, they usually suffer from a surplus of male singers. The most prestigious of these is the Freetown Choral Group, directed by London-trained Logie Wright, who heads the Music Department at Milton Margai Training College. This group (to

303

which I belonged) has two annual concerts—at Christmas and Easter—at which it performs such works as Handel's *Solomon* or Britten's *Ceremony of Carols*, as well as shorter pieces from the classical European religious repertoire. With the exception of a very few expatriates (one of whom served as accompanist in 1968–69), the members are Creoles who gained their musical experience in church choirs and schools. The choral group often performs on radio and television; for example, it broadcast a memorial concert for the late Creole governor-general, Sir Henry Lightfoot-Boston, featuring concert arrangements of traditional Creole "shouts." The seasonal concerts are well attended by Creoles, but sparsely by expatriates, from whom the group derives little support in general.

The music performed at Creole private ceremonies is, as I have noted and Jones has emphasized,[35] laced with African elements. There is a strong resemblance between Creole shouts and North American or West Indian black spirituals, which is hardly surprising, considering the origins of and influences on the Creole community. This music is performed spontaneously by nonspecialists: an individual starts the shout and the chorus is taken up by other mourners or celebrants, as the case may be. As noted above, shouts are sometimes incorporated into formal concert settings.

On the secular side, there is a great deal of musical activity beside the dances at which the Westernized bands play. There are informal groups that perform at Creole parties, dances, and weddings; occasionally they rove from house to house on public holidays. These are essentially rhythm bands and are known as *goombay* (or *gombay*) after the principal drum; they may or may not travel with a masked dancer. Goombay groups and a similar type of rhythm music called "milo jazz" frequently appear as alternate entertainment with popular bands at outdoor dances only.[36]

Another traditional Creole music form, called *maringa*, has melody, lyrics, and strophic form. The singer or singers are accompanied by groups of often improvised rhythm instruments (tins full of stones, for instance), guitars, banjos, drums, and—in one case—a plucked string bass. The two most popular groups of this type regularly appear on radio; the leader of one, Ebenezer Calender, is director of traditional music for Radio Sierra Leone and the only Creole member of the National Dance Troupe. Both groups performed a type of song cycle, alternating story and song elements in a continuous presentation, although the second band, the Rokel River Boys, performed only song at a private party given by an Englishman, for which they were hired.[37]

Popular Music: Bands and Occasions

A strong preference for Afro-Latin forms continued through the late 1960s; some of the most popular music, and most original compositions, were merengues and rumbas. By early 1969, United States soul music was becoming extremely popular, and the trend has continued. Since nothing brought dancers crowding onto the floor like an up-tempo merengue, soul music apparently owes some measure of its popularity to its extramusical implications of black solidarity.

In late June of 1969, there were eight civilian bands using electric guitars and basses, African and European rhythm, and—in one case—brass and woodwind instruments. One of these was composed of Fourah Bay College students playing on instruments borrowed from a professional band; they played only for the college community. Of the remaining seven, one has been dissolved[38] and the other six have each regrouped several times. In addition there were four bands that had formed in Freetown but were performing in other countries during 1968–69.

The environment in which these bands operated is typically urban, Western-oriented West African. They played for large public dances given as benefits, put on by social clubs or mounted by the bands themselves for fund-raising. The public learned of the dance through newspaper advertisements such as those quoted above or by public posters prominently displayed on buildings and utility poles (figs. 1–3). Although men were always charged admission, many organizations provided an incentive for women to attend by the notation "ladies by invitation" (meaning "no admission charge for women"). Higher fees for "patrons" usually conferred a ringside table upon the ticket holder.

Most dance-goers were young Africans under thirty. Dress for men was nearly uniform: a pair of solid-color trousers and a short-sleeve colorful shirt without tie. The women's clothes ranged from long skirts and blouses to the most extreme miniskirts; although

Fig. 1

SABANOH JAZZ BAND

AFTERNOON SHOW & DANCE

The Sabanoh Jazz Band

And The Famous Sabanoh Jazz Band Soul Sisters

Will Stage For The First Time

A Grand

DANCE

AT THE
FAMOUS CAPE CLUB

on SUNDAY, 22rd December 1968. at 9 p.m.

Entrance Fee - 50 cents FLAT

M.C's   Mr. Kobi Hunter

Please make the Ramadan A Memorable one by
Listening and Dancing to all the Hits. The Sabanoh
Jazz Band is Famous For. Dont Miss

"Sweet Bana"; "Now Now' and many others. You can be Sure this Day at the Cape
Club will be Well Spent.

M. Farewell
Secretary

Fig. 2

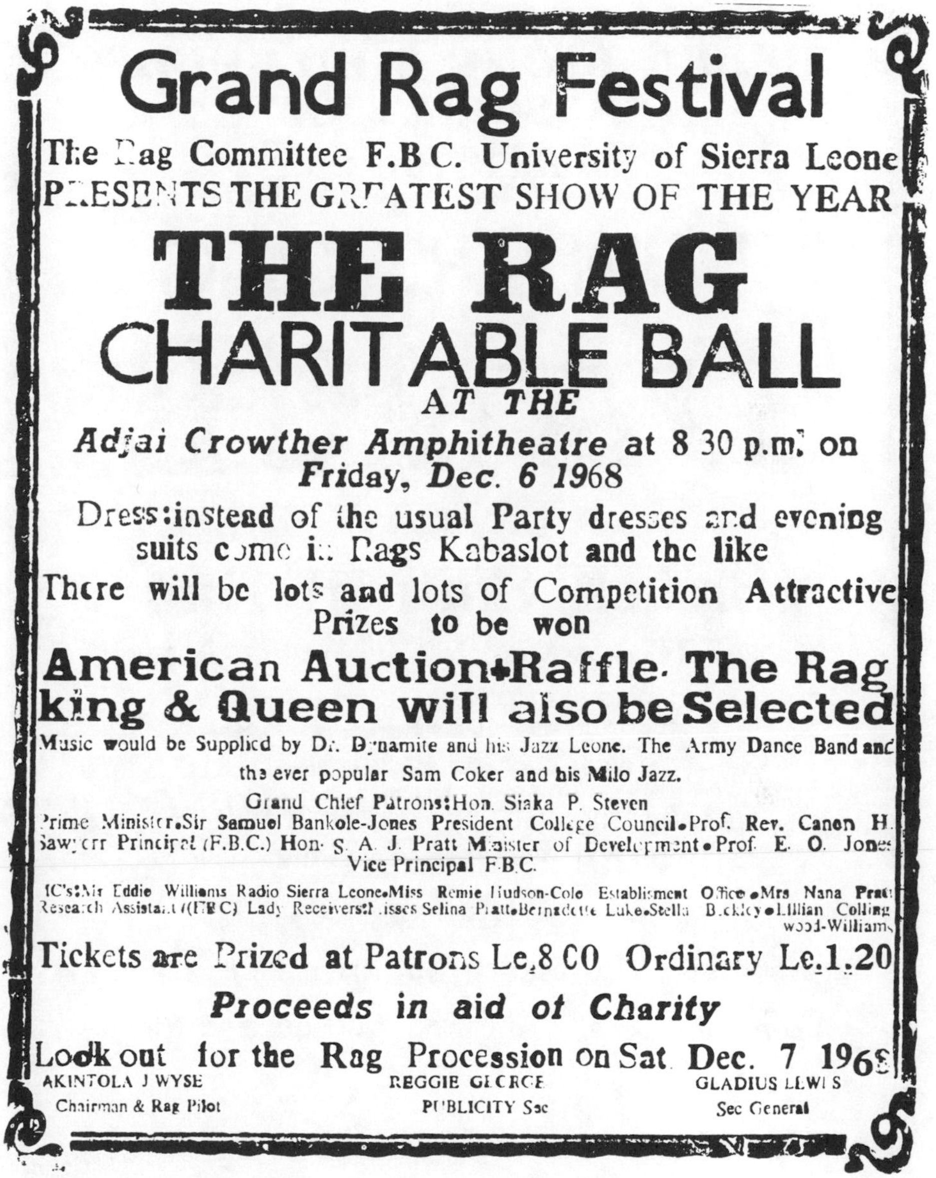

Grand Rag Festival

The Rag Committee F.B.C. University of Sierra Leone
PRESENTS THE GREATEST SHOW OF THE YEAR

THE RAG
CHARITABLE BALL

AT THE

Adjai Crowther Amphitheatre at 8 30 p.m. on
Friday, Dec. 6 1968

Dress:instead of the usual Party dresses and evening
suits come in Rags Kabaslot and the like

There will be lots and lots of Competition Attractive
Prizes to be won

American Auction+Raffle. The Rag
king & Queen will also be Selected

Music would be Supplied by Dr. Dynamite and his Jazz Leone. The Army Dance Band and
the ever popular Sam Coker and his Milo Jazz.

Grand Chief Patrons:Hon. Siaka P. Steven
Prime Minister•Sir Samuel Bankole-Jones President College Council•Prof. Rev. Canon H.
Sawyerr Principal (F.B.C.) Hon· S. A. J. Pratt Minister of Development•Prof. E. O. Jones
Vice Principal F.B.C.

IC's:Mr Eddie Williams Radio Sierra Leone•Miss Remie Hudson-Cole Establisment Office•Mrs Nana Pratt
Research Assistant ((FBC) Lady Receiverst:lisses Selina Pratt•Bernadette Luke•Stella Buckley•Lillian Colling
wood-Williams

Tickets are Prized at Patrons Le.8 00 Ordinary Le.1.20

Proceeds in aid of Charity

Look out for the Rag Procession on Sat. Dec. 7 1968

| AKINTOLA J WYSE | REGGIE GEORGE | GLADIUS LEWIS |
| Chairman & Rag Pilot | PUBLICITY Sec | Sec General |

Fig. 3

SIERRA LEONE GIRL GUIDES
ASSOCIATION
GUIDERS CIRCLE

FUND RAISING

DANCE

AT THE

British Council Hall

ON FRIDAY, 2nd MAY 1969 at 9 p.m.

Grand Chief Patron: The Honourable Dr. Siaka P. Stevens

M.Cs- Dr. Otis Pratt & Mrs. Tony French

Music will be supplied by the SABANOH JAZZ
BAND and an Amplifier.

Dress- Conventional or National Dress

Patrons: Le 10 Ordinary Subscribers Le 1.50c flat

There will be an American Auction and Raffle

by spring of 1969 one could see occasional bell-bottom trousers on women, pants were considered more indecent than a short skirt. Some women wore head ties: many wore wigs or processed hair, and a very few allowed their hair to assume a "natural" (or "Afro") style. Very seldom did dancers arrive as couples, yet many left thus; the dances clearly provided an opportunity for young people to meet members of the opposite sex in an acceptable way.

Most evening dances (the majority were held then) began at 9 P.M. or later and finished by 1 or 2 A.M. On the average, the featured band would play an hour-long set and take a break of about a half-hour, during which music would often be provided by one of the aforementioned amplifiers or a milo jazz group in the case of an outdoor event. Beer and soft drinks were sold in the hall by the club or band, and skewers of barbecued meat or liver were available from women concessionaires who frequented the dances. During breaks between sets, the musicians mingled with the dancers; but for the actual performance the band occupied a definite area at one end of the dance floor, separated from the audience.

Spoken communication and nearly all song texts were in Krio (language of the Creoles and the lingua franca of Sierra Leone). The exceptions were the direct imitations of imported songs: one band with women singers did note-for-note copies of Miriam Makeba's repertoire, while others regularly copied West Indian, British, and United States popular songs. The original compositions were always sung by men, the imitations by both men and women.

Support and publicity activities that contemporary American and European musicians consider indispensable were all but absent from the Freetown scene. There was no popular recording industry beyond a few local entrepreneurs, no music-publishing business, and scarcely any attention paid these bands by the broadcasting services. No booking agencies exist, although Freetown boasted one man who brought two singers in two years from outside the country. Each band had one member responsible for the band's instruments, publicity, transportation, and bookkeeping, much like an athletic team manager in school sports. Some bands acquired "sponsors," who underwrote the initial cost of instruments and costumes; but this arrangement was individual and usually clandestine.

The Musicians

Aside from being men, the popular musicians were quite distinct from all others in appearance, behavior, and, of course, in the music they played. With the exception of two women singers in one band and one in another, they were all men between eighteen and thirty. In this they differed from the players in Calender's band or the Rokel River Boys, who tended to be at least in their forties.

Whereas the middle-aged performers dressed offstage in conservative white or light-colored shirts and dark trousers, the younger musicians dressed colorfully—even flamboyantly—in bright shirts, fitted trousers (often flared), and the latest shoes. Many wore sunglasses outdoors; a few wore them inside and at night as well. The two women singers who performed together wore fashionable wigs and miniskirts as both daytime dress and performing costume. The bands wore matching shirts or jackets wherever possible. Most drink European alcoholic beverages; and there were rumors of hemp smoking, but no one ever suggested that anything stronger was used.

Popular bands are unique in that they are the only musical organizations in which Creoles and non-Creoles participate together voluntarily. Eldred Jones emphasizes this, using the players in the then Akpata Jazz Band (later renamed Sabanoh Jazz Band) to illustrate his point.[39] Although a young Creole has since joined the band, it was at that point entirely non-Creole, and Jones is right to state, "I do not think in the history of Western-style music in Freetown such a catalogue of names could be produced without a single Creole."[40] Nevertheless, the total population of these musicians contains a number of young Creoles disproportionate to the number of Creoles in Freetown. In 1967 they were less than 25 percent of the city's population;[41] yet of the names of fifty popular musicians who have been active during the period 1960–69, only eighteen are non-Creole, and ten of these are or were performers in the Sabanoh band. Clearly the Creoles have continued to produce more than their share of Western-style musicians, although they no longer have a monopoly.

The reasons lie in the performers' backgrounds. All have had Western schooling; most are secondary school–leavers (having completed the required number of years), although some completed O or A levels and a few have continued into postsecondary education. Nearly all were exposed to church music; for example, the leader of one band was a choirboy at the Wesley church. Music was stressed in the schools they attended to the extent that the four founding members of another band had played together in a school band, although not on the instruments they now play professionally. Church and school have always been important in Creole society, and it is logical that children from Creole families would be more likely to have access to these environments than would their non-Creole age-mates. Moreover, Creole children still have more exposure to Western or Euro-African music forms in their homes than do children from a particular African music tradition.

As I have explained elsewhere,[42] the young popular musician is, at best, barely making a living out of his business; the average income of a reasonably successful player is slightly below the average income for all occupations in Freetown and considerably below the average for people of similar background and education. The motivation can scarcely be economic, therefore. Beyond the creative urge, however—which is certainly an important but unquantifiable factor in the choice of an artistic career—lies the incentive to become a leader in one's peer group. Charles Keil made this point about black urban blues performers in the United States: they are culture heroes and role models for youth.[43] Popular musicians set style in Freetown and acquire regular followings and frequent imitators. Although much of their behavior is considered improper and even reprehensible by their elders, they are admired by their peers as cultural innovators.

This innovative role is clearly demonstrated by the critical part that the bands played in the introduction of soul music and associated black American cultural features to Freetown. So rapid was the growth of interest in soul music that its effects could be witnessed in just over a year. Hardly a natural hairdo was to be seen in the spring of 1969; yet by the fall the style was prevalent.[44] Likewise, there was a growing market for United States–manufactured cosmetics made by and for blacks.[45] The music clearly preceded these elements, and it was the bands that brought it.

Popular Musicians in Freetown Society

To deal with the problem of placing these popular musicians in the context of Freetown society, it is necessary to discuss the term *class*. It is often used to refer to a group that shares attributes such as income, lifestyle, standards, and aspirations. Certainly it has been used in this way in several classics of sociological literature such as the Lynds' Middletown studies and Warner's series on Yankee City. One point Warner brought out, of course, is that dissimilarities of income may be overlooked in the face of common origins and subculture—thus the distinction between "poor but respectable" and "nouveau riche."[46] Leo Spitzer emphasized the unity of Creoles across literacy and educational levels as the outcome of common experiences and values,[47] and the same could probably be demonstrated for other Freetown ethnic groups.

A lengthy examination of social class in Freetown is hardly appropriate here, but it will be useful to adopt Warner's six-level Yankee City model to describe the African population of Freetown—that is, the notion of three basic classes (upper, middle, and lower) that can each be divided in half.[48] I am avoiding Banton's more elaborate Freetown class analysis,[49] since only the distinction between Creole and non-Creole African within the three basic classes will be helpful here. From experience both in Freetown as an outsider doing research and in coastal New England (near the original Yankee City) as a native, I judge the use of the Warner model to be valid here, particularly with regard to the distinction between old, established families ("proper Bostonians" in Boston; Creoles in Freetown) and those with recently acquired wealth and political power (Irish- or Italo-Americans in Boston; Mendes and Temnes in Freetown). In both cases the "upper-uppers" see themselves as higher than the "lower-uppers," even though the latter may be far richer than the former. Usually the "lower-uppers" themselves are painfully aware of this distinction.

One can see a similar distinction made even within the middle and lower economic classes in Freetown. Although political and economic power do not always accrue to Creoles, they have the edge of respectability and become the upper halves of the six-level model. Musicians clearly are not numerous enough to constitute a class by themselves, nor are they isolated socially to form a caste-like segment of society. The questions then are: where may they be legitimately assigned in Freetown's class structure, and is this assignment related to their occupation?

Given that the majority of popular musicians are Creoles, we find them potentially drawn from either upper-upper, upper-middle, or upper-lower class Freetown. In actual fact, upper-class Creole families strongly discourage their children from either becoming or associating with popular musicians. The measures taken to accomplish this have ranged from forbidding children to be seen in the company of musicians to actually destroying an electric guitar.[50] The direct result is, predictably, that musicians are drawn from the ranks of the lower and middle classes; an indirect result is that many of them do not themselves see music as a respectable occupation and perpetually talk of "higher" career ambitions. A sizable number, however, have no other permanent jobs; nor are they apt to rise higher than a clerical job if and when they leave music. It seems likely that they will remain in approximately the same position in the class structure from which they came. Their lack of upward mobility is basically unrelated to their interest in music, however; it can rather be traced to their initial lack of access to the means of advancement, a solid secondary and post-secondary education. They come from and replicate families with non-upper-class education and means.

The non-Creole bandsmen, on the other hand, seem to be nearly all of middle-class origin. Like Creoles, upper-class non-Creole parents discourage such activities, and lower-class parents can rarely afford to send their children to secondary school.

In both cases, it is probably fair to state that even middle- and lower-class parents disapprove of popular music as a career, but—unlike upper-class parents—can offer their children no immediate alternatives that would provide as much prestige. Broadly speaking, it is possible to view popular musicians collectively as middle-

and upper-lower class individuals, but this is a cause rather than a result of musical activity. In other words, class affiliation is responsible for career choice in the case of the popular musician.

Regarding prestige, it seems useful at this point to refer to W. G. Runciman's distinction of class (he means economic class, or wealth), status, and power as the three significant variables in social inequality.[51] His analysis places individuals in a three-dimensional model, using these factors.[52] He states, "To bring the point out still more clearly, the three may be distinguished in terms of the kind of aspiration which they represent. To want wealth is not necessarily to want prestige or power; to want prestige is not necessarily to want power or wealth; to want power is not necessarily to want wealth or prestige."[53] Critical to his theory is the ability of an individual to rise high in one dimension without recourse to either of the other two.

Since Freetown popular musicians can hardly be said to be either rich or powerful, it remains to consider their status. Runciman himself said of the independence of status:

> Public entertainers furnish the most obvious example. How is the prestige accorded them to be shown to be either synonymous with or derived from one of the other dimensions? . . . In some cultures, artists and musicians are highly esteemed and well-rewarded; in others, they are recruited only from an inferior caste. But the cases where their status is curiously low cannot be traced to variations in power or wealth any better than the cases where their status is curiously high.[54]

This concept of status or prestige as an independent variable is clearly applicable to these young musicians. As noted earlier, they enjoy high status among the young people whom they entertain; this status is certainly unrelated to either economic position or power. Their prestige stems from their role as cultural innovators (or at least importers) and—unlike their social-class affiliation—is directly dependent upon their occupation. An entertainer's popularity is maintained by continuing public performance. Thus, although a person who leaves the music business may still dress and behave as before, he or she will soon lose the following enjoyed as a performer.

Popular Music, Nationalism, and Pan-Africanism

Looking beyond the particular relationships of Freetown's popular musicians to Freetown society, we may examine some of the ways in which the urban-music phenomenon has significance for an understanding of both nationalistic and pan-African consciousness in Sierra Leone. The distinction must be made between political movements with Western-educated leaders, which resulted in conferences and formal associations, and what might be called "grass-roots" pan-Africanism grounded in no particular philosophy but a recognition of affinity with black people on other continents or islands.[55] It is in this latter area that the West African popular music has relevance.

A common identity as Africans is hardly a new idea; it dates back at least to the first Pan-African Conference in London in 1900 and certainly earlier in the assorted writings of both literate Africans and Afro-Americans. Several factors have militated against its general acceptance by the rank and file, however, not the least of which are the mutually unpleasant images each has had of the other. African stereotypes in the media have been as available to Afro-Americans as to others, and most American and West Indian blacks had no wish to associate themselves with people identified as "primitive," "backward," or "savage." So strong was this prejudice that as recently as 1966 a linguist collecting versions of the "dozens" in Detroit encountered a small child whose ultimate insult was "Your forefathers come from *Africa!*"[56] This attitude has changed greatly, of course, as the popularity of African-inspired cloth, jewelry, and hairdos attests.

Looking at the other side of the equation, we must realize the extent to which United States blacks were rejected by Africans until recently. While condemned as racist by educated Africans, the subservient, shuffling, happy-go-lucky image seen in films and literature could hardly fail to create the same sort of reluctance to admit common goals or interests.[57] The current African enthusiasm for things black-American represents a major shift in perception; and the popularity of soul music is symptomatic of this, as well as partially responsible for it.

Although the more specialized literature may not be available,

even the non-elite Freetonian is aware of black solidarity movements outside the country. One of the local newspapers ran a
long series of articles on black power in spring, 1969,[58] and Stokely
Carmichael appeared in Freetown in conjunction with Miriam
Makeba's 1970 concert.[59] James Brown's "Black and Proud" was
a frequent radio request, and Liberian singer Louiza Sherman's
most popular number in Freetown was that same song, which she
performed in a Diana Ross–style dress and a natural hairdo.

Few discussions of pan-Africanism have dealt directly with the
arts or their practitioners. An exception is Chinweizu's recent criticism of African elites, *The West and the Rest of Us*, in which he
especially takes to task Western-educated African artists who have
assimilated European form and style. By contrast, he says, "the
vitality of modern Nigerian music, its popularity, and the inability
of European musical idioms to make significant inroads into it, in
spite of the prestigious patronage European music receives from
university, church and radio, may be partly accounted for by the
fact that literacy is not a prerequisite for participating in, enjoy-
ing or appreciating it."[60] While the "modern" music to which he
refers is doubtless not highlife, juju, or other urban Nigerian forms
played on Western instruments, he has nevertheless hit upon the
significance of these latter forms as well: they are not limited to
the upper-class affluent individual. Like his or her counterpart in
the United States, the average urban African seldom attends concerts of what is defined as art music or takes an interest in it; yet
the large public dances in Freetown overflow with young people
eager to hear not only the latest local songs, but also the latest
imports from other African and Afro-American traditions.

Identification with other Africans and black West Indians seems
to have been less difficult to deal with. Indeed, cooperation among
African popular musicians has historical precedent. The following
note in a 1921 newspaper only hints at what was apparently a
fruitful pan–West African collaboration: "The deepest sympathy
is extended this week all over the country to that fine band of
musicians, the Southern Syncopated Orchestra, which lost no
fewer than eight of its members in the disaster to the 'Rowan' on
the Scottish coast."[61] The rescued included a woman singer, Mrs.
Luke ("nee Dove"—both old Creole surnames), Mr. G. B. Martin
of Lagos, and Mr. W. M. Ofori ("one of the Ofori brothers, of

Kofiridau, Gold Coast"). A Sierra Leonean, Frank Lacton—the group's pianist—was not so fortunate. The article recalled his playing organ at two funeral services for West Africans in London; it was further reported that West Africans there were attempting to organize a benefit concert for the survivors. Regardless of the music they played, this orchestra clearly represented a collective effort by English-speaking West Africans and is entirely consistent with the de-emphasis on tribal or national affiliation evident in later popular bands. In addition to this relaxed attitude toward national boundaries, the West Indian origin of some Creoles and Sierra Leone's continuing contact with educated black West Indians have made West Indian music acceptable.[62]

If the contemporary bands have any political significance, it is their lack of ethnic enmity. In 1968 the Sabanoh Jazz Band performed as a unit at dances, traveled, rehearsed, and spent off-duty time together. Yet at the same time that Temne, Mende, Lokko, Creole, and Susu were thus commonly occupied, a national emergency was declared because Temne and Mende were engaged in serious political conflict up-country. If there were private conflicts within that band, they never surfaced. Similarly, visiting bands from other African countries were welcomed and judged by the same standards as the local groups, without regard for national origin.

The noteworthy feature of the Freetown popular-music scene thus appears to be a lack of true nationalism or tribalism. What identity exists is more that of loosely defined "Africans" or blacks. This is not to imply that regional or foreign music styles are not recognized as such; rather, they are not regarded as significant in any dimension other than musical. Nor should the question of conscious identification with other blacks obscure the probability that African-derived music from the Americas sounds better to the musicians and audiences and is therefore more likely to be imported than an unrelated tradition.

The American experience with jazz clearly demonstrates that much music can be assimilated without other cultural elements if the latter are regarded as undesirable; and had the Sierra Leone bands wished to do so, they could have used the music without the surrounding behavior. While their actions are perhaps less selective than those of a composer who sets out to write an "African

Symphony" or "African Cantata,"[63] these musicians have in fact succeeded in creating a pan-African musical culture that celebrates the African idiom wherever it occurs.

NOTES

1. Naomi Ware Hooker, "Popular Musicians in Freetown," *African Urban Notes* 5 (Winter, 1970), 11–18.

2. Michael Banton, *West African City* (London: Oxford University Press, 1957); idem,"Social Alignment and Identity in a West African City," in *Urbanization and Migration in West Africa*, ed. Hilda Kuper (Berkeley and Los Angeles: University of California Press, 1965), pp. 131–47.

3. Christopher Fyfe, *A History of Sierra Leone* (London: Oxford University Press, 1962); idem, *Sierra Leone Inheritance* (London: Oxford University Press, 1964).

4. Arthur T. Porter, *Creoledom* (London: Oxford University Press, 1963).

5. John Peterson, "The Sierra Leone Creole: A Reappraisal," in *Freetown: A Symposium*, ed. Christopher Fyfe and Eldred Jones (Freetown: Sierra Leone University Press, 1968), pp. 100–117; idem, *Province of Freedom* (Evanston, Ill.: Northwestern University Press, 1969).

6. Leo Spitzer, *The Creoles of Sierra Leone* (Madison: University of Wisconsin Press, 1974).

7. Rev. E. W. Fashole-Luke, "Religion in Freetown," in *Freetown: A Symposium*, ed. Fyfe and Jones, p. 127.

8. See Peterson, "Sierra Leone Creole."

9. Banton, *West African City*, chap. 9.

10. Leo Spitzer, unpublished research notes, 1965–66.

11. *Aurora* (Freetown), Sept. 24, 1921.

12. *Sierra Leone Guardian*, May 30, 1930.

13. For a good fictional description of Freetown during this period, see Graham Greene's novel *The Heart of the Matter* (London: William Heinemann, 1948).

14. *Daily Mail* (Freetown), Feb. 4, 1941.

15. Ibid., May 2, 1941.

16. Ibid., Aug. 30, 1941.

17. Ibid., Oct. 11, 1941.

18. Ibid., Dec. 6, 1941.

19. Ibid., Dec. 19, 1941.

20. *Sierra Leone Weekly News*, Jan. 13, 20, Feb. 3, July 7, 1951.

21. *Guardian*, 1930.

22. *Sierra Leone Weekly News*, June 30, 1951.

23. Thomas Decker, "This Is Freetown Calling," *Sierra Leone Studies*, n.s. 7 (Feb., 1956), 166.

24. *Daily Mail*, Jan. 2, 1961.

25. Ibid., 1961.

26. Ibid.

27. Ibid., Aug. 23, 1961. The holiday mentioned is the August bank holiday; the Flamingo has survived to the present under several different names.

28. Ibid., Aug. 26, 1961.

318

29. Ibid., Sept. 27, 1961.

30. Ibid., Aug. 26, 1961. The term *bajan* is Trinidad slang for a native of Barbados (see the Mighty Sparrow's calypso "Smart Bajan"); its use here, to describe a West African popular dance form, cannot easily be explained. I have not encountered the term elsewhere in the West African literature.

31. Ibid., Oct. 25, 1961.

32. Arnold J. Gooding, interview, Apr. 21, 1969.

33. Such renaming is curiously like the European Baroque musician's practice of "Italianizing" his name to increase the chance of success.

34. Geraldo Pino and His Heartbeats, "Oh Ye Charanga," Pino Records GP 7 (a) (matrix number GP 7 A + 1) (Freetown, 1965).

35. Eldred Jones, "Freetown—The Contemporary Cultural Scene," in *Freetown: A Symposium,* ed. Fyfe and Jones, pp. 199–200.

36. The term *goombay* provides a classic example of the confusion over origins; it is widely distributed in West Africa and the West Indies (even in travel brochures for the Bahamas).

37. The omission of Krio dialogue may be attributable to the presence of a largely non-Creole European audience.

38. Claire Easmon, personal communication, 1970.

39. Jones, "Freetown—The Contemporary Cultural Scene," pp. 202–3.

40. Ibid., p. 203.

41. *Household Survey of the Western Province,* Nov., 1966–Jan., 1968, vol. 1, *Household Characteristics and Housing Conditions* (Freetown: Sierra Leone Government, Central Statistics Office, 1967), p. 11.

42. Hooker, "Popular Musicians in Freetown," pp. 15–16.

43. Charles Keil, *Urban Blues* (Chicago: University of Chicago Press, 1966), p. 200.

44. LaRay Denzer, personal communication, 1969.

45. Ibid.

46. W. Lloyd Warner, Marchia Meeker, and Kenneth Eells, "What Social Class Is in America," in *Structured Social Inequality,* ed. Cynthia S. Heller (New York: Macmillan, 1969), pp. 177–78.

47. Spitzer, *Creoles of Sierra Leone,* p. 48.

48. W. Lloyd Warner, *The Social Life of a Modern Community* (New Haven: Yale University Press, 1941).

49. Banton, "Social Alignment."

50. Arnold J. Gooding, interview, Apr. 21, 1969.

51. W. G. Runciman, "Class, Status and Power," in *Social Stratification,* ed. John A. Jackson (Cambridge: Cambridge University Press, 1968), pp. 25–61; idem, "The Three Dimensions of Social Inequality," in *Social Inequality,* ed. André Béteille (1966; rpt., Harmondsworth, Middlesex: Penguin Books, 1969), pp. 45–63.

52. Runciman, "Class, Status and Power, p. 26.

53. Ibid., p. 31.

54. Ibid., pp. 39–40.

55. For a discussion of pan-Africanism as a nonpolitical movement, see Robert G. Weisbord, *Ebony Kinship* (Westport, Conn.: Greenwood Press, 1973), p. 7 n.

56. James R. Hooker, personal communication, 1971.

57. Weisbord, *Ebony Kinship,* p. 169.

58. *Unity* (Freetown), 1969.

59. LaRay Denzer, personal communication, 1970.

60. Chinweizu, *The West and the Rest of Us* (New York: Random House, 1975), p. 314.

61. *Aurora*, Nov. 5, 1921.

62. See Abioseh (Davidson) Nicol, "West Indians in West Africa," *Sierra Leone Studies*, n.s. 13 (1960), 14–23.

63. The titles are hypothetical.